D0110775

ALSO BY RICHARD BENYO

Superspeedway (1977)
Return to Running (1978)
Masters of the Marathon (1983)
The Exercise Fix (1989)
The Death Valley 300 (1991)

with Rhonda Provost
The Indoor Exercise Book (1980)
The Advanced Indoor Exercise Book (1981)
Feeling Fit in Your 40s (1987)

with Elaine LaLanne
Fitness After 50 (1986)
Dynastride! (1988)
Fitness After 50 Workout (1989)
Ear Right for a New You (1992)

as editor
The Grand National Stars (1975)
The Book of Richard Petty (1976)
The Complete Woman Runner (1978)
The Complete Runner II (1981)

Making
the Marathon
Your Event

Making the Marathon Your Event

RICHARD BENYO

 *RANDOM HOUSE   NEW YORK*

Copyright © 1992 by Richard Benyo
All rights reserved under International and
Pan-American Copyright Conventions. Published in
the United States by Random House, Inc., New
York, and simultaneously in Canada by Random
House of Canada Limited, Toronto.

Library of Congress Cataloging-in-Publication Data

Benyo, Richard.
    Making the marathon your event / by Richard
    Benyo.—1st ed.
      p.   cm.
    ISBN 0-679-73930-0
    1. Marathon running—Training. I. Title.
    GV1065.17.T73B46   1992   92-6335

Manufactured in the United States of America
9 8 7 6 5 4 3 2
First Edition

Illustrations by Pat Stewart

For Hal Higdon and Joe Henderson,
running writers whose work
illuminates the sport
and inspired a good many
of us slugs to give the marathon
a try Way Back When

Foreword

BY JOE HENDERSON
WEST COAST EDITOR, RUNNER'S WORLD

Runners live for the future. We look toward goals, such as running a first marathon or a faster one. We train for the day we might reach them, then reset them further into the future. Running writers cater mainly to this what's-coming-next thinking. But before Richard Benyo does this, let's take a quick glance backward to see where his ideas started.

If the complete history of running ever gets written, the year 1977 will carry a star. That's when the so-called "Running Boom" truly began.

Preliminary crackles and pops came earlier: with New Zealand coach Arthur Lydiard's training revolution of the early 1960s, with Dr. Kenneth Cooper's first *Aerobics* book in the late sixties, with Frank Shorter's Olympic Marathon victory in '72. They and others (such as physiology pioneer Dr. David Costill, the shoemakers at Tiger and Nike, magazine publishers Browning Ross and Bob Anderson, and the women and masters who expanded the sport's boundaries) were foundation layers, to be sure. But these separate sparks didn't all combine to create the real boom until 1977.

The New York City Marathon had just completed its first citywide run late in 1976, giving the country its first mass marathon without qualifying times. New York and Boston produced the first heroes and the new generation:

Bill Rodgers, who could win while still seeming like "one of us," and Miki Gorman, who could still beat all women after her fortieth birthday.

In 1977, Jim Fixx released his *Complete Book of Running.* It would sit atop the best-seller lists for more than a year.

The Honolulu Marathon Clinic began exporting its plan for turning new runners into marathoners in less than a year. That program boasted a 98 percent success rate.

Jeff Galloway, an ex-Olympian, expanded outward from his running shop and into running camps and clinics. He formulated a marathon training plan along the lines of Honolulu's.

In 1977, *Runner's World* magazine published its first marathon training schedule. It didn't prescribe the *most* running that runners could tolerate but the *least* they needed. It drew more reader response than any other article published to date.

Richard Benyo came to work for *Runner's World* in 1977. He had run in high school and college, but that was fifty pounds earlier. He could have carried that weight in his old job as a car-racing writer, but not when the subject was running and all of his audience ran. Benyo became both a product of the Running Boom and a player in it. He quickly uncovered the athlete under all that flesh, ran the Boston Marathon less than a year later, then wrote a book about that year called *Return to Running.*

That was almost fifteen years ago. Benyo still writes and runs. His running and fitness books now number more than a dozen. His runs haven't stopped at the marathon distance, but have reached as far as 300 miles.

Fifteen years into the boom, the marathon enjoys better health than ever before. Nineteen ninety-one was its biggest year yet in terms of entrants in U.S. races.

Another number means even more. That's the percentage of marathon *finishers.* Fifteen years ago, about 80 percent of the starters would survive the typical marathon. Left uncounted were those who trained unwisely and broke down before reaching the starting line, and those who couldn't or wouldn't run again after the race ended. But the finish rate at the New York City Marathon has been as high as 98 percent in recent years, and one group that trained together for the Los Angeles Marathon started 505 of its runners and finished 503.

Marathoners today are infinitely smarter than they were in 1977. Their collected wisdom is all here in Richard Benyo's book.

Preface

This book is not written for the elite or the elitist runner; not for the will-o'-the-wisp who can ghost past at the track while doing five-minute miles, and it's not for the runner born with national- or world-class genes. It is written for those of us who are slow of step and lumbering of foot, who have more will than wisp, and whose genes are weighted more heavily in the realm of perseverance than speed.

It is written for the new runner who wants to aim long-term at doing a marathon, for the returning runner who wants to reapproach the marathon from a more logical standpoint and at a more humane pace than the last go-around, and for the long-term runner who wants to become as comfortable with the marathon distance as it is possible to be.

It is written from the point of view of a training partner who's made literally every mistake *for* you and who, being your friend, hopes to lead you around some of the obstacles over which he stumbled. It is not written in the didactic form of "Just do it!" This isn't the army and it isn't a TV commercial. A running partner explains *why* the hard/easy or hard/easy/easy training principle works, explains *what* you should expect to feel during the final two weeks leading up to marathon day, and explains the consequences of deviating from the prescribed training regimen. Marathoners are an intelligent lot. If the would-be marathoner understands *why* he or she is doing a specific workout, that runner is more likely to approach that workout with more confidence and relaxation.

This book does not contain any shortcuts to the marathon. There are *no* shortcuts, and anyone who says there are has obviously been cutting the course. There are no miracle nutritional hijinks in this book that will knock fifteen minutes off your marathon time. My philosophy about nutrition is similar to my philosophy about the final two weeks of training leading to a marathon: If you've consistently trained well, the only thing you can do during the final two weeks is mess up the previous fourteen by experimenting. Nutritionally, you should employ a well-balanced diet at least 90 percent of the time; if you are living the marathon lifestyle, you can afford to fudge your diet 10 percent of the time. If you attempt to manipulate your diet during the tapering phase in hopes of finding a shortcut to better performance, you're likely to undo all your hard work.

In an increasingly unfit world, once you work yourself to the level of the marathon lifestyle, you lodge yourself in the top one-tenth of one percentile of fitness in the world. Although it may take 120 horsepower to move a car up to 55 miles per hour, once the car is at speed, it can maintain that speed by using 12 to 15 percent of its available horsepower; similarly, once you've put in the effort to become a marathoner, it becomes more painful to curtail the training than to continue it.

But of course, getting up to speed is half the fun. I suspect the ancient Greeks would agree.

—RICHARD BENYO
Forestville, California

Acknowledgments

Marathon running is a constantly evolving art. It owes its current level of development to a long line of athletes willing to experiment, to coaches intuitive enough to understand what works and what doesn't, and to scientists who pick through the entrails. The programs in this book are evolved from the teachings of one of the greatest of coaches, Arthur Lydiard, whose wisdom and insight allowed me to safely pass through many successful and satisfying marathons.

I would also like to acknowledge the invaluable input to the evolving manuscript of this book by Rhonda Provost and Tom Crawford.

Thanks also to Kenny Herbert of The Al Gordon Library of the New York City Roadrunners Club for his help in preparing several of the Appendixes.

Contents

Making the Marathon Your Event

Introduction:
The Marathon Lifestyle

> Fitness is what you pass through on the way to a superior physical and mental and spiritual state. Beyond fitness is also a new and demanding, albeit infinitely rewarding, life-style.
>
> —GEORGE SHEEHAN, M.D., *Dr. Sheehan on Fitness*

Nearly every time you pick up your daily newspaper, there's another story on yet another study concluding that the level of fitness of the typical American is truly abysmal. Take, for example, two studies that came out in May 1991:

- A Louis Harris and Associates survey conducted for *Prevention* magazine found that 64 percent of adult Americans (some 98 million people) are overweight. This is up from 61 percent the previous year, and from 58 percent in 1983, the first year of the survey. Nearly one-third of these overweight Americans do not admit to being overweight. The survey also reports that some two-thirds of Americans are experiencing noticeable stress in their lives.
- The U.S. Department of Agriculture, using a sophisticated live-in laboratory called a "calorimeter," which studiously and impartially counts calories that test subjects ingest, found that the long-running claim by some overweight peo-

ple that their problem stems from a slower metabolism than that of their slim friends is, in fact, unfounded, and that the extra pounds come from a combination of sneaking extra snacks and too little exercise.

Visit any sports bar and you'll find that most sports fans are overweight and couldn't run a mile in eight minutes if their lives depended on it—which, in effect, they do.

Visit any elementary or high school during fitness assessment tests and you'll be appalled at how many children are unable to do one pull-up. The number of overweight youngsters is staggering—and is steadily growing worse.

Yet in this sea of pitiful fitness and appalling health assessments, there are islands of sanity and occasional mountains of people who are fit in mind and body.

As part of its twenty-fifth anniversary celebration, *Runner's World* commissioned a survey of the exercise habits of a select group of people in high-stress and high-visibility jobs. Some 86.6 percent claimed that they are exercising as much or more today than they were a decade ago; 55.1 percent claim they feel mentally better than they did a decade ago; while 46.9 percent claim they feel better physically than they did ten years ago, even though they are a decade older. The primary exercise in which the respondents participate is running.

Research into what was once considered the inevitable process of aging now claims that Jack LaLanne's famous phrase of 1936—"Use it or lose it!"—was on target. The negative effects of aging *can* be attenuated by a regular program of exercise and good nutrition. We are increasingly reminded of this by images of older people acting as though they were half their age. George Foreman comes out of retirement to trade punches with a boxer young enough to be his son. Nolan Ryan pitches a seventh no-hitter at age forty-four. Johnny Kelley, eighty-four years old, completes his fifty-eighth Boston Marathon.

What do these unusual and special people have in common? They *work* at staying young. George Foreman faithfully put in many miles of roadwork each day for his comeback. Nolan Ryan spends hours a day on his stationary bicycle before *and* after pitching. Johnny Kelley runs 50 miles a week.

While most Americans look at these people as freaks of nature, more and more of us want to emulate them. Americans are taking note of the good effects of a fitness lifestyle and are embracing fitness as a personal statement of taking control of their own lives.

The most public and extraordinary statement of your intention to get fit, retard aging, and take control of your life is to run a marathon—and then maintain what has come to be called the "marathon lifestyle."

The successful completion of the marathon distance is an endeavor that can raise the average individual to heroic dimensions. It requires hard work, dedication, self-control, perseverance, careful pacing, delayed gratification, sacrifice, and a willingness—even a passion—to go against the grain.

This elite group (less than one in one thousand Americans ran a marathon last year) stands on the pinnacle of the fitness pyramid. By training to become a marathoner, and then by maintaining a fitness level that allows the runner to, at will, drop into a sixteen-week marathon-training program, the marathon lifestyle guarantees an arsenal of physical and psychological benefits that is overwhelming, especially at a time when the average American's lack of basic physical fitness is a national disgrace.

To master the marathon requires a training discipline and a dedication that goes well beyond other avocations and hobbies. The pursuit of the marathon requires a person to become fit even *before* embarking on a typical sixteen- or twenty-week-long program specifically geared to carrying the runner safely and well through the 26.2-mile distance. It is not a single-minded pursuit, however. It can—and should—become more than merely striving for a finishing certificate or medal, and certainly more than a onetime statement of purpose. People who embark on a running program simply with the goal of running a marathon often fall out at the other end disappointed, disillusioned, and disheartened—and sometimes embittered and hobbled by the entire experience.

Those who do well, who make the marathon a regular or recurring goal in their lives, come to the distance gradually, and not necessarily as an end in itself. Covering 26.2 miles successfully under your own power becomes a secondary goal to the act and art of long-term long-distance running. For these runners, the ultimate pursuit is to live the marathon lifestyle: a dedication to ongoing physical, spiritual, and mental conditioning through running, and an enjoyment of the benefits that flow from that lifestyle and add to the quality and quantity of one's life.

The marathon lifestyle is *not* a dedication to obsessively running every day. It does not require membership in a running club or a fitness group. It does not require running a specific number of marathons per year. What it is instead is a dedication to long-distance running as an integral part of everyday life. It is running at a level where, with sixteen weeks' notice, the runner is able to increase training sufficiently to run a credible marathon based on sex, age, and past performances.

Of course, some people attempt to maintain a training level so ambitious that they can comfortably run a marathon at a moment's notice.

But the marathon lifestyle can be maintained on as little as 25 miles a week and can successfully pass through periods of time when the runner takes an entire week or two off without significantly jeopardizing involvement in the sport.

In fact, as will be discussed in later chapters, it behooves the long-distance runner to schedule annual easy periods during which the body can heal itself from the physical stress it has undergone during those periods when the running schedule is directed toward a specific marathon. Some of the more successful long-term marathoners interrupt their regular training with a week's worth of backpacking or cross-country skiing—or with doing nothing physical whatsoever. Rest is a prime ingredient of a successful training program.

. . .

Some would argue that running long distances is an unnatural act. To some extent those people are correct. Although primitive man kept game on the table by running animals to the ground, there is no need for modern man to run 30 or 40 miles a week on an ongoing basis.

But the fact that the largest muscles and bones in the human body are those in the legs indicates that the human animal was designed to move under its own power. And certainly there is a mountain of evidence that associates disease with a sedentary lifestyle (the antithesis of the marathon lifestyle), which further indicates that the human being *should* be engaged in some form of regular aerobic exercise for health reasons.

A human being can enjoy a battery of physical benefits from running slowly for twenty minutes four times a week, and many people do just that. But a twenty-minute run is typically more of a chore than a joy, and is generally done as a prophylactic against heart disease. It is out beyond the half-hour run that the body warms up and the primitive joy of physical movement begins, where the psychological benefits accrue, and where the physical benefits are more profound and more finely honed. Running doesn't become fun until you reach the point where you can comfortably run forty minutes at a time (though even then, some days it still takes a real effort to get out the door).

Running *is* hard work and, at times, maintaining the marathon lifestyle is *damned* hard work, but it harkens back to the age-old axiom that the harder you work for something, the more precious it is. Certainly, on some days the running comes so smoothly and beautifully that it is like receiving a divine and unexpected gift. Occasionally a runner will enjoy several of those days consecutively. But other days the running joy doesn't come, the run *is* hard work, and the runner wonders afterward if the effort was worth it. The temporary runner is the one who asks that question one too many times. The marathoner is the runner who continually searches for the perfect run and, in the process, is more than satisfied with the physical and psychological benefits the marathon lifestyle bestows during the process of the quest.

Physical Benefits

It is not our purpose here to embark on lengthy discussions of the physical benefits of a regular long-distance running program. Such information is available in any number of books about aerobic exercise that have appeared during the past decade. (Some of the most readable ones are those written by Dr. Kenneth Cooper, the father of aerobics.) Rather, I will briefly explain some of the benefits.

High serum cholesterol is a proven indicator of incipient heart disease. High cholesterol typically indicates that the walls of major arteries are slowly but inexorably being occluded by plaque formations, until ultimately the blood supply to the heart is compromised, causing pain (angina) or death of the heart muscle—what is commonly referred to as a heart attack. Cholesterol can typically be lowered in three ways: (1) by diet manipulation, (2) by drugs, and (3) through aerobic exercise.

Aerobic exercise increases the production of high-density lipoproteins (HDL), the "good" cholesterol that essentially scrubs the bad cholesterol (low-density and very-low-density lipoproteins) from the walls of the arteries.

In his 1989 "The Case Against Cholesterol" contribution to the *Encyclopaedia Britannica Medical and Health Annual,* Peter D. Wood, D.Sc., Ph.D., of Stanford University, wrote about aerobic exercise as a contributor to HDL: "Although dietary modification is frequently projected as the only important hygienic approach to improved serum lipoproteins, several other important life-style changes clearly have worthwhile effects, especially on the HDL fraction, and should not be neglected. In sedentary, moderately overweight people—about one-third of the American population—increased exercise on a regular basis, and the loss of body fat that goes with it, results in increases in the serum HDL-cholesterol."

Regular aerobic exercise also lowers the resting pulse rate, an indicator of a strong heart. Aerobic exercise temporarily increases the pulse rate, thereby exercising the heart, which subsequently increases its strength, endurance, and stroke volume. As a result, under resting conditions, the heart muscle is not called upon to beat as often to supply the body's needs, since each stroke is significantly stronger and of greater volume. An analogy would be to replace a car's 2.0-liter four-cylinder engine with a 3.2-liter six-cylinder engine. The engine works less to provide greater results.

Regular aerobic exercise lowers blood pressure. In a study reported in the *American Journal of Medicine* in 1984, jogging was used (without any medication) to markedly lower blood pressure in patients with hypertension. Blood pressure was studied before the program began and again three months later, when the subjects had gradually progressed through a walking program and into a 2-mile-a-day jogging program. Blood pressure readings on the diastolic side fell an average of 15 points.

Running lowers body fat content. Aerobic exercise, especially if it is done slowly and for extended periods of time as it is in marathon training, burns body fat by slowly converting it to the energy needed for the continuation of the run. At the same time, the exercising increases muscle strength and endurance and increases muscle tone. In a person who is not overfat to begin with, this muscle development can actually increase the person's total body weight, since muscle weighs more than fat. (It should be stressed that when you exercise regularly *muscle does not replace fat.* Fat and muscle tissues are not interchangeable. What happens is that fat molecules are reduced while muscle molecules increase in size.) The regularly exercising body slowly adjusts its proportion of fat to muscle. This process also improves posture because fat, which sags toward the ground, is counterbalanced by muscle, which enables the human skeleton to defy gravity. Incorporating a regular program of upper-body strengthening—especially one concentrating on the abdominal, back, shoulder, and upper-arm muscles—will further improve posture. It should also be noted that a regular aerobic program causes the body to metabolize fat and calories for many hours after the activity ends—essentially no-strain fat loss.

The loss of excess body fat and the increase of body musculature decreases the stress on bones and joints simply by lessening gravity's pull on the body and increasing the body's ability to resist gravity.

The exercising body is also able to increase ingestion of nourishing foods with impunity from a body-fat standpoint. Marathon training burns a tremendous number of calories. This increased metabolism of calories allows the marathoner to consume a wider range of beneficial foods, thereby more thoroughly providing the body's daily needs in vitamins and minerals and trace elements that are not necessarily available to the person attempting to regulate body fat through restrictive dieting. A marathoning program makes dieting obsolete.

There is a saying among those who exercise regularly that "energy begets energy." This is certainly true. A body can be expected to function only in ways it has been trained to function. Therefore a body that is taught to expend tremendous amounts of energy running at a marathoner's level week after week is trained to generate tremendous amounts of energy when needed. The marathoner's potential energy stores increase tremendously.

Conversely, a person engaged in regular marathon training finds it easier to fall asleep and enjoys restorative sleep more regularly than the person who does not exercise. (Overtraining-induced insomnia is covered in Chapter 10.)

Regular aerobic exercise relieves common muscular stress typically centered in the shoulders, neck, and back. Massage therapy is helpful here, too.

Regular exercise also increases flexibility in the extremities, the back, and the shoulders. As we age, a sedentary lifestyle wreaks havoc with the body's flexibility. Like a rusting gate hinge, the human body stiffens and becomes unyielding. Fortunately, the human body is one of the only machines known that improves its function with use. I'm especially partial to

Jack LaLanne's philosophy: "I'd rather wear out than rust out!"

Many arguments are waged against running because of its alleged negative effects upon aging bones. Nothing is further from the truth: Running retards degenerative bone maladies. In a 1986 study titled "Long-Distance Running, Bone Density, and Osteoarthritis" published in the *Journal of the American Medical Association,* forty-one long-distance runners aged fifty to seventy-two were compared with a control group to "examine associations of repetitive, long-term physical impact [running] with osteoarthritis and osteoporosis." The conclusion? "Runners, both male and female, have approximately 40% more bone mineral than matched controls."

A regular program of distance running also promotes regularity of bowel movements, an ongoing concern to many Americans. Sluggish bowel movements are associated with various types of cancer and can cause chronic abdominal discomfort. A sedentary lifestyle, bad posture, and the typical American diet contribute to irregularity. A regular program of aerobic activity moves fecal matter through the intestines and promotes regularity, especially over the age of forty. In most cases, irregularity is a condition not of life but of lifestyle: insufficient fluid, roughage, and physical activity.

Psychological Benefits

By embracing the challenge of training for and running a marathon and subsequently maintaining the marathon lifestyle, specific psychological benefits also accrue.

The primary benefit is a tremendous increase in self-esteem and self-confidence. When you cross the finish line of a marathon, you feel you can literally conquer the world. Numerous stories abound of the positive effects generated in a person's life in the wake of training for and successfully running a marathon. It is an opportunity to embrace a physically and mentally tough challenge in a world sadly bereft of physical challenges. By adopting the marathon lifestyle, you can apply the physical and mental toughness needed to run the marathon to your daily life: commitment, self-discipline, focus, pacing, and the ability to use power and energy efficiently to achieve goals.

The simple act of training for sixteen weeks to attain a goal increases mental toughness, hones motivational skills, and increases your short- and long-term planning skills. Training for a marathon is much like climbing a ladder. Each rung is a short-term goal that must be met in sequence in order to reach the long-term goal at the top of the ladder. The ability to set short-term goals leading toward a long-term one appears to be a vanishing skill in an era more renowned for its obsession with immediate gratification and taking shortcuts. Skills built by methodically reaching one short-term goal after another can be appropriately applied to your daily or professional life.

The act of running is a purging experience, a process wherein the seemingly overwhelming cares of the day are, mile by mile, placed into a logical priority list. The mind is cleared; problems are stripped of their camouflage and verbiage, and can be suddenly perceived as simple enough to solve with a minimum of effort. The psychological release that comes with physical activity has a reviving effect and is more beneficial for some than psychotherapy. In fact, since the 1970s, psychologists have recommended physical activity, such as running, rather than psychotherapy as a form of psychological release. For the average individual faced with the daunting dilemmas of today's society, a good run four or five times a week is better than a comparable amount of time spent with a therapist—and it's a lot cheaper and brings with it many physical benefits that lying on a couch does not.

Engaging in a marathon lifestyle also provides a sense of well-being and equanimity, both because the physical act of running clears the head and because the release of endorphins in the brain has a calming effect. It is difficult to come back from a forty-minute run in the same frazzled state of mind you were in when you left.

Many of us do not have an opportunity on a regular basis to engage in healthy competition. Many of us, in fact, may be turned off by what passes for competitiveness, whether in the workplace or as we huddle over the sports section. Some personalities seem to thrive on bald competition, the louder and the rougher the better. Others engage in almost maniacal surrogate competition by spending time following a favorite sports team. Ultimately, however, the most difficult competition a person can take on is with him- or herself. This is true because most of us are built so that once we achieve a particular goal, we can set the next goal even farther out. Marathon training and running provide one of the best arenas for competing with yourself. It is very much an individual sport. If you set up a training schedule and meet it, you know at the center of your soul whether or not you managed to hold to it and just how much work you put into it. By the same token, if you goofed off at some point, you are the first one aware of it and the last one who will forget it.

Marathoners concentrate on what they refer to as "PRs," or "Personal Records"—performances against their own best records, adjusted for age as they mature. This form of personal competition has obvious advantages when translated to the workaday world.

Few of us grew up with a strong body awareness. That commodity seemed to be reserved for the high school football star and the head cheerleader. Most of us grew up awkwardly, not sure if our bodies were our friends or our enemies. By age thirty, the body begins to go bad at an inexorable rate, and does, in fact, seem to be the enemy. However, the marathon lifestyle provides an opportunity to turn your body around, to make it outstanding for its age. Remember, very few bodies can run 26 miles under their own power at any age. At the age of forty-five or fifty-five, such a feat becomes even more astonishing.

It has always been particularly gratifying to see women engage in marathon training. It is typical for women beginning a running program to want to work out in a baggy, shapeless, drab gray sweatsuit and to run at those times of the day or night when there are few people on the street to see them. There is a certain reluctance to take the old body into public. But little by little, as the fat melts away and the muscle tone increases, these same women seem to emerge from a cocoon; their new body awareness and fitness give them the confidence to change into a sleek, designer warm-up outfit as they go gliding along on their 10-kilometer workout. The marathon lifestyle can literally introduce you to the physical side of yourself that has been begging for decades to be allowed to run wild.

The primary relationship most Americans have to the world of sport is that of spectating, but many sports fans would have trouble puffing their way once around the block. Instead of expanding to embrace as many people as possible at a time when they could well use the exercise, sports continually becomes more and more elitist. We pay more and more money to watch fewer and fewer people engage in sport. The exorbitant salaries of professional athletes and the fact that so many people pay so much money to engage essentially in voyeurism verges on the pornographic.

The marathon lifestyle promotes doing rather than watching, which is a refreshing change of pace from the direction sports is taking. By adopting the marathon lifestyle you can confront your own lions, be your own hero, fight your own battles, challenge yourself. Then, when you are ready to step up to the starting line, you can do so knowing that, unlike in other sports, where you'd never get to pitch against the American League batting champion, block for the 49ers quarterback, or set Michael Jordan up for a shot, you *can* and *will* line up with the best marathoners in the world.

When Monday morning comes, you can stiffly walk into the office and ask Joe Jock what he did over the weekend.

"Hey, I watched the big game on the tube. . . . What did you do?"

"I ran in a marathon against Frank Shorter, Bill Rodgers, and Grete Waitz."

I

How to Lay
the Groundwork

1

The Greek Ideal in Our Century

> The marathon is not the most arduous sport, as it's commonly known, but the most perfect sport for the human organism.
>
> —MANFRED STEFFNY, *Marathoning*

Western civilization flows from the ancient Greeks. The Greek ideal of the balanced physical and mental development of the individual infused Athenian culture in the ancient world. In today's terms, we would probably represent the Greek ideal like this: A fit mind in a fit body. The Greek ideal today would best be represented by the concept of the scholar-athlete.

It is not surprising, then, that the concept of the marathon also comes to us from ancient Greece, for to them, physical pursuits were as worthy as those mental.

In 490 B.C. the Greek city-state of Athens faced a huge Persian army on the Plains of Marathon, about 22 miles from the city of Athens; in fact, the very survival of Athens hung in the balance. The Greeks, not waiting for the Persians to set up their massive offensive machine, attacked, and the enemy was routed.

Legend has it that a Greek messenger (a *hemerodromoi* or "all-day runner"), Pheidippides, was dispatched to Athens to report the startling victory. Pheidippides ran the 22 miles, proclaimed "Victory!," then collapsed on the steps of the city and died. Scholars claim that the tale of Pheidippides' death didn't appear in the literature until some eight hundred years after the event, and that it was then embellished by Robert Browning's 1879 poem "Pheidippides."

In reality, there *was* a Pheidippides, but he ran from Athens to Sparta at the behest of the Athenian generals who were seeking military help to face the Persians. The trip from Athens to Sparta was roughly 132 miles, and Pheidippides made the trek with no apparent trouble. A trip of merely 22 miles from Marathon to Athens would have been child's play for the average *hemerodromoi.*

When the Olympic Games were revived in 1896, a special marathon commemorated the run from the Plains of Marathon to Athens. (It was the only track event won by a Greek that year.) New York and Boston spectators at the Games were so enthralled by the challenge of the marathon that they started their own marathon races in the United States. New York held a marathon in late 1896 and Boston held its first marathon in 1897—an event that is now the longest-running marathon race in history. It was not until 1924 that the now-standard 26.2-mile distance was put in place—though it took a while for it to be accepted.

In A.D. 1991, the twenty-second annual New York City Marathon fielded nearly 30,000 runners (and boasted 25,797 finishers), making it the world's largest marathon. Even so, organizers had to turn away 23,890 more. Figures from California marathons testify to a growth spurt in the latter half of the 1980s:

	1986	*1991*
Napa Valley Marathon	590	1,687
California International Marathon	1,804	2,015
Big Sur International Marathon	1,760	2,445
Los Angeles Marathon	10,787	18,380

The big-city marathons report that 38 to 50 percent of their entrants are first-time marathoners, and that much of the recent growth in the size of the field comes from the group aged thirty to forty-nine. A staggering 68 percent of the 1990 New York City Marathon entrants were in that age group.

In the midst of reports that the youth of industrial nations are woefully out of shape and patently unfit, a notable number of their elders are finding the energy to train for and run the marathon distance—a significant undertaking at any age.

As recently as 1962, there were only 231 entrants in the Boston Marathon. In 1991 there were 8,600. What occurred within the intervening thirty years to swell the Boston starting field more than thirty-five times?

The first major blip on the seismograph of fitness came in 1968 when a former air force doctor, Kenneth Cooper, put together a physical fitness program that used running as its backbone. Cooper's *Aerobics* went up the best-seller charts as middle-aged men who faced the increasing prospect of dying of heart disease took to Cooper's very formal—but voluntary—program of aerobic points. The business and professional people who followed Cooper's program saw their blood pressures and resting pulse rates drop, their cholesterol levels drop, and their body fat evaporate, and they felt better than they had in years.

From 231 entrants in 1962, Boston swelled to 1,335 in 1969. A significant number of the newcomers that year were Cooper aerobics graduates who took their running program one step further. In addition, college runners who felt confined by track races saw Boston as a worthy goal. For instance, Amby Burfoot, the only American to win Boston in the 1960s, was a senior at Wesleyan College when he triumphed in 1968. Burfoot was born in 1946, at the cusp of a generation that would embrace running in huge numbers.

The next blip on the graph came in 1972 when Frank Shorter became the first American since Johnny Hayes in 1908 to win the Olympic marathon. Like Burfoot, Shorter, who was born in 1947, was a Baby Boomer. He made his marathon victory at Munich appear almost effortless. When the pace seemed too pedestrian for him, he squirted out of the pack and took a lead that was never challenged. Many of the runners who took up the marathon during the mid-1970s claim Shorter inspired them.

"Winning the marathon in Munich made my running, in the eyes of others, legitimate," Shorter later observed. "Suddenly it was okay to be a runner, to train for two and three hours a day. There was a purpose behind it, something to be gained. My running had been looked upon as a diversion, as a peculiar habit for a grown man. After all, it was not done on behalf of a university team. It was not earning me a decent living. It was not even making me look manly, skinny guy that I really was."

By the time the Montreal Olympics were televised to larger audiences in 1976, the first wave of Baby Boomers was entering their thirties. Many Americans, passing into their fourth decade of life, looked in the mirror and saw that holding on to their youth demanded an ongoing effort. The marathon suddenly seemed a viable—and noble—vehicle for grasping a fading youth.

In 1976 there were 1,898 entrants in the Boston Marathon. In 1977 there were 2,766. In 1978 there were 4,000. And in 1979 there were 7,800.

The marathoners were the tip of the pyramid of literally millions upon millions of sloggers, joggers, and runners who took to the streets. When, in 1976, the New York City Road Runners Club moved its marathon out of Central Park and onto the city streets in conjunction with the year's bicentennial celebrations, the race grew from hundreds to thousands. Meanwhile, *Runner's World* magazine, which was not even available on newsstands until 1977, saw its circulation rocket from less than 50,000 in 1976 to more than 250,000 by 1979.

Why running? There were many reasons: It was simple; you could do it anywhere; *anybody* could do it; it was inexpensive; you didn't need to schedule a court or even have a partner.

Why marathoning? It was the next logical step for a generation's first wave that had been grounded in long-term goals, in delayed satisfaction, in dreams of ultimate excess—the promise that if you worked hard and behaved yourself, you'd far outstrip your parents in all things.

In turn, the running revolution spawned the many-headed fitness revolution, which took off around 1980. Many who had begun with running moved to other, more chic forms of fitness: aerobic dance, the triathlon, working out on high-tech equipment in health clubs, and so on. For many, running just wasn't chic anymore. As far as the trendy were concerned, one of running's early attractions—that it was so simple—became its undoing.

It seemed, therefore, that running peaked during the early 1980s.

But then came 1984. The cusp of the Baby Boomer generation was staring down the muzzle of turning forty, the fabled and feared territory of middle age. And many of them again took a *long* look in the mirror: at their careers, at their families, at the crow's-feet around their eyes, at spreading waistlines. And they didn't like what they saw.

Life had become too complicated. They wanted to simplify. They wanted their lives back, and in a simpler mode. So running (just put one foot in front of the other) began to look mighty attractive again—even to those who had given it a try before but been discouraged by injuries caused by the wrong kind or amount of training or by inefficient pacing or ill-fitting shoes. Now better shoes (to more effectively prevent injury) were available, and many forty-year-olds had finally learned a little more about proper pacing.

Others who had never run took it up, spurred by its simplicity—and its economy. Why should they pay for a health spa membership when there are hundreds of thousands of miles of perfectly good streets and roads available to run on for free?

Schooled, however, in creating short-term goals as stepping-stones to long-term goals, many late 1980s marathoners took years to build up to the marathon, ran fewer marathons per year than their counterparts had in the late 1970s, and attempted to make a high-level fitness program a permanent part of their lives.

They had learned that through pacing and patience, even a thing of seeming excess can, in the end, be a moderating force.

I've always been more impressed watching a fully loaded moving van lumber along an interstate highway at 50 miles per hour than a Ferrari doodle along at 100 miles per hour. While the Ferrari seems to defy inertia, the moving van is impressive because it faces inertia head-on and overcomes its inherent immobility.

During the early days of the running revolution, a number of elitist runners complained bitterly of the invasion of their sport by the out-of-shape "moving van" masses; at the same time, they were quite willing to accept the suddenly generous prize money races were able to offer as a result of the infusion of thousands of "also rans." Fortunately, road racing has been blessed with some very understanding and sympathetic elite runners. Interviewed after one of the four consecutive New York City Marathons he won in the late 1970s, Bill Rodgers stood watching runners struggle to break four hours. His interviewer asked him what he thought of these sloggers. Rodgers said: "I've got a lot of respect for those runners. I don't think I could stay out there for four or five hours. It's a lot easier getting it over with in two hours and ten minutes. They're the heroes."

Running on a regular basis is hard work, especially if you aren't whippet-thin. Tom Crawford, a Santa Rosa, California, running friend, organizes two local 50-mile races annually and has thrice run from Death Valley to the top of Mount Whitney in the middle of summer. "Why do you think there's been a drop-off in running lately?" reporter Bruce Meadows of the *Press Democrat* asked Tom back in 1984.

"First of all, I'm not sure there is," Tom Crawford said, "but when people drop running it's usually for one of two reasons: They run unwisely and hurt themselves, or they find out that it's more work than they thought it would be."

If plain running is hard work, marathon running is in a league by itself. It is a special kind of running that requires a commitment many people are unable to make. While it takes a fourfold dedication to become a marathoner after you've become a runner, the rewards are commensurate.

Run your first marathon and you've moved to a plateau inhabited by one in a thousand. Run two marathons and you're one in ten thousand. But there's more to it than joining such a small group or getting a finisher's medal or T-shirt. When you are able to rise to and maintain the level of fitness that is referred to as the marathon lifestyle, your self-esteem rises, as does your self-confidence: Anything in life suddenly seems possible. You also develop very special relationships that could be forged nowhere else than on the demanding roads and trails on your way to the marathon and beyond.

2

Basic Training

> No matter what your natural physique, or how poor your starting condition, you can improve. . . . The time required, and the absolute magnitude of the change achieved, are the variables.
>
> —JOAN L. ULLYOT, M.D., *Running Free*

Where sprinters compete on nerves, marathoners compete on patience. It takes time to become a good marathoner. For instance, although observers in the late 1970s felt Alberto Salazar's physical strength and his low, ground-eating running style were ideally suited to the marathon (and although many of Salazar's workouts were similar to classic marathon training), his coach, Bill Dellinger, would not allow him to compete at the distance too early in his career. Once Dellinger felt Salazar had matured enough both physically and mentally, he unleashed a talent that was overwhelming and that dominated the marathon in the early 1980s. Salazar's debut marathon in New York City in 1980 was an amazing 2:09:41.

Many runners entering the sport in the late 1970s and early 1980s were not nearly so talented or so patient: They exhibited an ignorance of the unique demands of the marathon and an arrogance about their own physiology. These runners began a modest running program and in no time at all were training for and running their first—and usually last—marathon. The negative experience that awaited them beyond 20 miles, combined with the physical beating they took from being improperly trained, frequently led to an early retirement from the sport and often to nagging foot, leg, knee, hip, or lower-back injuries. Naturally, their post-race theory was that people weren't built to run such distances.

In actuality, the fault lay with the arrogant supposition that they could beat their body into shape to perform beyond its *current* ability. I stress the word *current* because in most cases, if these now-hobbled ex-marathoners had first evaluated their physical condition and then laid out a long-term training program building toward the marathon distance, they would likely still be running—and enjoying—the distance.

As with any endurance sport, marathon training is a process of stress and rest repeated endlessly but carefully.

A muscle's endurance is increased by carefully stressing the muscle and then allowing it to rest and repair itself so that when next it is stressed, it begins the training process just slightly stronger than it did the last time. A muscle that has not been regularly stressed in twenty years begins the process at a very low level.

In order to develop that muscle safely, one must stress it slowly. The muscle tissue must be meticulously strengthened, and the collateral blood supplies that are formed to feed and repair it must be allowed time to develop; muscles must follow this cycle in order to be transformed into the muscles of a mobile animal. This applies to the long muscles of the legs as well as to the muscle of the heart. Too many people who take up running arrogantly expect a body they have ignored at best and abused at worst for twenty years to make a miraculous turn around in a few months just because they want it to. It took years to get out of shape—expect it to take years to get completely back into shape.

The human body is a complex organism, and only the person who has the greatest respect for it will benefit when he or she makes the decision to take up the marathon lifestyle. A running program leading to the marathon does not have to involve a physical thrashing. The patient runner may experience the occasional discomfort and tired muscle but seldom pushes it to the extent that to move is an agony. The patient runner is not so distracted by the discomfort of getting into shape that he or she is blinded to the enjoyment—and the little accomplishments and landmarks of the process. (The impatient runner, attempting to get it into shape quickly, thrashes his or her body, and the body fights back as though resisting. This person suffers aches and pains that make it almost impossible to face the next workout.)

A running program can and should be fun. Not knee-slapping fun, but there is a joy of movement, a feeling of power, and a feeling of accomplishment as one's body gradually changes to that of a runner.

If you are about to embark on a long-term running program, have a photograph taken in as few clothes as modesty permits. Then, every six months, have another photograph taken. In the course of several years, you will see the contours of your body shift—in some instances, the shifts will be significant.

Keep a daily log of your training program as it evolves, and keep an album of your evolving physical stature. Several years down the road, you will be astonished at how the miles have changed you—and at how you have been able to change your perception of the miles. I occasionally run with a woman who bikes to her job. Ten years ago, she felt it took a lot of effort to get to work in the morning because the 3-mile trip was "uphill." The uphill she was referring to was an elevation gain of less than 50 feet over the 3 miles. Having patiently worked her way through 5Ks, 5-milers, 10Ks, 20Ks, marathons, and 50-milers, this woman is currently in training for her first 100-mile race. Her complaints about pedaling her bicycle 3 miles "uphill" a decade ago are now a regular source of amusement to her.

Your Fitness Evaluation

Before embarking on a running program leading to marathon training, you must evaluate your current level of fitness and health. Regardless of whether you have never engaged in a running program before or were a star on the college cross-country team a decade ago, the best way to do this is to get a complete fitness evaluation, including a stress test.

There has long been controversy regarding this subject, so by now there are many arguments why a complete physical isn't necessary:

1. You might find out something you'd be "better off not knowing." The persistence of this hoary nugget, which obviously stems from the days when there was literally nothing to be done about certain diseases, is mystifying. These days it goes without saying that the sooner a suspicious spot on an X ray or a tendency to high blood pressure is identified, the better.

2. A doctor who evaluates the results of your test might attempt to discourage you from running. If that concerns you, I recommend screening your prospective physicians before you visit them. Ask whether they subscribe to a "fit" lifestyle. Don't be afraid to be specific. Any enlightened physician will understand. If he/she doesn't, you don't want him/her as your physician anyway.

3. It's expensive, and a lot of health insurance plans don't cover the costs of doctor's visits and tests when they concern "wellness" rather than a specific illness. Even if you have to pick up the cost yourself, considering the fact that running is the cheapest fitness activity there is, the cost of such testing is up-front money well spent.

4. Running is such a relatively inexpensive sport when compared with other options—bicycling, triathloning, skiing, etc.—that it would be well worth the initial investment of approximately $250 to put yourself through a stress test at a local medical or fitness center and have the results interpreted by a doctor who is conversant with the implications of such results.

5. You don't need such tests if you are thirty-five years old or younger. Autopsies done on eighteen- and nineteen-year-old military casualties of the Korean War revealed that some

young men already suffered from the relatively well advanced arterial plaque buildup that is an indicator of creeping heart disease.

The best attitude toward fitness evaluations and stress tests can be compared with another automotive analogy: You wouldn't plan to take your car on a drive across the country and back without dropping it by the shop to have its current status evaluated, would you?

You are about to embark on what will hopefully be a lifelong, intense fitness program. It is to your benefit to have your body tested and to have those tests results explained to you by a professional. These results can guide the speed at which you begin a running program.

The typical evaluation includes the following:

1. Blood test
   Total serum cholesterol
   High-density lipoprotein (HDL)
   Low-density lipoprotein (LDL)
   Very low density lipoprotein (VLDL)
   Uric acid
   Glucose
   Sodium
   Potassium
   Iron
   White blood cells
   Red blood cells
   Hemoglobin
   Hematocrit
   Mean cell volume
   Mean corpuscular hemoglobin
   Mean corpuscular hemoglobin concentrate
2. Muscular endurance test (usually tested on Sybex or similar machine, on arms and legs)
3. Flexibility tests
4. Body fat evaluation (skin fold test or hydrostatic test)
5. Stress test (on treadmill or bicycle or both)

VO2 max
Electrocardiogram
Maximal heart rate
Blood pressure
Breathing characteristics
Maximal work capacity

Many clinics that regularly administer fitness evaluations and stress tests will give you a complete book summarizing the results after they've been explained to you. If you are about to begin a running program, items such as VO2 max, resting pulse rate, blood pressure, percentage of body fat, and blood chemistry serve as excellent indicators of your best beginning work level; they also serve as a baseline. Take the tests again at regular intervals (e.g., every two or five years) and compare the numbers to see the physical benefits your marathon lifestyle generates.

The Slow Build

Many well-respected distance coaches feel that in order to avoid injury, an athlete should not increase his or her training more than 5 percent a year. Of course, since most national- and world-class runners have been competing since grade school, they may, at twenty-two years of age, be at 100 miles per week. Consequently, a 5 percent increase would allow them to add another 5 miles per week and/or a 5 percent increase in speed.

For the person just beginning a running program, however, the 5 percent rule is impractical. Although we will use careful and cautious methods of getting around the 5 percent rule, the lesson we should take from such caution is that it is unwise to push too much too soon.

Whether you have been sedentary all your life or are returning to running after a substantial layoff, your body has had time to adapt to the lifestyle of the past ten years. Our bodies can adapt to what we demand of them, but the speed of adaptation to a marathon-training program varies with age, sex, previous athletic experience, current physical condition, and genetic predisposition.

The fitness evaluation and stress test give you a realistic picture of where you are at this point and what challenges you face in pursuing the marathon lifestyle. The program presented in Chapter 4 is based upon time put in on the road instead of on distance. It is also time adjusted to take into account the option of a combined walk/run program for the beginner.

While the concept of walking is odious to some hard-core runners, I think walking is a good way to extend one's range and capabilities, and not a defeat.

Combining walking and running may be the best way to begin a running program for the complete beginner. It's also a good way of extending one's range on longer workouts. Programming some walking into a long run or into the marathon itself can effectively extend the athlete's range and effectiveness, while it also minimizes sore muscles and injuries. The farther an athlete goes, the more effective walking becomes. Tim Twietmeyer, who consistently places in the top five of the Western States 100-Mile Endurance Run and who won the 1992 edition of the famous race, claims that he typically walks 15 percent of the course. In fact, walking in ultramarathons is an accepted method of competing. No one *runs* over Colorado's Hope Pass (12,600 feet) in the Leadville Trail 100—not even the leaders.

And if you set a camcorder out at the 20-, 22-, and 24-mile points of the typical marathon, you would see 40 percent or more of the participants walking. Unfortunately, their walking at that point is usually due to their inability to continue running. They would have been much better off—and would probably have finished earlier—if they had programmed in a bit of walking along the way to keep their legs fresh.

Remember that on the long workouts (and the word *long* is a very relative term), the object is to keep moving and to get time on your legs. In the programs that follow, we will make haste slowly in order to go the distance.

The Aerobic Path

In his 1968 book *Aerobics,* Dr. Kenneth Cooper put together a fitness program whose backbone was jogging. His term *aerobics* has been simplified to mean "with oxygen" as opposed to "anaerobic," which means "without oxygen."

In anaerobic exercise, glycogen stored in the muscle can be converted to glucose and then used for energy. This, however, is a very inefficient means to produce energy; because the energy is produced quickly, it lasts only briefly (depending on the power generated by the effort, from a few seconds to a couple of minutes).

Even for the highly trained athlete, sprinting 400 meters around a track is done anaerobically—that is, beyond the athlete's body's ability to keep up with the oxygen demanded of the working muscles. The athlete goes into "oxygen debt."

Pushing Back the Anaerobic Threshold

The object of a marathon-training program is to effectively increase the capacity of the runner to do more work longer while staying within the aerobic envelope. In order to run faster, longer, or both while staying within your aerobic capacity, you must push back what is referred to as the "anaerobic threshold." (This point is also called the "lactate threshold" or the "lactate turnpoint," although scientists are not completely satisfied with any of the three terms.) The anaerobic threshold is that point in your workout when you convert from aerobic to anaerobic forms of metabolism for your energy. When this happens, the remaining capacity for muscular work is severely limited. We reach and exceed our anaerobic capacity when our ability to take in sufficient oxygen to meet the needs of our working muscles ends—we begin to breathe harder and faster, we ultimately begin to gasp, our muscles begin to revolt on us, and we burn out.

Think of the aerobic threshold as the endurance version of resistance training in a gym: You exercise a muscle against resistance in order to strengthen the muscle enough so that next time it takes a bit more resistance to retard the muscle's effort.

While the anaerobic thresholds of a highly trained marathoner and a rank novice are very different, a beginner can build an impressive aerobic capacity by methodically pushing back the anaerobic threshold.

This is accomplished by carefully venturing into anaerobic territory during one or two training sessions per week. It does *not* mean running too fast too soon, so that one is thrust into the nightmare world of oxygen debt (the kind of bad experience that turns novices off).

In a careful, long-term marathon-training program, the object is to *nudge* the anaerobic threshold farther and farther away. As it gradually requires more and more effort to reach the threshold, the aerobic capacity correspondingly increases.

The anaerobic threshold can be pushed back in three ways: (1) by running farther, (2) by running faster, and (3) by running farther *and* faster.

The long run and the speed workout are the two workouts that consistently push back the anaerobic threshold. The long run is the backbone of any running or marathon-training program. But the term *long run* is relative. For a novice, a 3-mile run may be a long run, while for the veteran, it may take a 20-miler to qualify as a long run. By the same token, a ten-minute mile may be a speed workout for a novice while a national-class marathoner may need to do a 4:20 mile to achieve the same effect.

The anaerobic threshold can be pushed back by combining long runs and speed workouts. If you do your long run fifteen seconds per mile faster than usual, it nudges the anaerobic threshold farther away, and if you increase the number of repetitions in your regular speed workout, the threshold is again nudged farther out.

The exciting thing for runners just beginning a program and for would-be marathoners moving from a basic running program to a marathon-training program is that there are huge gains to be made in pushing back the anaerobic threshold. (National- or world-class athletes have pretty much reached their anaerobic threshold and there's not much they can do to improve it without courting injury and exhaustion.) Nevertheless, everyone should be patient here. In order not to turn off would-be marathoners by the discomfort and work typically involved in pushing back the anaerobic threshold, the programs in this book build very gradually and with a minimum of discomfort and pain. Who wants to suffer unnecessarily? The "sprint-and-upchuck" track training so common in high school and colleges during the "Dark Ages" turned off enough potential runners. Our track workouts will be essentially painless. If you hurt during the track workouts prescribed in this book, you're running too fast.

With a little patience, you can take the sting out of getting acquainted with the anaerobic edge of workouts.

Where the Rubber Meets the Road

If there is one subject that seems to confound runners, it is the matter of running shoes. There is so much fancy advertising by shoe manufacturers and so many confusing claims about what miracles specific shoe models can perform that runners can be excused if their heads are spinning in circles every time the subject is raised.

In the "Dark Ages" of running, choosing a pair of shoes was much easier: There were only a half-dozen companies, each with only two or three models. But for some runners this primitive footwear provided precious little protection against the thousands of strides taken in each day's workout.

These days, running shoes should first and foremost be practical. The purpose of a running shoe is to protect the runner against the damaging effects of the impact that occurs when the foot strikes the ground, and to counteract any existing biomechanical peculiarities the runner exhibits, such as overpronation.

When choosing a running shoe, the marathoner should embrace the theory that "less is more." By that I mean, buy as simple and as basic a shoe as you can, considering your particular running characteristics. It should be obvious that the object of buying a running shoe is not to see how much money you can pay; nor is it to see how high-tech a shoe you can find.

You can immediately eliminate one entire segment of running shoes. Racing flats may be extremely light and snazzy-looking, but they offer very little impact protection, and the slight advantage you may pick up in speed will be more than offset in sore calves and Achilles tendons. You need impact protection, good wear characteristics, and serviceability.

You can also eliminate the training flats that are heavy on gimmicks (such as air pumps) and definitely forget the bargain-basement knockoffs you find in department store sales bins. Shop at a reputable running-shoe store and make it plain when you walk in that you want to start with low-tech and low-buck shoes and work up from there.

Several of the major running-shoe manufacturers still offer very simple, durable running shoes for $75 or less. In order to stay competitive, these manufacturers find it necessary to continually release new models even though they are not necessarily improvements over the older models. So, look at recently discontinued models as well—they'll be heavily marked down, and many of them are good shoes.

If you do not have any gross biomechanical problems, begin with a fairly neutral shoe model that offers good stability and motion control and adequate heel cushioning. Several shoe companies offer width sizing, which is beneficial for runners with very wide or very narrow feet. Your running shoe should be long enough that your big toe has at least a half-inch of space between the tip of the toe and the inside front of the shoe's toebox. This extra space is necessary for two reasons: on downhills, your feet will slide forward a bit and you don't want to jam your toes against the inside of the shoe; and on longer runs, your feet tend to swell an extra shoe size.

Try on a number of shoes that meet your needs. If the store

does not happen to have your size in a model you like, don't compromise by buying a size that is too small or too narrow, since you'll be putting in a lot of hard miles in the shoes and you want them to protect you—not turn on you. When you've narrowed down your choices to one or two, go outside and run in them for a hundred yards or so to make certain they feel good to run in. Any reputable running-shoe store will encourage you to do this, as long as it's not pouring outside.

Once you've bought the simplest shoe that meets your needs, monitor how well it holds up to the kind of miles you put on it. Keep track of any persistent aches that you feel are associated with the shoe. When you go to buy your next pair of running shoes, take your current shoes with you. A knowledgeable running-shoe salesperson will be able to give you valuable input on the type of shoe you should purchase next by interpreting how and where your old pair of shoes have worn down. You may benefit from greater rearfoot stability or from additional impact protection.

As you increase your mileage, it's a good idea to have more than one pair of running shoes so that you can alternate them. This increases the longevity of the shoes and tends to protect your feet and legs from injury by altering—even if by only a fraction of an inch—the angle of impact. Runners tend to duplicate almost exactly their impact stride after stride, thereby stressing the feet and legs the same way a thousand times or so per mile. By alternating the shoes you wear, you can distribute the angles of impact between two days' worth of running and thereby retard the injury potential of the extremely repetitive impacts.

You can increase the life of your running shoes and help them to protect you from overuse injuries by taking good care of the shoes. Keep them clean. When they get wet, stuff newspapers in them to help them dry and do not dry them near high temperatures, since the heat can compromise the glue that holds them together. Don't just throw them into a corner; store them flat.

Be careful to monitor wear on the soles. When the sole begins to show excessive wear, you have three choices: Put the shoes aside and purchase a new pair; extend their life by applying Shoe-Goo to the areas of wear on the soles, especially in the heel area; or have them professionally resoled (but don't do this more than once per pair, since the mid-sole will become too compressed by that point to offer much impact protection).

Running is one of the least expensive sports you can pursue. Your running shoes constitute the single largest expenditure you are likely to have, but by running on well-maintained shoes, you can avoid very expensive visits to the podiatrist or the orthopedic surgeon.

Occasionally a runner finds that the mid-sole compresses long before the outer sole wears down. If you are increasingly feeling less impact protection from the insole, it is time to invest in a new pair of shoes, even if the outer sole is still relatively intact. When you *do* find a shoe model that works for you, it may be worth your while to stockpile a half-dozen pairs in case the shoe manufacturer suddenly decides to discontinue it.

When you have amassed enough used running shoes to fill a good-size shipping box, pack them up and send them to World Shoe Relief, P.O. Box 423, Trabuco Canyon, CA 92678. They'll be reconditioned and distributed to needy youngsters. Why throw away what were $75 running shoes when they still have some mileage left in them that will be appreciated elsewhere?

Again, when dealing with running shoes, remember that less *is* more.

The Sane Way to Train

Training involves a process of Stress + Rest = Performance, which is commonly referred to as the hard/easy training principle. The hard side of the equation refers to a workout that is performed faster or longer than the average workout at your current level. The easy side refers to a training session that is done at a slow speed or at a short distance, an easy workout in an alternate aerobic sport, or even a rest day.

Both hard and easy training is important. If you only stress yourself, you'll become injured; if you only rest, you'll see no improvement.

Except for high-performance training when you're gearing up for your best marathon, I recommend taking the hard/easy method one step further to the easy side. Many weekly workouts in this book are thus based on a hard/easy/easy formula. I propose this formula not to trivialize workouts, but because overtraining will short-circuit a marathon-training program. When in doubt, do less. Overtraining typically leads to injury, which disrupts a training program and jeopardizes your future running. The object is to stay fresh and healthy, and the way to do that is to go easy while your body is recovering from the key hard workouts.

Although training principles all evolve from a few basic concepts, each runner is unique in the way his or her body responds to workouts. Some bodies are able to take a tremendous amount of hard work and in fact need what may seem to be excessive hard work in order to perform to potential. Other runners perform better on more rest and less hard work. For instance, at the height of their careers in the early 1970s, Frank Shorter was able to take on tremendous loads of training while his 1972 Olympic teammate Kenny Moore learned that he performed best using the hard/easy/easy approach. Moore's body required more recovery time than Shorter's. Yet both realized very impressive performances. In the 1972 Olympic marathon, Frank Shorter won while Kenny Moore placed fourth. During one period, Moore won the San Francisco Bay-to-Breakers race seven years in a row using a hard/easy/easy.

In most of the basic programs in this book, then, we will make use of the hard/easy/easy method of training, preferring to err on the side of undertraining rather than gamble with the dire consequences of overtraining. This also acknowledges that most of you have lives to live, jobs to do, families and friends who like to see you occasionally. The programs will use five days per week of training and two days per week of rest, and will never require more than 55 miles per week. The object of training for the marathon is to make and keep it a positive experience; embracing the hard/easy/easy formula does much to assure it will be.

To Breathe or Not to Breathe

People who have not grown up immersed in athletics tend to approach a sport determined to do everything just right, certain that there is one correct way to do everything. In particular, people who take up running and who want to train for the marathon are obsessed with doing things correctly, whether it's in their daily lives, their job, or their training.

So in spite of the fact that running is among the simplest of sports and in spite of the fact that these people have been breathing all their lives, some people feel there is a proper way to breathe that must be learned in order to run well. To some extent, their concern is well founded, because there *are* correct ways to breathe. But what people need to realize is that they are probably already doing it correctly.

At a running symposium in the late 1970s, a would-be marathoner in the audience asked Frank Shorter, "What are your feelings about breathing?"

Shorter answered, "I'm all for it."

In fact, there are only four basics to keep in mind concerning breathing.

Blow Out, Suck In

It is difficult if not impossible for two substances to occupy the same space at the same time. I hedge on that because although it is impossible for two solid objects, it is a different matter when it comes to gases. When you breathe, you are performing two functions: You are expelling or exhausting waste gas (carbon dioxide) and you are inhaling air (which contains that very precious commodity, oxygen). When a person feels the need for more oxygen, the first response is to inhale some air. Unfortunately, for efficiency's sake, that's the wrong response. Your body wants oxygen because it already has an oversupply of carbon dioxide. When you suck in oxygen, you are attempting to force it to occupy the space already occupied by two lungs full of carbon dioxide. Consequently, you severely inhibit the amount of oxygen you can take in because there is already something occupying its space. Instead of gasping in oxygen first, expel the built-up carbon dioxide, thereby making plenty of space in the lungs for the oxygen you're about to take in. Try it. Exhale carbon dioxide, inhale air.

Relax

The most valuable skill a marathoner can learn is to relax. A relaxed runner performs a comparable amount of work with less effort, thereby expanding the range the runner can cover using a specific amount of energy. It is understandable that a novice runner finds it difficult to run relaxed: Obsessions about doing everything right cause stress. As far as breathing goes, when you are running, allow yourself to breathe comfortably, primarily through the mouth (since the mouth has the ability to move much more air than the nose does). Your body will tell you by its effort how much air it needs to take in to continue the current running activity. If you are breathing too hard, are about to go anaerobic, and have 2 miles left of a workout, back off the pace, relax, and roll with it.

Belly Breathe

The more oxygen you can process in each breath, the better. The better you get at running, the more you will be able to process oxygen. But you can help yourself initially by perfecting your belly breathing. Most people already belly breathe, whether they know it or not. Unfortunately, some people shallow breathe, never using their diaphragm to guarantee a maximum expansion of the lungs. Belly breathing involves taking such deep breaths of air into the lungs that, as the lungs expand, they press against the diaphragm. When you exhale, your abdominal muscles push back against the diaphragm, which helps expel the carbon dioxide from the lungs.

Here's a simple test to see if you are already belly breathing. Find a heavy book, lie on your back on the floor, and place the book on your abdomen. Now, exaggerate your breathing. If you are belly breathing correctly, the book should rise and fall noticeably with each breath. If the book is not rising and falling, your breathing may be too shallow, which means that you are not making full use of your lungs. In that case, use the same technique to learn to belly breathe—simply lie on your back and raise and lower the book on your stomach.

It should also be noted that when you run, you should run with your back straight and shoulders back. This allows for full expansion of the lungs, which is not possible if you bend or slouch forward.

Orchestrate Your Breathing

Stay in control of your breathing—don't allow it to control you. We tend to attempt to suck in as much oxygen as our bodies are demanding for the work they are doing. What we sometimes fail to remember is that we are in control of how fast we are running. The faster we run, the more oxygen we will need to process. Unless you are specifically doing speed workouts aimed at pushing back the anaerobic threshold, run within your body's capacity to keep up with the oxygen demands of your running.

Monitor your breathing and regulate the rate of breathing your body needs. If you feel your body is about to require a bit more oxygen for an approaching hill, deliberately kick up your rate and depth of breathing a notch *before* you reach the hill so that your oxygen needs are met as they are due.

The Elements of Marathon Training

Whether you are a sub-2:09 marathoner or a rank novice runner, the four elements of training you need to juggle are the same: endurance, strength, speed, and rest. For the novice, strength and speed can wait on endurance and rest, so the equation becomes even simpler.

There is nothing mysterious about these elements of training. As you learn to listen to the signals your body sends, you will be able to customize them into a program that perfectly meshes with your strengths and weaknesses.

Endurance

Our muscles are ready, willing, and able to accommodate sustained work. The capacity for endurance in the muscles of a human being lies at the molecular level, at the mitochondria of the muscles, where glycogen has been stored in the muscle prior to exercise to fuel the muscles in their efforts. The mitochondria must be trained to "fire" more effectively and to fire longer and longer without wearying. What this firing does is contract the muscle, in much the same way that the trigger on a mousetrap fires, releasing the stored up energy of the mousetrap's spring. Even though the untrained muscle is capable of firing for short periods of time, that ability to fire time after time is quickly exhausted and the mitochondria sputter to more of a weak spasm than an efficient contraction. Endurance is built by easy, aerobic, repetitive firing of the muscles in the hard/easy or hard/easy/easy manner of training. As the repeated activity is increased, the mitochondria within the muscle gradually become more adept at effectively using fat for fuel.

Endurance training also encourages the body to develop additional collateral capillaries to deliver blood more effectively to the working muscles, including the heart. Blood contains the oxygen that the muscles need in order to function. These collateral blood capillaries significantly increase the marathoner's endurance capacity and increase the general health of the body through what could be called superoxygenation.

Rest

Rest is the one element of marathon training on which most runners come up short. For the marathoner who is not a professional runner, rest is a commodity that is usually at a premium. Yet without adequate rest, a marathoner's training is severely compromised. If the endurance workouts are not followed by adequate rest, the muscles are unable to rebuild themselves, are always working to play catch-up, are continually stressed, and are more likely to suffer injuries. Muscles that are inadequately rested can never function as well as those that are. The wise marathoner respects the complex functions that are being demanded of the in-training body and accommodates the natural rhythms of work and rest. Because rest is so important but so overlooked, the programs in this book will stress it beyond any of the other elements.

Strength

Strength in marathoning refers to the ability of a muscle to continue to function with power. The central point of the buildup of strength in the marathoner is in the quadriceps on the front of the thighs. On each stride, the quads lift the leg and throw it forward to extend the body's progress. In a long endurance event such as a marathon, the quads tire first. Once this happens, the runner's stride becomes shorter and choppier. Consequently, the runner is covering less ground with each stride and, by running less efficiently, is using more of his or her precious resources to accomplish less.

The best way to build up strength in the quads in endurance training is by doing hill work. The exaggerated lifting of the quads required to run up hills increases their capacity to lift when on a level course. While many runners fear hill training almost as much as they hate track running (perhaps because they envision a steep mountain), uphill running on a relatively gentle slope isn't painful and enables you to continue at a good tempo.

Speed

Speed obviously allows you to get your marathon over with faster and to run more efficiently. A runner will not be able to run faster in a race if he or she does not *practice* running faster. The best place to learn to do this is at a track, which also allows you to learn pacing, an essential skill in quality marathoning. Besides doing speed workouts at a track, a runner can incorporate speed into workouts by doing fartlek running (throwing speed surges into a road workout), by incorporating "burners" into regular workouts (more on these later), and/or by regularly scheduling short races into an overall workout program. If a runner builds speed skills gradually, it never becomes a painful or feared training element.

You may hear the terms *slow twitch* and *fast twitch* in reference to muscles. We all have both slow and fast twitch fibers in our muscles. The proportion of slow to fast twitch fibers is determined genetically: some of us are born with a preponderance of slow twitch fibers, which are beneficial for endurance sports, while others are genetically endowed with a good supply of fast twitch fibers, which benefits the sprinter. The marathoner must slowly develop the slow twitch muscle fibers in order to go the distance while also bringing along any fast twitch muscle fibers in order to finish the marathon faster. Incredibly, some marathoners never bother to develop the fast twitch fibers with which they are endowed because they have a mental hang-up against doing speed work. The marathoner's ultimate potential can never be truly realized until the available fast twitch fibers are developed through a regular program of speed workouts, primarily at the track. Regular speed workouts allow the marathoner to develop the fast twitch fibers to the point where the marathon distance is not merely run, but raced.

• • •

Strength and speed are not elements that must be worked on fifty-two weeks out of the year. Again, we will initially emphasize endurance and rest. As the runner evolves into a marathoner, the strength and speed elements will be worked into the overall program in specific increments.

On Becoming Faster

The runner who has ambitions to become a marathoner typically harbors two goals: to successfully complete the marathon safely and to run it quickly. The wise runner will keep those two goals in their proper sequence. Only after any would-be marathoner completes a marathon safely and is familiar with the distance should he or she turn to setting realistic goals to run a faster time.

A runner can increase speed in only three ways: (1) increase stride length, (2) increase leg speed, and (3) increase both stride length and leg speed.

Because each increased-length stride carries you farther, you'll get to the end of the marathon course faster. If you are running eight-minute miles and increase your stride by one half-inch, and all other factors remain static, you can potentially knock three minutes off your time, and a 3:29 is always more satisfying than a 3:32.

Unfortunately, many people come to running with strides (or with ideas of strides) that are long enough already. A runner who overstrides can cause injuries to the knees and hips that can short-circuit a running program within a matter of weeks.

The safer method of increasing speed is to learn to increase the rate of leg turnover, or the leg speed.

The ideal method of increasing speed is to find the optimum effective stride length for your particular body by analyzing your running style at a track using a camcorder and tripod. At the point of impact, you should be able to draw a vertical line through your ankle, the trunk of your body, and onward through your ear. Your leg should be slightly bent to accept the impact like a loaded spring or lever and should not be straight at the maximum moment of impact. *Then* begin a regular program of speed workouts designed to gradually and gently increase your leg speed by pushing your speed at shorter standard track distances—200, 400, and 800 meters—and eventually employing mile repeats.

By the time the typical person embarks upon a running program, his or her biomechanical limitations are already in place. This is not necessarily bad, however. If you have been even modestly active, your always-adaptive body will have come up with effective compromises based upon your biomechanical characteristics, and any attempt to change those characteristics could do more harm than good.

For example, in the early 1980s, Dr. Peter Cavanagh of Pennsylvania State University ran some computerized running tests on Bill Rodgers. Cavanagh found that Rodgers moved one arm in a rather inefficient way relative to the other arm. Nevertheless, after analyzing the computer information, Cavanagh advised Rodgers not to make any changes to this seemingly inefficient arm swing. The reason? Over the years Rodgers's body had made adjustments to the exaggerated arm swing, and why mess with something that was apparently working (in the two years before this test Rodgers had won twenty-two consecutive races)?

The more you run and the more you become relaxed in your running, the more likely your body will be to adapt to the process in a way that is most efficient for you. Weekly trips to the track can then serve to improve running style and speed by further refining what has been efficient for your body. The more efficient you become, the more likely the legs will be to gravitate to their own best stride length, and the more you can concentrate on increasing leg turnover to build more speed.

Running Efficiency versus VO2 Max

VO2 max is a measurement of the efficiency by which a person takes in and uses oxygen while performing a specific physical task. And for years it has been used as a measurement tool of a runner's ability to perform. VO2 max, one of the measurements taken in a fitness appraisal and stress test, is the number of milliliters of oxygen used per body weight per minute under maximum workloads. It has been theorized that, for the most part, VO2 max is genetically determined. Vigorous training can increase VO2 max only 5 to 15 percent, and it automatically *decreases* with age: about 9 percent per decade after age twenty-five for inactive persons and about 5 percent per decade in active individuals.

Scientists who like things to be nice and neat and who like to have everything fall into categories have long pushed the concept of VO2 max as a limiting factor of what an individual can accomplish in endurance sports. Some runners with relatively low VO2 max have been able to turn in sterling performances on a par with or beyond athletes who have a VO2 max as much as 15 points higher. Running efficiency, the ability to transport your body mass while expending a minimum of energy, helps explain why.

Let's briefly consider two examples:

	VO2	*Personal Marathon Best*
Gary Tuttle	82.7	2:17
Derek Clayton	69.7	2:08:34

American Gary Tuttle had what could be considered the classic runner's profile: His running style was graceful, he seemed to float above the ground, and his body fat was once measured at less than 2 percent. Australian Derek Clayton was pretty much the opposite: He was well over six feet tall, well muscled, and ran very low to the ground, his legs shuffling along the ground rather than floating above it, and his body fat was typically in the 5 to 7 percent range. Yet in spite of Clayton's inferior VO2 max (some 13 points lower than Tuttle's), he set two world records in the marathon (1967 and 1969, the latter lasting a dozen years) and ran the marathon nearly nine minutes faster than Tuttle.*

In his 1980 autobiography *Running to the Top*, Clayton explains what happened to him when he took up marathon running.

> When I started training for marathon distances, my style changed naturally. Running 20 miles a day cut down on my stride length. It also eliminated the tendency to lift my knees. Gradually, my power stride evolved into one of economy. Despite the energy-draining action of my upper body, I developed a very natural leg action I call the "Clayton shuffle." Through miles and miles of training, I honed my leg action to such a degree that I barely lifted my legs off the ground. The "Clayton shuffle" is probably the best thing that ever happened to my running. It was economical and easy on my body.

We can learn a great deal from studying elite runners like Clayton. We must learn to allow ourselves to find *our* most efficient style instead of attempting to force our bodies to adapt to a running style that we admire or idealize.

Other Aerobic Sports

Despite the number of runners who converted to the triathlon when it became popular in the early 1980s, most runners remain resistant to taking up other forms of aerobic fitness, even when they are injured and can no longer safely pursue their running.

"I tried bicycling, but it wasn't for me" is a common enough lament as a runner anxiously waits through an overuse injury caused by running. "Other aerobic sports just don't give me the same lift as running does—and bicycling takes so

*An excellent discussion of this phenonomenon appears in Dr. Tim Noakes's comprehensive book, *Lore of Running*.

much more time to gain the same benefits. And there's the bicycle itself: You have to change flat tires and the chain comes off. I got into running because it's simple."

Many people *do* get involved in running because it is so simple: You can do it virtually anywhere; you can do it at any time of the day or night; you don't need to schedule a court; you don't need to find a partner; and there is no equipment involved beyond a pair of good running shoes. And, let's face it, running takes very little talent: If you can walk, you can usually figure out how to run.

As someone who has faced his share of overuse injuries from running, however, I've found that a "retreat" to other aerobic exercise can be beneficial. During the period when I was running year-round at a relatively high level, the connecting tissue between my calf and my Achilles tendon would give out every year. The only question was whether it would be the connecting tissue of the right or left leg.

When running on my damaged leg would send spears of red pain up my leg, I bought a bicycle. I began pedaling cautiously at first, but as the leg healed I got to the point I could alternate between an easy 1-mile jog on a dirt track one day and a 10-mile bicycle ride the next.

As long as I kept my pulse up by pushing the pace, I was impressed by the quality of workout I could get from the bicycle. Therefore, when I went into training in 1989 to run the 300-mile course from Death Valley to Mount Whitney and back in midsummer, I used the bicycle for my second workout of the day; this gave my leg muscles and connecting tissue time off from the usual pounding they received. As a result, I suffered no major injuries during weeks that hovered around 200 miles of combined workouts (80–100 run/walk miles plus 120 bicycle miles), and I managed to complete the out-and-back course.

While putting in 80–120 miles a week of bicycling to complement my running, I learned that the hours on the bicycle translated to much stronger quadriceps (thighs). I was able to run faster and stronger during track tempo sessions because of the upper-leg workouts required by bicycling two or three hours straight.

Another time, when I had a twisted ankle, I found that training in a pool was beneficial. I gently ran in deep water while holding on to the side of the pool, which helped me maintain a fitness level without placing additional strain on the injured ankle.

There is also much to be said in favor of training on the stair-climbing machines. They build the legs and increase aerobic capacity without the ceaseless impact of running.

At least one session per week doing a circuit-training program, where you go from one exercise machine to the next without resting, keeping your breathing aerobic by using modest weights but high reps, is an ideal supplement to running. Jack LaLanne and other fitness gurus developed this training method in the 1930s and it is still appropriate today. Sebastian Coe, the outstanding British miler of the 1970s and 1980s, was a faithful circuit-training enthusiast, and it obviously worked well for him.

Other forms of aerobic exercise may not be as enjoyable to the experienced runner, but by incorporating them into the off-season, or when injured, they can significantly preserve and extend your career.

In several of the training programs in this book, you'll find nonrunning aerobic exercises offered as alternative workouts. Once you are well into your marathon lifestyle, you may not prefer any other type of aerobic exercise, but the complete marathoner likes to have options available—just in case.

3

Twenty Questions

> For complete cardiovascular fitness, all you need to run is
> 12 to 15 miles a week.
>
> —KENNETH H. COOPER, M.D., *Running
> Without Fear*

It is essential to a successful marathon-training program that
we have a thorough knowledge of how the human body
responds to progressive training loads.

How does my age affect my prospects of running a fast
marathon? Should I be concerned about running along roads
where automobile exhausts are heavy? Should I run in the
morning, at noon, or in the early evening? How good am I at
establishing short- and long-term goals? Does my current job
lend itself to taking on an ambitious running and marathon-
training program at this time? How close is the nearest track?

Answers to these and other questions will give you a better
idea of how a training program will fit into your life, how
quickly you can physically afford to move the program along,
and where the needed resources are situated in your community.

What is your sex and your current age?

Although it is illegal in the United States to discriminate
against people based upon sex and age, nature does discriminate.

Males have proportionately more muscle than females; females have more body fat than males. As a result, males tend to have higher VO2 max values than females and are able to run faster. The current world marathon record for men is 2:06:50 (Dinsamo), 2:21:06 for women (Kristiansen). Dinsamo's VO2 max is 80.6, Kristiansen's is 71.2. As far as age goes, as we grow older, our VO2 max and our ability to efficiently do physical work deteriorates.

Both men and women are discriminated against as far as genetics go: Elite athletes are simply more naturally endowed with all the good tools they need than the rest of us.

But remember that runners and marathoners are not required to compete head-to-head against those who are physically far superior. Within a marathon, males race against males, females run against other females, and there are numerous age-group divisions so that twenty-six-year-olds run against other twenty-six-year-olds and not against forty-six-year-olds, although many forty-six-year-olds _do_ beat twenty-six-year-olds.

Older marathoners have usually developed a refined sense of patience and pacing, essential tools of successful marathon running, and tools that are seldom found in the young.

Also, the beauty of the marathon and of running in general is that you needn't race against anyone but yourself. If you want to run the marathon merely to cover the distance, you're welcome to do that.

One of the great by-products of the marathon is that the tens of thousands of participants in the sport have radically altered the way the medical profession regards both sex and aging. Female runners have shown that they are capable of turning in some extraordinary performances at any age. One of the most incredible marathon performances I've ever seen was when Marci Trent of Anchorage, Alaska, ran the 1988 Napa Valley Marathon in 4:11:54; she was seventy years old at the time. In fact, increasing research with older runners points to the marathon lifestyle as a prime factor in retarding aging.

Your sex and your current age should be an indicator of how slowly and carefully you should embark on a basic running program, but sex and age should never be a factor in preventing you from taking up the running life—or excelling in it.

How many excess pounds are you currently carrying?

Most Americans are overfat, meaning they are carrying too much body fat for their height. We use the term *overfat* as opposed to *overweight* because the latter can be misleading. A bodybuilder such as Arnold Schwarzenegger would be considered "overweight" based upon the standard height/weight tables, even though his body fat is less than 10 percent, which is well below what is considered ideal for men. Arnold's "overweight" comes from well-developed muscle mass, and he certainly does not qualify as "overfat."

It would be valuable at this point to check your ideal weight relative to your height (See Tables 3.1 and 3.2). If you are within 7 pounds of the ideal weight for your height, you can be considered within the ideal range, and are likely not overfat.

If you are more than 7 pounds over the ideal weight, you would benefit greatly from an ongoing fitness program. You may find it slightly more difficult to progress through the running and to the marathon program simply because you will be carrying too much weight. However, if you are carrying too much body fat, you will probably see dramatic improvements relatively quickly. By contrast, while a person who is already at the ideal body weight will find it easier to run the necessary miles, the changes in body image will be less perceptible.

When I decided to return to running at age thirty in 1977, I was carrying 207 pounds on a 6-foot frame, compared to an ideal weight of 154–170. Obviously, I had my work cut out for me. Psychologically, I could not face running while weighing more than 200 pounds, so I embarked on a weight-loss program. I cut out the Roy Rogers roast beef sandwich, large fries, and chocolate milkshake at lunch and instead ate an apple and took a 2-mile walk. It took nearly two months to drop to 199 pounds, but the day I did, I began my running program: a slow lumber twice around the block. A year from the day I started running regularly, I weighed 162.

Once again, taking a photograph of yourself every six months is a good way to monitor the progress of your physical reincarnation. You can also take body measurements every month or so at strategic locations, such as the chest, waist, hips, thighs, and so on. Keep in mind that once you begin a running program geared toward the marathon, body fat will decrease and muscle will increase; muscle weighs more than fat, so merely using a bathroom scale to chart your progress may be very misleading—you may, for a time, weigh *more* than you did before you embarked on your program, thanks to the buildup of muscles.

Your current level of body fat should serve as an indicator of how fast or slowly you begin your program. If you are significantly overweight, it will be easier to keep with the program if you opt for the walking workouts whenever that's an option, at least until you drop some weight. The bones and ligaments need quite a bit of time in a training program (usually several years) before they are strengthened to the point that they will be able to bounce back from supporting excess body weight in a workout. Don't expect your body to adapt overnight. Treat it gently at first. Take the long view, begin easy, and stick with it.

There are numerous examples of people who were overfat and who, by sticking with a running/marathon-training program, managed to drop the weight and make the transition. All it takes is patience and dedication—to your training program and to yourself.

Table 3.1 Ideal Weight Range for Adult Women

Height*	Small Frame	Medium Frame	Large Frame
4'10"	92–98	96–107	104–119
4'11"	94–101	98–110	106–122
5'0"	96–104	101–113	109–125
5'1"	99–107	104–116	112–128
5'2"	102–110	107–119	115–131
5'3"	105–113	110–122	118–134
5'4"	108–116	113–126	121–138
5'5"	111–119	116–130	125–142
5'6"	114–123	120–135	129–146
5'7"	118–127	124–139	133–150
5'8"	122–131	128–143	137–154
5'9"	126–135	132–147	141–158
5'10"	130–140	136–151	145–163
5'11"	134–144	140–155	149–168
6'0"	138–148	144–159	153–173

*Wearing shoes with a 2-inch heel.

Table 3.2 Ideal Weight Range for Adult Men

Height*	Small Frame	Medium Frame	Large Frame
5'2"	112–120	118–129	126–141
5'3"	115–123	121–133	129–144
5'4"	118–126	124–136	132–148
5'5"	121–129	127–139	135–152
5'6"	124–133	130–143	138–156
5'7"	128–137	134–147	142–161
5'8"	132–141	138–152	147–166
5'9"	136–145	142–156	151–170
5'10"	140–150	146–160	155–174
5'11"	144–154	150–165	159–179
6'0"	148–158	154–170	164–184
6'1"	152–162	158–175	168–189
6'2"	156–167	162–180	173–194
6'3"	160–171	167–185	189–199
6'4"	164–175	172–190	182–204

*Wearing shoes with a 1-inch heel.

What, if any, experience do you bring to running?

The more experience you already have with running, the more of a jump you have over the novice, right?

Although one would assume that to be the case, it is not necessarily so. One who is a novice to a running/marathon program may have an advantage because he or she has no bad habits that need to be unlearned before new habits can be incorporated. In many instances, ex-runners are ex-runners because they took a wrong turn during their first try: too much training too soon, spotty training, training that was ill-founded or ill-advised, an inability to relax during the running process, persistently ignoring signs of impending injury, and so on.

In fact, overdoing it is the principal reason that people stop running. Many runners were led astray by well-meaning but ill-informed running friends who overlooked the fact that not everyone is physically created equal and therefore not everyone can—or should—train the same.

If you have no previous running experience, you have no bad memories left over from the first time around. For example, Patti Catalano of Quincy, Massachusetts, was overfat and woefully out of shape. She began running in the late 1970s to get into shape, and within a few years was a national-class road racer. She possessed genetic qualities that she had been totally unaware of until she employed them in her running.

If you are a former runner who is returning to the sport, you, too, have an advantage: You pretty much know what to expect and you have at least a rough idea of your potential. The programs in this book will no doubt be considerably gentler and easier than those you used for your first try at running, and it is possible that the slower buildup will better allow you to maximize your talents and experience.

If you are already running, and are reading this book to take the next great step into the world of marathoning, some of what you find here may reassure you that you have been on the right track with your modest running program, or may allow you to realize more benefits from less strenuous effort than you anticipated.

Each person brings a unique set of talents to a running program. Strengths in other areas, such as a talent for long-term planning, translate very nicely into marathon training and can contribute to your realizing tremendous accomplishments in the sport.

What is your resting pulse rate?

Your pulse rate, which you can feel at your wrist or at your neck, is your fitness tachometer. The pulse rate marks the beating of the human heart as it circulates oxygenated blood around the body to nourish the cells and organs while receiving used blood for reprocessing. When you become active, your heart beats more quickly to meet the needs of the working muscles, and the pulse rate rises. An increase in your pulse rate occurs when you tell your body to crawl out of bed in the morning, when you get up from a chair and walk across the room, or when you run to catch a bus. The greater the effort, the higher the pulse rate.

Under maximum workloads, such as those reached during a maximal stress test or indicated by the theoretical maximum, the human pulse rate reaches a point where the body's efficiency begins to deteriorate (among other things, aerobic activity is replaced by anaerobic). The pulse rate/tachometer is typically at idle first thing in the morning when you are still in bed. This rate is referred to as your "resting pulse rate."

The more fit you are, the lower this resting pulse rate. Some well-trained marathon runners have resting pulse rates in the thirties. What this indicates is that their hearts are extremely efficient in supplying the needs of their bodies while they are at rest. This efficiency comes in large part because the heart of the endurance athlete has been trained to pump a much larger volume of blood on each stroke, thereby allowing it to pump fewer times per minute.

The resting pulse rate is a major indicator of aerobic fitness and of general health. It is also a valuable training tool because a decrease in your resting pulse rate reflects increases in fitness, and a rise in your resting pulse rate can indicate when you are overtraining.

Additionally, by using your "maximum heart rate" against a simple set of computations you can use your "working heart rate" to gauge the severity of your regular workouts and stay within a safe range.

It would be valuable at this point to have several pulse rate figures at your fingertips. So, tomorrow morning before you get out of bed, take your resting pulse rate. To do this, lay your right index finger over the pulse on your inner left wrist, or against one of the pulse points in your neck, and count the number of beats in one minute. That number is your resting pulse rate. Fill in the number on the first line below. Try to remember to check your resting pulse rate six months from now and a year from now, and you'll be able to have a record of your progress here.

Date	Resting Pulse Rate
_____	_____
_____	_____
_____	_____

For the workouts in the early chapters this book, you will need to know your working heart rate at certain percentages of effort. This is also easy to do.

1. Begin with the number 220.
2. Subtract your age (we'll use 45). That gives us 175. This is known as your Maximum Heart Rate.
3. Calculate 50 percent, 60 percent, 70 percent, and 80 percent of your Maximum Heart Rate. (For a rate of 175, the corresponding percentages are 50 percent = 88 beats,

60 percent = 105, 70 percent = 123, and 80 percent = 140.)

Place your own rates in the spaces provided below:
My heart rate at 50 percent is _____ beats.
My heart rate at 60 percent is _____ beats.
My heart rate at 70 percent is _____ beats.
My heart rate at 80 percent is _____ beats.

These four figures will serve as the prime tachometer points for the basic training that follows—up to and including your first marathon effort.

You may wish to put these four numbers on a 3 × 5 card for easy reference and then use the card as a bookmark for this book so it's readily available.

If you have taken your stress test, you will also have a Maximum Heart Rate under laboratory conditions. It should correspond fairly accurately with 220 minus your age. Your Maximum Heart Rate is of little interest in your training toward a marathon, since in order to reach it you would have to push deeply into an anerobic effort, which doesn't get you through a marathon.

Are you injury prone or biomechanically unsound?

As mentioned before, not everyone is created equal. Some people are taller than others, some are big-boned, some are slight, some are quick, some are slow. When it comes to long-distance running, good biomechanics go a long way, while poor biomechanics make sports-medicine specialists rich.

Biomechanical considerations begin with the skeleton. Are the bones straight where they're supposed to be straight? Are they curved where expected? Are they aligned with the other bones, radiating primarily from the spine? Are the bones of good density?

Bones are held together and hinged by a variety of tissues: cartilage, ligament, tendon. Are these connecting tissues soft and properly flexible or are they dried out and stiff from lack of use or from disease?

The skeletal muscles provide power to move the skeleton and can have a profound effect upon the bony foundation. Over a period of years, a well-developed quadriceps opposed by a weak hamstring can actually contort the huge femur bone in the upper leg, throwing off the biomechanics of the entire leg, ankle, and foot. In a similar fashion, a small problem in the foot can radiate problems upward through the ankle, lower leg, and knee.

Your body is a marvelous machine, but like any machine, it can get out of alignment and can be negatively affected by misuse or disuse.

Disuse usually comes in the form of a sedentary lifestyle. Sitting down too much can deform the spine and cause hip problems, and the additional weight usually associated with a sedentary lifestyle can put undue strain on the legs and feet. Misuse can extend to accidents (a broken leg in a childhood bicycling accident), bad habits of posture (curling the same leg under you when you sit), chronic tension (a distortion of the shoulders from unrelieved stress in the neck), or disease (scoliosis).

Fortunately, your body is very adaptable. Many biomechanical peculiarities end up being accommodated by the body's willingness to make certain provisions, as we have seen with Bill Rodgers's elaborate arm swing.

Some biomechanical shortcomings do not become problems for runners until the mileage is significantly increased or until the runner begins to experiment with stride length or with undertaking major increases in speed.

In running, most biomechanical shortcomings above the waist are tolerated quite well. All you need do to verify this is to watch some film of the great Czech runner Emil Zatopek. Above the waist Zatopek was a disaster. His head would roll from side to side, his tongue sometimes lolling from his mouth; his arms would flail madly. It was actually painful to watch him run. But below the waist, where the running action really happens, he was smooth, his legs working like pistons. He remains the only athlete to win all three distance events (5,000 meters, 10,000 meters, and marathon) in one Olympics.

Many biomechanical deficiencies from the waist down are countered by wearing the proper running shoes and by paying attention to staying off particularly jarring surfaces as much as possible, especially concrete roads or sidewalks. By its very practice, long-distance running is a torturous activity involving thousands of repetitions of the same movements of the legs, each repeating the same impact to the feet, ankles, legs, and knees. The effects of these thousands of repetitions must be minimized as much as possible by wearing the correct shoes for your particular biomechanical needs, running on surfaces that are less jarring, and not running when there is an indication of impending injury.

Most biomechanical shortcomings below the hips can be diagnosed by good orthopedic surgeons, good podiatrists, and good running-shoe salespeople if they examine the wear patterns on your running shoes or watch you run.

If you feel you have some biomechanical problems, it is advisable to consult with a podiatrist who specializes in sports medicine for advice on exercises you can do to strengthen specific leg and hip functions, appliances you might be able to use in your shoes (lifts or, in more severe cases, orthotics), and particular shoe models that are designed to address your problems. It is imperative to take care of any biomechanical shortcomings as early in the game as possible because marathon training will only exacerbate the problems.

As for being injury prone, although some biomechanical problems do set certain people up for accidents or injuries, the same can be said for people who do not pay close attention to what they are doing. For example, you can go over on your ankle because a biomechanical shortcoming makes you prone to do so or simply because you were not paying attention when running off a curb. Once you have gone over on your ankle, there will be an increasing tendency to repeat the same accident because the muscles and tendons in the ankle have been stretched beyond their usual range of motion and, once stretched, seldom return to their original tone.

Many running accidents and injuries can be prevented simply by paying more attention to the condition of your running shoes, to how and where you run, and to any indications that an overuse injury is imminent. In this last case, take care to back off on your workouts. In addition, learn your own peculiarities. For instance, if your left leg is a mite shorter than the right, you might be able to avoid injuries by running on the right side of the road, while you could aggravate injuries by running on the left side of the road.

Have you quit smoking cigarettes within the last two years?

If you answered yes, you're probably concerned about the damage cigarette smoking may have done to your lungs. Actually, except for lung cancer and scar tissue on the lungs (neither of which can be reversed), the lungs have a startling ability to heal themselves—even after years of abuse from cigarette smoking. Within two years of quitting cigarette smoking, the average person enjoys nearly 100 percent use of the lungs.

A considerable number of ex-smokers and ex-substance abusers take up long-distance running and transfer their drug addiction to a running addiction. This is something that occurs when the runner feels he or she *must* get in that next run even if common sense dictates otherwise.

The addicted runner will embark on the next scheduled workout even if suffering from a nagging injury that will only worsen in the wake of the run. In essence, the addicted runner is prepared to abuse his or her body in order to get the good feeling that comes with the next run.

Some attribute this phenomenon to the fact that during an endurance exercise (and under certain other circumstances), your brain releases endorphins, which are naturally occurring opiatelike drugs. It is theorized that these endorphins are present to ameliorate discomfort and pain that can come with extended physical endeavors. (Theoretically, in prehistory, these endorphins made it more likely that a hunter could push through the pain and discomfort of a long hunt in order to catch game and put meat on the table.) In research for my 1990 book, *The Exercise Fix,* it became clear that the endorphins (and the related enkephalins) can also be stimulated by a number of other events: acupuncture, pain, stress, psychological disturbances (such as schizophrenia and depression), sexual activity, or suggestion.

This good feeling that comes to certain runners during prolonged workouts has come to be referred to as "the runner's high." Some elitist runners claim this is a fabrication, since in spite of all the miles they have put in they have never experienced it. Psychologists who have studied the runner's high feel it is unavailable to runners who run with a critical eye toward their workout, which would include those who are professionals. It isn't that the endorphins aren't pumping in the professional runner; it's just that the runner is too self-critical during his or her run to perceive the good feeling.

This feel-good result can have an addictive effect upon those who are prone or susceptible to addictions to begin with, so that a person transferring from one addiction (nicotine, cocaine, etc.) to long-distance running (endorphins, enkephalins) may be leaving the frying pan for the fire.

The typical end to a running addict's career, of course, is a major injury through which he or she can no longer force an abused body to run.

A person who is withdrawing from nicotine or other drug dependency should approach a running program cautiously and might want to limit such a program to a level well below that necessary to run a marathon.

Do you have an obsessive/compulsive personality?

Aerobic sports, with their reliance on compliance to a regular schedule, are custom-made for people with obsessive/compulsive personalities.

On the one hand, this is a real plus, because the success of a long-term running program, and especially of a marathon-training and marathon-lifestyle program, relies on what can most kindly be described as a faithfulness to purpose. Remove the regularity and consistency from a marathon program, and the entire structure collapses.

However, there is a danger that the obsessive/compulsive tendencies will undermine the effectiveness of the program by dictating that it be adhered to even in the face of exacerbating a potential injury due to overuse.

A runner who is overly obsessive/compulsive will want to fill in the workout on the page in the running log even if to do so involves limping through a workout, which in turn jeopardizes future workouts. A little of the obsessive/compulsive goes a long way in marathon training, but too much goes nowhere.

The challenge, then, is to maintain the wider view beyond today's scheduled workout. A skipped or modified workout today might allow a sore tendon to heal, while a regularly scheduled workout might push the soreness into injury. The wise marathoner knows when to run short in order to go farther.

Do you have the genuine support of your family and friends in your marathon endeavor?

Embarking on a modest (à la Ken Cooper) running program does not consume a great deal of time. To run 2 or 3 miles three or four times a week requires at most a commitment of 4 hours of the 168 hours in a week, a mere pittance when compared with the health benefits bestowed.

Training for a marathon, however, requires an ambitious commitment of time, energy, and money. As the marathon date approaches, the commitment of time increases significantly, as does the time required for recovery. Where a runner can jog through 2 miles and then mow the lawn before taking a shower, a runner training for a marathon does not typically return from a track workout of 5 repeat miles eager to take out the garbage or make supper. The more typical reaction is that he or she is going to want to be horizontal for a few hours. A marathon-training program also brings on the urge to go to bed an hour or two earlier in the evening than is normal. All of this means time is taken "away" from family and friends.

Some people who embark on a marathon-training program do so with utter disregard of how it will affect family and friends. However, not taking them into consideration is unfair. Ultimately, it's also unfair to the would-be marathoner, making him or her extremely one-dimensional. A marathon program can fit smoothly into one's life without overwhelming it.

If your family is resistant to your marathoning goals, you can avoid a huge number of conflicts down the road by using some creativity and coming up with some compromises. For instance, if you want or need your family to come along on your scheduled shorter races, pick races that are near places or events they want to attend; after the race is finished and they offer you congratulations, you can reciprocate by spending the rest of the day with them at a crafts fair, an amusement park, or at Aunt Martha's.

It's important to be creative and considerate of your family and friends during your marathoning program so you don't have to face an archenemy of running at home.

Are you a lark or an owl?

Because of circadian rhythms, different people have different peak energy times during every 24-hour period—some of us are early risers and others are night owls. Conversely, each person has a time of the day when lassitude prevails and energy is in short supply.

Therefore, it makes sense that you should try to schedule your workout at or near your peak time of day. Because a workout increases the rush of adrenaline and oxygen-carrying blood through the body, thereby reviving it and providing an energy lift, the workout can be fit into the day to both maximize the training effect and provide an energy boost for the next several hours.

For example, if your prime time for creative work is 8 A.M. until noon but you bog down by midafternoon, a workout over the lunch hour would take advantage of your prime time to maximize the quality of the workout; at the same time, turbocharged adrenaline and oxygen transport to the brain will energize you to get you efficiently through the rest of the afternoon.

On the other hand, if you have trouble crawling out of bed before 10 A.M. but come alive after dark, you might want to schedule your workout for 6 P.M.

One more thing to keep in mind is that you should avoid workouts within 2 to 3 hours of when you plan to go to sleep, since the increased flow of adrenaline may make sleep difficult.

By identifying your peak energy time of the day, you will be able to increase the quality of your workouts while also using the exercise session to augment your regular work and social functions.

What are the restraints on your time and energy due to your job?

The dictates of a job, whether it be a sales job involving extensive travel or that of a mother who spends most of her day trying to keep up with a toddler, have a tremendous impact on when, how, and even whether you can train effectively for a marathon.

Even professional runners, who have the luxury of scheduling everything else in their day around their run, sometimes have problems shoehorning in their workouts. For the average person, putting together a viable training program on top of everything else in the day requires some creative approaches.

If your workday involves the classic nine-to-five format, schedule workouts before you leave for work (if you're a lark) or before dinner in the evening (if you're an owl). Many progressive companies offer fitness-center membership and flexible lunch hours to accommodate employees who wish to pursue their fitness goals.

Salespeople who do a lot of traveling can use the arrival at a new city as an opportunity to change into running clothes and go out on a run to reconnoiter the area while also stretching the legs and getting the blood and oxygen pumping before they begin their business calls. This is especially effective if you typically drop by the hotel to freshen up before seeing clients. There's nothing like arriving at a client's office radiating fitness and the goodwill brought on by a successful workout.

Airline pilots who are also marathoners know some of the most out-of-the-way courses near every major airport in the country and overseas. Airport perimeters are perfect for long workouts.

Mothers with small children have increasingly shown their creativity by using their running as a means of transportation through an obstacle course of errands, pushing their youngsters in front of them in a Baby-Jogger (which also doubles as a cart for transporting packages home).

For those who are truly booked up for most of the day, flexibility seems to be the key word. A workout squeezed in when you begin to bog down mentally is usually a good pick-me-up that makes you more effective for the remainder of the day.

For many larks, the ideal workout is one that comes very early in the morning, when only the newspaper delivery person is about. The world is a very special—and very private—place at 5 A.M. However, on those days when it seems just plain impossible to get in a workout, you will not be the only person in the world doing so at 9 in the evening. Such a run can provide a perfect coda to a busy and/or harrowing day.

What is your VO2 max?

At one time it was believed that the VO2 max was the one factor that once and for all quantified a person's performance abilities. However, your VO2 max should not be regarded as a limiting factor. As we have seen in Chapter 2, some runners with relatively low VO2 max outperform contemporaries with significantly higher VO2 max figures.

Runners of equal VO2 max who engage in identical training can have vastly different results simply by one runner employing a more efficient style than the other. Therefore, use your VO2 max only as a yardstick in annually or biannually measuring your progress toward the marathon lifestyle.

Are you patient enough to delay your gratification?

No long-term running program, and certainly no marathon-training program, is successful if it is based upon instant gratification. In fact, it is the ideal model of delayed gratification: You build your running program to an acceptable plateau, then pick a marathon four, five, even six months down the road, and train patiently toward that distant goal.

If you are used to instant gratification, perhaps you would be better advised to train for sprint events. They, too, take training and dedication, but you can run them more often and the results are available almost instantly.

Marathoners must take the long view. (It's no coincidence that such a high incidence of well-educated people run marathons; a formal education is another form of delayed gratification.) The closest a marathon-training program comes to instant gratification is when a regular workout goes particularly well or when a shorter race scheduled as part of the training program is singularly successful.

The marathoner glories as much in the process of training as in the end results.

How available are your weekends?

A determined would-be marathoner can make effective use of a training program whatever his or her work, family, or social schedule happens to be. A training schedule can be customized to virtually any schedule if you are determined to fit it in.

The typical marathon-training schedule relies on a backbone of a long run each week. The long run is usually done on the weekend, since most people function on a five-day workweek and use the weekend for chores and leisure. Consequently it is easier and causes less strain to the training body to schedule the long run on a Saturday or Sunday. You also increase the chances that you will be able to find other runners with whom you can do part or all of your long run if you are so inclined.

Virtually any marathon-training program can be adjusted by a day or two to accommodate those who have weekdays available for the long run instead of weekends. However, it is easier to fit the training program into the typical week, thereby reserving the weekend for the long run—especially since the marathon toward which you are aiming will be held on a Saturday or Sunday (unless it's in Boston, which is run on a Monday), and the schedule will therefore dovetail much more effectively if long runs are keyed to weekends.

The process is more challenging for the would-be marathoner who must fit the long workout in during the week because of weekend commitments. It may merely require a bit more creativity and determination (two characteristics that cannot be in too much supply for any marathoner).

Does your schedule allow you to travel to races on weekends?

Most races are held on weekends, for obvious reasons.

The would-be marathoner needs to develop a fair familiarity with running in races of 5K to half-marathon distances as part of the ongoing program of building toward the first marathon.

Runners for whom the marathon is their first race line up at the starting line at a distinct disadvantage because of their unfamiliarity with prerace rituals. Fortunately, most parts of the country have one or more races available nearly every weekend. You will therefore need to make certain weekends available, and may also have to travel a ways to participate in shorter road races. Local running clubs often send carloads of their members to races in nearby cities and frequently have room for additional runners who need a ride and some companionship along the way.

How good are you at setting long-term goals and reaching the short-term rungs of the ladder along the way?

Some people find it very difficult to put together and follow through on long-term goals. Yet a successful marathon-training program demands that the runner set long-term goals and then work toward them faithfully. There are no shortcuts to success in the marathon.

If you are not particularly good at setting and sticking to long-term goals, you are not automatically excluded from the ranks of the marathoner or the long-term distance runner. You merely have to fashion a method of reaching your goal—the marathon—that will work for you.

The simplest way to do this is in terms of a ladder. If you have an apple tree where the best fruit is at the top, you can still get to them using a ladder. Each rung of the ladder brings you closer to the apples. In the same way, a person who has problems dealing with a goal sixteen weeks away can often achieve his or her aim by dealing with one rung of the imaginary ladder at a time.

*How well does your busy lifestyle
accommodate achieving quality rest?*

Of the four elements of marathon training—endurance, strength, speed, and rest—rest is the most important. The art and science of marathon training involves a constant process of breaking down the body, then resting it so that it comes back stronger than it was before. The more effectively this process works, the more likely you are to reach your goals.

Without adequate restorative rest, you may go into your next training session playing catch-up: The muscles are still broken down, without having had time to adequately recover, and then you break them down again.

Fortunately, the very act of training demands a high level of rest. The in-training marathoner feels almost blissfully tired after a satisfying workout. In fact, to be a successful marathoner, you must make space in your life for this additional rest, just as you will for additional training. You may find it necessary to cut back on some of your social commitments. Your body will be more than willing to tell you how much rest and sleep it needs to recoup from workouts. But it becomes your responsibility to your body and to your marathon-training program to listen to and find the time to satisfy those needs.

Where do you live?

In order to maximize their training year-round, and therefore increase their earning power, professional runners follow the sun. When winter comes to the Boston area, Bill Rodgers moves to Arizona to continue his training unencumbered by bad weather. Grete Waitz, Norwegian marathoning champion, also packs her bags and travels to warmer climates in order to keep training. But most of us do not have those options and are forced to modify our running efforts to fit the seasons in which we find ourselves.

Some would think of this as a limiting factor. For the amateur runner, the change in seasons acts as a natural governor on one's running, dictating down periods during which the body can rest and recuperate from its training efforts.

Runners who live in ideal climates such as Northern California often find themselves training too hard too long and racing too hard too often. They tend to end up on the injured list more often than runners in Iowa, where winter's snows force a slowdown.

For the marathoner, this cycle of forced rest followed by a buildup toward another racing season is not only natural but necessary.

It is no accident that most marathons are scheduled in the spring and fall. The ideal weather for a marathon is overcast (to minimize radiant heat), 55–65 degrees, and 50 percent humidity.

If you live in a temperate climate, allow the seasons to dictate your running load. Build your mileage as winter breaks and spring arrives, cut back in the heart/heat of the summer, and build again as autumn comes and the temperatures fall.

If you live in a climate that allows running all year, it is still advisable to follow the cycle of the temperate zones. For the average marathoner, one quality marathon in the spring and one in the fall is plenty. Don't push your body to go against nature.

As will be seen in the next chapter, a process of building and then cutting back keeps the running fresh and the body healthy. The object of a marathon lifestyle is to take advantage of its benefits, not to be its slave.

Do you live in an urban, a suburban, or a rural area?

The way you approach your marathon-training program, the way you put together your all-important long runs, will be dictated in many ways by where you live. While those who live in rural areas will find it extremely easy to design a long-run course, those living in urban areas will not. On the other hand, tracks are usually far more available in urban areas.

For long runs, would-be marathoners who live in urban

areas may have a hard time finding a course that is both varied and unencumbered by breaks in the rhythm of the run—stop lights and traffic. Fortunately, most urban areas also come equipped with parks that are ideal, such as Manhattan's Central Park, Philadelphia's Fairmount Park, or San Francisco's Golden Gate Park. Public transportation in major metropolitan areas allows an easy way to travel to park areas that aren't close at hand.

If you are pressed for time in an urban environment and can't travel to the local park to run 5 miles, you may find yourself circling the block a few dozen times. Although such courses tend to become boring, they are easily measured. Make sure that you run on asphalt and not on hard concrete sidewalks and that you round corners to minimize knee strain rather than cutting it sharp.

The suburbanite has his or her own set of challenges. Many suburban areas have long stretches of connecting roadways where there is no provision made for pedestrians. More modern suburban developments, however, often have walkways and green corridors designed into them; these allow pedestrians and cyclists pleasant connecting pathways that are safely removed from traffic.

The ideal environment for the marathoner, however, is the rural setting, where there are miles upon miles of roads uninterrupted by traffic lights. The runner always needs to be aware of vehicular traffic, especially where roads are narrow and curving. It is odd how frequently on a lonely rural road two trucks will pass each other at the exact spot you happen to be.

The runner should always attempt to run on the left side of a roadway, facing traffic, except in those instances when to do so presents hazards, such as embankments that extend through blind curves where you face the possibility of being struck by an automobile because there is no safe escape space.

Is a good track available?

No matter where you live, if you are going to be any kind of a runner, you should know the location of the nearest track (and if the nearest track is in decrepit condition, you should know the location of the nearest *good* track). "Good track" does not necessarily mean a Tartan all-weather track. It can be a sand compound, dirt, or asphalt track, but it should be one where you will be able to run unimpeded by ruts, puddles, and clumps of weeds coming up through the track surface. For the purposes of learning pace and discipline, and for honing leg speed, a track is an invaluable tool.

Many people who come to marathoning without a track background will rant and rave at its mere mention. They feel that a track flies in the face of the freedom and wanderlust that road running provides. And certainly there are some good marathoners who have never in their lives gone to a track to work out.

On the other hand, those who are most successful do have some track training. Even Bill Rodgers went to the track once a week with his Greater Boston Track Club teammates to run timed miles in the 4:25 range.

The track is an integral tool for any runner. It is not something to be feared. Find a good local track and be prepared to go there at least once a week to have some fun with your pacing and to build your leg speed.

What are the local pollution levels?

There is a certain irony in the fact that in your pursuit of fitness and health, you may end up damaging yourself more than the person who is sedentary.

This point comes home when you consider the fact that marathoners, who put out tremendous amounts of energy each week pursuing their lifestyle, do most of their workouts on the same roads clogged by automobiles, the largest single source of air pollution in the country. Invariably, since the marathoner is processing tremendous volumes of air, he or she is also processing tremendous amounts of air pollution. Naturally, the more traffic along the streets and highways you run, the more potential air pollution you'll be sucking into your lungs.

The severity of air pollution is affected by more than just the amount of traffic. If you live in an area such as Washington, D.C., which is in a natural bowl, you will find that the air pollution gets stuck inside the Beltway and is added to each day, turning the atmosphere from pale yellow to brown within a week. You can go for days at a time without enough wind to move out last week's pollution, so that the accumulated mess is merely added to on a daily basis until it becomes fairly lethal.

One positive trend is the fact that a 1970 car pumped out forty-seven times the air pollutants as does a comparable 1990 model, and some cities, among them Los Angeles, plan on increasing air-quality standards over the next decade.

In the meantime, however, the best rule of thumb is to minimize air pollutants when you exercise. Get up earlier in the morning to run—pollution levels are fairly low before the morning rush hour. Or you may want to run in the evening just after dark. If you live in an area of high air pollution, the worst time to run is near noon—the rays of the sun mutate the air pollution into a deadly brew.

If at all possible, run in park areas where the trees may have some positive effect upon the city's air pollution. In a suburban area, run away from the main commuter arteries, and in rural areas avoid running near fields where the crops have recently been sprayed.

Remember that as an athlete you are building your capacity to process oxygen to accommodate your running. Consequently, while you are running, you are moving tremendous amounts of air through your lungs—amounts that would astound a sedentary person. The more air you process through your lungs, the more volume of available pollutants you process at the same time.

4

Ground Zero

Even for the free man, life is a dangerous and difficult game. Man, the player, must train long and hard before he can move through life with the simple, certain, leisurely grace of the expert. Still, it is the only game in town.

—GEORGE A. SHEEHAN, M.D., *Dr. Sheehan on Running*

The marathon is not an event for the impetuous. A successful marathoner is patient and has developed a sense of perseverance tempered by pacing.

It is no accident that Alberto Salazar did not run his first marathon until the age of twenty-two. He was physically capable of an outstanding marathon debut years before his coach Bill Dellinger decided he was ready psychologically. Dellinger wanted Salazar to mature into the marathon, to be wise enough to run it well.

When Salazar lined up at the start of the 1980 New York City Marathon, he had an advantage most first-time marathoners do not enjoy: He had physically built to the distance over more than a decade of competitive running. His muscles and joints and ligaments had been gradually stressed to the marathon distance. He was primed in every aspect, mentally and physically.

Most of us come to marathoning later in life than Salazar. Consequently, we typically have one advantage and one disadvantage. The advantage is that we have usually successfully gone through enough of our life to have learned some basic pacing principles, so we aren't as likely to run the first 5 miles of a marathon at a 10K race pace. Our primary disadvantage is that we are not as physically trained to the marathon distance as Salazar was; our joints, tendons, and ligaments have not had the years of mileage gradually applied to them through high school and college the way his did.

Too many of us begin to run and almost immediately set our sights on the marathon instead of taking the short steps of 8K, 10K, 5-mile, and 10-mile races. However, it is essential that a potential marathoner establish a firm foundation of distance training before taking on the very ambitious marathon-training programs that follow. This chapter presents a one-month training schedule that is built upon the hard/easy/easy training method and based upon your WHR (Working Heart Rate) and modest time goals.

If you can build to and comfortably maintain this program for three consecutive months with no negative physical problems, you are ready to progress to the marathon programs presented in Part II. Or, if you merely wish to maintain a good fitness level through running, you can repeat this training schedule indefinitely. Let's review the two basic elements that drive the program.

Hard/Easy/Easy Training

You'll remember from earlier that the bodies of animals (man included) are just about the only machines that improve their function the more they are used. Your body improves when careful stress is applied. Stress the muscles of your body, then back off to allow it to repair itself; when you again apply stress, your body will be capable of more work than when you first stressed it. Stress . . . rest . . . stress . . . rest . . .

The hard/easy or hard/easy/easy method of training stresses your human machine, and the subsequent rest allows you to recover and adapt stronger.

In the programs that follow, we'll use the hard/easy/easy method of training more often than the hard/easy one.

If we were to plot the hard/easy method of training for a week it would resemble an eccentric staircase.

One-Week Schedule of Steps

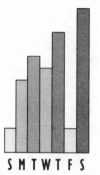

S M T W T F S

It goes up, then goes down before going up again. Extend this training theory week after week, however, and the bigger pattern begins to emerge:

Four-Week Schedule of Steps

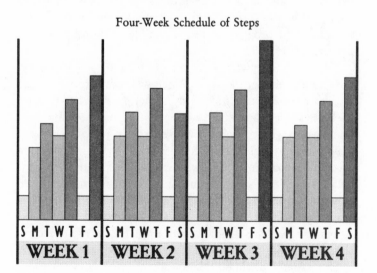

| S M T W T F S | S M T W T F S | S M T W T F S | S M T W T F S |
| WEEK 1 | WEEK 2 | WEEK 3 | WEEK 4 |

You can see that the volume of work is very gradually increasing, even though each hard workout is followed by several days of lesser effort. The last week falls back in order to allow an easy end to a four-week cycle (but it does not fall back as far as the first week began.

By this method, you are able to increase your workload while minimizing the chance of injury.

Working Heart Rate (WHR)

You'll remember that your heart rate (pulse rate) indicates the strain on your heart. In marathon training, most of your workouts are done at a relatively low range: 60 to 70 percent. The fact that your heart is lightly stressed for long periods of time accounts for the incredible cardiovascular benefits of the marathon lifestyle.

If you haven't yet determined your Working Heart Rate, turn back to pages 57–58.

The monthlong hard/easy/easy basic running foundation program features workouts based upon time and WHR, not upon time and distance. (The exception is track workouts, where your goal will be a specific distance at a specific WHR.) This allows for the program to be compatible with anyone at any age and ability.

When you begin your workout, do so by jogging gently. Do not go out the door in a flash. When you move from a resting state to an active state, your body's reaction will be to prepare itself for a strenuous effort; consequently, your breathing will immediately go anaerobic until your body realizes that you are exercising gently, at which point it will change to the more tolerable aerobic level. You will want to take your WHR just before you begin exercising and again about five minutes later. You do not need to be obsessive about hitting every number perfectly. If the workout calls for a 60 percent effort and your 60 percent WHR is 105, anything from 100 to 110 is acceptable. Eventually you'll become so acquainted with your level of effort that you will be able to estimate your WHR without taking your pulse rate. To begin with, however, take it five minutes into the workout and again at fifteen minutes and every quarter hour after that. So as not to interrupt the workout, take your WHR for ten seconds and multiply by six for a quick estimate.

If you miss a workout, *do not attempt* to make it up the next day by combining workouts. If you miss a workout, just skip it. However, if you begin to regularly skip workouts, begin the program over at a point when you feel you can remain at least 95 percent faithful to it.

If you can follow this one-month program for three months comfortably, you will be ready to proceed to Part II. If you *cannot* comfortably do it for three consecutive months, drop back and begin again until it becomes comfortable.

Your Basic Running Program

Weeks 1, 5, and 9

S   Rest day
M   20-minute run at 60% WHR
T   25-minute run at 70% WHR
W   25-minute run at 60% WHR
T   Track workout: 3 repeat miles* at 70% WHR
F   Rest day
S   Long run: 60 minutes at 60% WHR or a 10K race at 70–80% WHR

Weeks 2, 6, and 10

S   Rest day
M   25-minute run at 60% WHR
T   30-minute run at 70% WHR
W   25-minute run at 60% WHR
T   Track workout: 3 repeat miles* at 80% WHR
F   Rest day
S   Long run: 45 minutes at 60% WHR

Weeks 3, 7, and 11

S   Rest day
M   30-minute run at 60% WHR
T   40-minute run at 70% WHR
W   25-minute run at 60% WHR
T   Track workout: 4 repeat miles* at 70% WHR
F   Rest day

S Long run: 75 minutes at 60% WHR or a 10K race at 60–70% WHR

Weeks 4, 8, and 12
S Rest day
M 25-minute run at 60% WHR
T 30-minute run at 60% WHR

W 25-minute run at 60% WHR
T Track workout: 3 repeat miles* at 70% WHR
F Rest day
S Long run: 60 minutes at 60% WHR

(Note: The long workout on Saturday and Sunday's "rest" day can be switched in order to accommodate family obligations or any 5K or 10K races being substituted for the long workout.)

Your Training Journal

The habit of maintaining a training journal is a vital one to get into no matter what form of exercise you enjoy. It is an invaluable record of your program that allows you to see what did and did not work for you during your training.

Training journals come in many shapes and sizes; the form I like to use, which is shown on page 000, is a simple one set up to cover one week on two pages. If you like this format, make copies of these pages and keep them in a three-ring binder. Here's what I do.

My Working Heart Rate   This is a convenient way of keeping your WHR percentages/pulse rates handy. At each birthday, however, you should refigure the numbers in order to stay accurate.

---

*When doing your track workouts, jog one mile as a warm-up. Walk one lap between timed miles, and walk one-half mile as a cool-down following your track workout.

Resting Pulse Rate   Take your pulse rate each morning before you get out of bed.

Scheduled Workout (or Rest)   Record in this block the workout you were scheduled to do for this day.

Scheduled Working Heart Rate   This box allows you to transfer from the workout schedule the WHR you should use as your tachometer during the workout.

Weather Conditions   Weather conditions, especially extreme ones, can have an effect upon your workout. You do not need to make elaborate notes here, but temperature, humidity, precipitation, and wind conditions may be worthy of note.

Cool-Down   This block acts as a reminder. Ideally, to cool down, you should walk ¼ mile for each 5 miles you ran.

Upper-Body Workouts   You needn't worry about this block at first. We'll get more into the benefits of an upper-body workout as you move further into the marathon-training schedules (see pages 128–29).

Notes/Comments   This is where you detail how your scheduled workout went. Did you feel you could have run another 2 miles at the end of your workout? Were the weather conditions particularly brutal? Did you try a new course? Did the workout begin badly but halfway through turn around and end up positively? If you find you have a great deal to jot down, turn the page over and continue on the back.

Keeping a journal can be one of the most beneficial aspects of your training program. All that happens to you in your ongoing running program can be tracked back to what you have done before in building toward a successful race. The journal provides an ongoing history of yourself as a runner— and ultimately as a marathoner.

My Working Heart Rate	WEEK OF _____ TO _____, 199__		
60% = __ bpm 70% = __ bpm 80% = __ bpm 90% = __ bpm	SUNDAY	MONDAY	TUESDAY
Resting Pulse Rate	____ bpm	____ bpm	____ bpm
Scheduled Workout (or Rest)			
Scheduled Workout Working Heart Rate	____%	____%	____%
Weather Conditions			
Cool-Down	[ ] Yes [ ] No	[ ] Yes [ ] No	[ ] Yes [ ] No
Upper Body Workouts	__ Sit-ups __ Push-ups __ Arm curls __ Chest openers	__ Sit-ups __ Push-ups __ Arm curls __ Chest openers	__ Sit-ups __ Push-ups __ Arm curls __ Chest openers
Notes/ Comments			

WEDNESDAY	THURSDAY	FRIDAY	SATURDAY
____ bpm	____ bpm	____ bpm	____ bpm
____%	____%	____%	____%
[ ] Yes [ ] No	[ ] Yes [ ] No	[ ] Yes [ ] No	[ ] Yes [ ] No
__ Sit-ups __ Push-ups __ Arm curls __ Chest openers	__ Sit-ups __ Push-ups __ Arm curls __ Chest openers	__ Sit-ups __ Push-ups __ Arm curls __ Chest openers	__ Sit-ups __ Push-ups __ Arm curls __ Chest openers

5

Short Takes

> The difference between the mile and the marathon is the difference between burning your finger with a match and being slowly roasted over hot coals.
>
> —HAL HIGDON, *On the Run from Dogs and People*

As I've mentioned earlier, a startling number of people who enter a marathon without ever having run in a race before fail to reach their goal, and of those who do, few run another step. There are two major reasons that the first marathon may mark the end of a running career.

First, novices don't understand how much the marathon is a unique event—one with its own language, customs, and protocol. Running in some shorter races first won't teach you everything you need to know, but chances are you won't then be overwhelmed to the point that running 26 miles takes second place to finding the starting line.

Second, the starting line has plenty of its own potential pitfalls. There's an air of excitement around the start area on marathon day, and many first-timers get swept up in it, so that, once the gun sounds, they get sucked into going out too quickly and expend too much energy too soon. Those charged moments before the race begins can be so confusing that the novice's best-laid plans are forgotten (or not remembered until the 5-mile point, when it's too late). In addition, many beginners line up too far forward at the start line (which not only reinforces any tendency to go out quickly but can also impede the faster runners behind).

I cannot overemphasize how much the world of the road race must become second nature before the novice racer can feel comfortable amid the seeming chaos.

Like anything else, the road-racing world is easier to learn by starting with the basics. And the basics in this case are best learned in a small, low-key, local 5K or 10K race. Arrive at least forty-five minutes before the start if you have yet to pick up your bib number or at least thirty minutes before if it was mailed. Mingle a bit, get a feel for the starting area so you know in advance where the *starting line* is located, warm up by jogging five to ten minutes, do a little stretching, and then do a few quick strides to loosen up the large muscles in the legs.

With ten minutes to go, gravitate toward the spot where you wish to line up. If you are uncertain, ask the runners around you what minute-per-mile pace they plan to run. Runners are generally helpful to the novice. However, don't ask them questions requiring detailed answers twenty seconds before the starting gun.

If the race for which you are lining up is your first, and you are not capable of holding a five-minute-per-mile pace, it is usually customary to line up at the back of the pack and run the race at a comfortable, nearly jogging pace. In this way, you can get a feel for how the race unfolds and you will invariably pass some runners as the race progresses, which is always an uplifting experience.

In addition, 5K and 10K races can both act as your long workout on alternate weekends and provide a second speed workout.

The more comfortable you can become running shorter races (and you don't need to go beyond a 10K until you advance to weeks sixteen to twenty in your marathon-training program), the more relaxed you will be when lining up at a full marathon. And the more confident of your environment and the more relaxed you can be at the starting line, the better you will feel when you have 3 miles to go in the race.

You'll also meet other runners of similar interests and abilities. If they live nearby, they may be willing to join you on your longer workouts, which can make workouts fun. Talking to veteran road racers is a great way to pick up advice on training and on other races.

Five Rules of Easing into the Road-Racing Scene

1. Begin by running races close to home. This saves you time and money. Many local newspapers carry a list of upcoming races, and local running clubs are a tremendous source of information.

2. Once again, when it's appropriate, use the race as your weekend long run.

3. Begin with short events, such as the very popular _5K and the standard 10K._ Don't move up to 10-milers, 20Ks, or half-marathons at this point. You'll find out how to integrate races longer than the 10K into your marathon-training program later.

4. When you cross the finish line, do not immediately stop. If you stop immediately after strenuous exercise, you send mixed signals to your heart, and its response can be physically dangerous to you. Doctors at Harvard and Tufts universities in Boston conducted studies of healthy men between ages twenty-two and thirty-five and came to some startling conclusions about the importance of the cool-down phase of exercise. "The worst possible strategy for exercise cessation would be to have the patient abruptly stop exercising and stand [still]," the doctors concluded. "The best strategy would be for the workload to be diminished gradually." After you cross the finish line of a 5K race, walk a quarter mile, gradually slowing. Once again, the rule of thumb is for each 5 miles raced, walk a quarter mile.

5. Do not overrace. A 10K every other weekend at this point is enough. Too much racing can—and usually will—

cause staleness and/or injury. Your weekend workouts should be based on the hard/easy theory of training, just as your entire program is: If you race one weekend, do your long workout the next weekend at a slow, steady pace.

Shorter races are an excellent tool for fortifying and rounding out your training program, but use them sparingly.

II

The Training Blueprint

6

Pick Your Race Carefully

> The marathon, like most things worth doing, offers risks and rewards. Because it gives a chance to go beyond usual boundaries—and at least an equal possibility of failing—the race both attracts and frightens runners.
>
> —JOE HENDERSON, *The Complete Marathoner*

Before the running revolution in this country, a runner who wished to enter a marathon had the choice of roughly a dozen races. Today, with more than two hundred marathons offered annually in the United States alone, you have any number of options in picking a marathon that meshes with your life and then building a running program toward it.

Marathons come in all sizes and styles: from mega-marathons such as New York, Los Angeles, and Boston, to small, intimate, and out-of-the-way races, such as the Equinox in Fairbanks, Alaska, the Tupelo in Mississippi, and the Big Sur along California's magnificent Pacific Coast Highway. There are also marathons at virtually every altitude, from the nose-bleed Pike's Peak "Marathon" to the relatively flat Jacksonville Marathon in Florida.

When picking a marathon for your first—or for your best—consider these ten factors:

1. Major versus Minor

Are you interested in a marathon that is huge and generates a lot of hype, one in which you can simultaneously become lost in the crowd while feeding off the spectacle? Or are you interested in an out-of-the-way marathon with a relatively small field and inspiring scenery to help you through your first or best effort? A pair of marathons held two weeks apart illustrate the world of difference.

For some runners, the New York City Marathon is the logical choice because there is a certain electricity that emanates from nearly 30,000 runners and 2 million spectators that turn this marathon into a block-by-block party. Of course, you do tend to get lost in the crowd, the expedition to New York City is expensive, and if you hit a bad patch around 18 miles, running through Harlem isn't likely to do much to lift your spirits and get you back on pace. And for some, the hoopla and the sensory overload is the last thing they need for concentrating on keeping to a planned pace. In addition, it seems to take forever to reach the starting line at such a mega-marathon.

At the other extreme, the giant redwood trees around Weott, California, instill a sense of calm and the Six Rivers Running Club keeps the Humboldt Redwoods Marathon very low key. You aren't likely to expend valuable energy as you line up for this combined half-marathon and marathon. On the other hand, when more than three-quarters of the field turns off to run toward the half-marathon finish while you head back into the redwood groves with 13 miles left to run, you can suddenly feel very alone.

The important thing is to pick a marathon that you feel will complement your personality by providing an environment in which you will feel most comfortable and inspired.

2. Urban versus Rural

The primary considerations in picking urban versus rural marathons centers not on the hype or the crowds but more on the character of the course. Once again, this choice comes down to your personality. You may be more comfortable with an urban environment if that is the area in which you do most of your training. Conversely, you may want a change of scenery. Some people are comforted by the rows after rows of buildings, while others feel closed in and trapped. By the same token, the urban runner may feel cast adrift running along the bucolic Silverado Trail, scene of the Napa Valley Marathon.

Urban events usually fall into the category of major marathons—large fields, large crowds of spectators, and lots of hype. But this isn't always true—for instance, maybe because of the number of running events held each year in the Bay Area, the San Francisco Marathon has never grown to the size of Boston or New York.

If you favor both urban and rural settings, a number of urban marathons (City of San Francisco, Grandma's, City of Pittsburgh) wind through city parks and thus give you a bit of both.

3. Hot versus Cold

For most marathoners, the ideal temperature is neither hot nor cold, which is why most marathons are scheduled for spring and fall. However, some runners have found that they run well in more extreme temperatures. Frank Shorter, for instance, does fairly well in hot weather, which contributed to his winning the 1972 Olympic marathon (traditionally held under very warm conditions); at the other extreme, Bill Rodgers is notoriously bad in heat, although by running conservatively, he was able to win the rather warm New York City Marathon of 1979.

The running experience you bring to this point—especially your response to a variety of climatic conditions you faced in training and racing to date—should have established your comfort zone as far as running and racing are concerned. If you are one of those extremists who are comfortable in very cold or very hot conditions, you can compete at a high level in races where other runners with a narrower comfort zone will crumble.

Cold-weather specialists should consider two races held each January: the Englewood Reserve Marathon in Englewood, Ohio, and the Great Valley Marathon in Chambersburg, Pennsylvania.

On the hot end of the spectrum, the Grandfather Mountain Marathon in Boone, North Carolina, is held in July and the Rainbow Marathon in Flushing Meadows Park in Queens, New York, takes place in August.

Considering the number and variety of marathons offered in the United States these days, you should be able to find one that's ideal for your perceived comfort zone.

4. Hills, Rolling, or Flat

At first consideration, a flat marathon would seem to be the ideal for maximizing performance. After all, running up hills, even small ones, requires a certain amount of energy expenditure.

Ironically, for most marathoners, flat is not always fast. A course that is perfectly flat tends to use and reuse the same muscles over and over in the same limited range of motion, which inexorably tires these muscles so that by the time the marathoner reaches 18 or 20 miles the leg muscles are sore and dead.

A course that is gently rolling is much more runner-friendly. The change in angle of attack on the runner's legs allows them to stay fresh longer because the major leg muscles are not limited in their range of motion. On the occasional downhills, the runner can even stretch out the leg muscles a bit, thereby offering at least a modicum of massaging action that will help the legs stay fresh longer.

Of course, the more significant hills a marathon course features, the more challenging and difficult it is. The Big Sur Marathon along California's rugged coast draws thousands of runners for the scenery but not for the ease of the course; between miles 10 and 12, the course climbs 500 feet. The scenery from the top of the climb is breathtaking, but so is the effort required to get there.

Although the Boston Marathon is an overall downhill course (especially during the first 5 and last 6 miles), the infamous Newton Hills (a series of three hills) arrive at mile 18.

For those who thrive on challenge, the Pike's Peak Marathon is the ultimate hill-climbing race, which gives it its famed position as the mother of all marathons.

If you find that you do well on a hilly or rolling course, search one out for your first marathon. Go with your strengths and avoid the pitfalls of the seemingly easy flat courses.

5. Ability to Train Properly

As previously noted, scheduling a twenty-week training program on top of your already busy life can be stressful. And just as the length and severity of the workouts increase and you find your body pleading to go to bed a half hour to an hour earlier than usual, it sometimes happens that a major family or work crisis rears its ugly head.

If your life during the twenty weeks you plan to train toward your marathon promises to be hectic and chaotic, make sure you enter a local, low-key marathon. If your training schedule is then disrupted, you'll feel less obliged to force yourself to run the marathon because you have not invested $1,000 in plane tickets.

If your training is severely interrupted and you face going into the marathon undertrained, you can still salvage a valuable experience by lining up for the low-key, local marathon. Instead of going the distance, use the race as a long workout and plan on dropping out at a convenient spot—say mile 18 or 20. By doing that, you can still get a good, but not exasperating or painful, 20-mile performance from your weeks of training; just as important, you will have gained the experience of running in a marathon field. Two months before my first marathon effort in 1978, I entered a local club marathon that consisted of five laps of a 5-mile course. I dropped out after 15 miles with a good workout under my belt and the experience of running in a marathon field. This made me much more comfortable at the starting line of my planned first marathon.

6. Travel/Time/Time Zones

Another consideration when choosing a marathon is the amount of travel required to get there, and also the time zones that must be made up once you arrive.

The simpler you can make your plans for travel to and from your first marathon, the less exhausting the experience will be and the quicker you'll bounce back to begin planning for your next one. Of course, some people travel better than others. If you are a person who is used to travel because of your business, planning your first marathon in New York City while you live in Hawaii may be a breeze. But for the person who does not travel a lot, a marathon that's a 90-mile drive from home may be a major undertaking and a physical and mental drain.

Give yourself every advantage you can for your first marathon. If you know that you travel badly, pick a more local race for your first effort, or arrive several days in advance so that you can settle in a bit before the race. You can always build toward one of the mega-marathons—New York, Chicago, or Los Angeles—further along your marathon career.

If you do plan to cross the country for your first marathon, pay the extra $20 for a direct flight instead of taking one that changes in Dallas or Chicago; it's worth the peace of mind to get the direct flight and keep things uncomplicated.

If you are planning to cross time zones, the rule of thumb is that it takes one full day to adjust to each hour of change—or else don't bother adjusting at all. If you are flying from Los Angeles to run the New York City Marathon, you should plan to arrive two to three days in advance. Three days will allow you to adjust to the changes in time zones, while arriving as close to the marathon start time as possible is, according to experienced travelers, a way of shortchanging the time differences. Of course, at some point your body will demand retribution, but hopefully it won't come at the 23-mile mark.

In order to prevent a catastrophe if the airline loses your baggage, carry your race outfit and shoes on the plane as carry-on luggage. By using a flexible athletic bag for this purpose, you can efficiently stow it in your baggage on the return trip.

By doing a little research into the options with your travel agent before you make your commitment and begin your training program, travel stress can be minimized and you can concentrate on the enjoyable aspects of the experience.

7. Combine Your Race with a Business Trip or Vacation

If you are a fledgling marathoner and travel regularly as part of your job, it may be possible to schedule your first marathon around a business trip that can be planned well in advance (e.g., an annual convention or conference). If you go this route, try to get your business done *before* the marathon. You'll want to recuperate after the race rather than work.

The same type of planning can be done to combine a marathon in a distant city with a family vacation. In this instance, however, the marathon should be scheduled for the beginning of the vacation so that you can get it out of the way without your vacation tiring you out so much that you are exhausted on race day.

The ability to combine your first marathon with a business

trip or family vacation significantly increases your options, from both a time and expense standpoint, since you can do double duty on one dime.

8. The Expense of Travel

The choice of which marathon to run can be limited by money. Expenses *can* be cut by going to the marathon with a running partner and thereby sharing at least hotel expenses.

Certainly rural marathons are much less expensive than urban events. Some rural marathons often send out lists of nearby campgrounds or even offer a location where runners can bring a sleeping bag and sleep with a bunch of other runners in a barrackslike setting for $5 a night. Typically, there is also an inexpensive carbo-loading pasta dinner the night before at the local fire company or some similar building.

To put the range of expenses into their proper perspective, at a race such as the New York City Marathon, your entry fee may well be the least of your expenses, while at a race such as the Humboldt Redwoods Marathon in Northern California, the entry fee will probably be your single largest expense.

No matter what your finances, among the more than 250 marathons per year in the United States, you should be able to find one that's right for you.

9. Type of Course

There are three basic types of running courses: point to point, out and back, and loop. Your preference for a specific type of course should affect which marathon you pick as your first.

Point to Point   Many of the largest marathons (New York, Boston) are point-to-point courses, as are some of the most scenic (Napa, Big Sur). The benefit of this type of course is that you never see the same scenery twice. The drawbacks are that your sweats and other gear must be transported from the start to the finish in some manner, and you must usually take a bus or some other transportation to the starting line. To some purists, a point to point is not a legal marathon, because there can be an overall altitude loss and runners on such a course can be wind-aided if they run on a day when there is a tailwind.

Out and Back   A simple out-and-back course runs out 13.1 miles and then reverses itself. On a double out and back, such as the Avenue of the Giants Marathon in Northern California, you run out 7 miles, turn around, then run 6 miles in another direction, and then back. There are other variations. The benefit of such a course is that you can park your car at the starting line and it is at the finish line when you are through, so you are assured your sweats and other clothes will be waiting for you; an out-and-back course looks different on the way back than it did on the way out, so it seems as though you are traversing different territory; the course is accepted by purists as a legal course because all altitude losses are equaled by altitude gains, and if there is a tailwind on the way out, it is neutralized by a headwind on the way back. However, even if the course looks different on the way back, it's still the same course you went out on, and if you're having a bad time at mile 23, you don't necessarily want to recall how good you felt at that same point when it was mile 3, seemingly half a dozen hours ago.

Loop   The loop course can be anything from a 26.2-mile loop through rolling countryside to twenty-six loops of a 1-mile course in Central Park. Here, too, you can park your car at the starting line and it will be at the finish when you are through, as will be your clothes. The loop course is accepted by purists because all altitude losses are offset by equal altitude gains, and the wind factor will also be neutralized. On a "pure" (single-loop) 26.2-mile loop course, you pass new territory until you come in sight of the finish line. The only drawback to a loop course comes when multiple loops are used to equal a full marathon, which periodically places you within sight of the finish line when you might have another 13.1-mile loop to go. My least favorite variation used to be the Silver State Marathon (just north of Carson City, Nevada): besides being in the high desert (5,000-foot elevation), the course used an 18-mile loop around Washoe Lake and then sent runners on an additional 8-mile loop into the hills above the lake after allowing the runner to literally smell the finish line as one loop ended and the other began.

By learning, during your basic training and your racing on shorter courses, which type of course you prefer, you can give yourself a marked psychological advantage on the day of the race (and on race day, you need every advantage you can get).

10. Expectations/Amenities

Your choice of a first marathon site can also be dictated by expectations beyond the type of course or the time of year the event is run. It can just as easily be dictated by the amenities offered—or by the amenities *not* offered.

If you are used to traveling first class and you enjoy fancy hotels and room service, your choice of a marathon will probably revolve around those offered in urban areas, where the amenities are extensive—but so is the bill.

On the other hand, if you spend twenty weeks of training in the urban setting where you live, you may be looking forward to renting a little cabin in the woods and getting away from it all for the week leading up to a marathon.

Perhaps you want the rural setting but you still want the amenities. The Big Sur Marathon offers a campground under the redwoods at one end, and the chic town of Carmel at the other—the best of both worlds.

Narrowing Down the Field

With more than 250 American and Canadian marathons from which to pick, your choices are far from limited. Use the checklist below to better decide on what you are looking for in a first marathon; then, using that information, peruse the information presented for U.S. and Canadian marathons in Appendix I.

1. [ ] Major/huge
   [ ] Intermediate/average
   [ ] Small/low-key
2. [ ] Urban
   [ ] Urban/suburban
   [ ] Suburban
   [ ] Suburban/rural
   [ ] Rural
3. [ ] Hot: summer
   [ ] Cold: winter
   [ ] Mild: spring, autumn
4. [ ] Hills
   [ ] Rolling
   [ ] Flat
5. [ ] Far away, bucolic
   [ ] Far away, frenetic
   [ ] Local, bucolic
   [ ] Local, frenetic
6. [ ] Great amounts of travel
   [ ] Modest travel
   [ ] Little travel
   [ ] Same time zone
   [ ] One time zone away
   [ ] Two time zones away
   [ ] Three time zones away
   [ ] More than three time zones away
7. [ ] Combine with work travel
   [ ] Combine with vacation travel
8. [ ] On the cheap: under $100
   [ ] Moderate: $100–400
   [ ] Expensive: $400 +
9. [ ] Point to point
   [ ] Out and back
   [ ] Loop
10. [ ] Low expectations/amenities
    [ ] Modest expectations/amenities
    [ ] Moderate expectations/amenities
    [ ] Great expectations

7

Your First Goal: To Finish Safely

> Anything to which one totally commits betrays the deepest attitudes and convictions. The inevitable difficulties one encounters in training for a marathon—the long stretch of roadway and the intense effort expended to complete the course—flush to the surface true feelings, true desires, true faces.
>
> —JIM SHAPIRO, *On the Road: The Marathon*

If you are running a marathon only to get a feel for what it's like to run *in* a marathon, it's senseless to line up at the starting line. For the first-time marathoner, finishing safely should be the first priority. There is little sense of putting in sixteen to twenty weeks of training if you have not in the process maximized your chances of completing the distance.

The most important thing to do is to run well within your abilities, conserving a good portion of your energies for the challenging final 10K. "Run within your abilities" means to pace yourself properly, to hold your enthusiasm in check (to allow it to run wild will get you into trouble), and to call upon your reserves at the appropriate time.

Keeping this in mind almost guarantees success to both the amateur marathoner and the professional runner. Neither can run beyond his or her training. The body can perform only to the extent that it was trained to perform.

The first-timer's *career* as a marathoner is almost always determined by the taste that first race leaves in the mouth. If the first was hard work but a satisfying experience, you are likely to come back for more. If, on the other hand, the experience was horrendous, you almost immediately become an ex-marathoner. There are a million ways to turn a marathon into a horrendous experience and only a handful of ways to make it successful and memorable. The fact that sixteen or twenty weeks of hard work comes down to walking such a high wire is what makes the challenge so alluring.

Pace

Pacing is the most important tool to a successful marathon performance, whether it's your first marathon or your fiftieth. That pace is determined by your 10K performances. If your best 10K performance within the past six months is under forty minutes, you are prepared to jump into the sixteen-week marathon-training schedule. If your best 10K performance is over forty minutes, use the twenty-week marathon-training schedule, which allows you to more thoroughly build your strength through hill workouts and your speed through track workouts. Once you have embarked upon your training schedule, your best subsequent 10K performance will determine your marathon race pace and will also be used to set a pace for your long training runs and for your mile repeats at the track.

Key 10K races or time trials are built into both of the training schedules that follow.

Hill Workouts and Track Workouts

Even though hill and track workouts are integral parts of a well-rounded program, both suffer from bad press. Runners associate track workouts with the archaic "sprint and up-chuck" philosophy of training. Hill workouts suffer from the same misplaced mentality: the image of some poor masochist struggling up a 6-mile hill that a four-wheel-drive truck would give up on.

When they are used carefully and well, the track and the hills make the would-be marathoner well rounded and prepared to more easily handle the challenge of the marathon distance.

Repeat miles at the track should be done at a speed that keeps them comfortable and that does not fill the runner with dread of the next scheduled mile. Repeat miles should be done based upon Working Heart Rate, as listed in the sixteen- and twenty-week schedules.

Unless you've picked the Pike's Peak Marathon as your first effort, hill workouts should be done only on long hills with gentle grades (3 to 5 percent); this way you can maintain a strong, steady pace. The uphill portion of a hill workout builds leg and cardiovascular strength while the downhill part increases leg speed and improves stride efficiency. If you feel punished during a hill workout, you are using a hill that is too steep or you are attacking it too vigorously.

*The Sixteen-Week Marathon-Training Program**
For Sub-Forty-Minute 10K

Week 1

S   Rest day
M   4-mile run at 60% WHR
T   1-mile jog, 2 hill miles at 70% WHR, 1-mile jog
W   3-mile run at 60% WHR
T   Track: 4 repeat miles at 70% WHR
F   Rest day
S   10K race

Week 2

S   Rest day
M   5-mile run at 60% WHR
T   1-mile jog, 2 hill miles at 80% WHR, 1-mile jog
W   3-mile run at 60% WHR
T   Track: 4 repeat miles at 80% WHR
F   Rest day
S   10-mile run at 70% WHR

Week 3

S   Rest day
M   5-mile run at 60% WHR
T   1-mile jog, 3 hill miles at 70% WHR, 1-mile jog
W   3-mile run at 60% WHR

*See the notes on page 110.

T   Track: 4 repeat miles at 80% WHR
F   Rest day
S   8- to 9-mile run at 80% WHR or 10K race

Week 4

S   Rest day
M   4-mile run at 60% WHR
T   1-mile jog, 2 hill miles at 70% WHR, 1-mile jog
W   3-mile run at 60% WHR
T   Track: 3 repeat miles at 70% WHR
F   Rest day
S   12-mile run at 70% WHR

Week 5

S   Rest day
M   5-mile run at 60% WHR
T   1-mile jog, 3 hill miles at 70% WHR, 1-mile jog
W   4-mile run at 60% WHR
T   Track: 4 repeat miles at 70% WHR
F   Rest day
S   10K race

Week 6

S   Rest day
M   5-mile run at 60% WHR
T   1-mile jog, 3 hill miles at 80% WHR, 1-mile jog
W   4-mile run at 60% WHR
T   Track: 4 repeat miles at 80% WHR
F   Rest day
S   14-mile run at 70% WHR

Week 7

S   Rest day
M   5-mile run at 70% WHR

T   1-mile jog, 4 hill miles at 70% WHR, 1-mile jog
W   4-mile run at 60% WHR
T   Track: 5 repeat miles at 70% WHR
F   Rest day
S   10- to 11-mile run at 80% WHR

Week 8

S   Rest day
M   4-mile run at 60% WHR
T   1-mile jog, 3 hill miles at 70% WHR, 1-mile jog
W   4-mile run at 60% WHR
T   Track: 4 repeat miles at 70% WHR
F   Rest day
S   15-mile run at 70% WHR

Week 9

S   Rest day
M   5-mile run at 60% WHR
T   8-mile run at 70% WHR
W   4-mile run at 60% WHR
T   Track: 5 repeat miles at 70% WHR
F   Rest day
S   10K race plus a 10K recovery jog

Week 10

S   Rest day
M   5-mile run at 70% WHR
T   1-mile jog, 4 hill miles at 80% WHR, 1-mile jog
W   4-mile run at 60% WHR
T   Track: 5 repeat miles at 70% WHR

F   Rest day
S   16-mile run at 70% WHR

Week 11

S   Rest day
M   6-mile run at 60% WHR
T   8-mile run at 70% WHR
W   4-mile run at 70% WHR
T   Track: 5 repeat miles at 80% WHR
F   Rest day
S   11- to 13-mile run at 70 to 80% WHR

Week 12

S   Rest day
M   5-mile run at 60% WHR
T   1-mile jog, 4 hill miles at 70% WHR, 1-mile jog
W   4-mile run at 60% WHR
T   Track: 4 repeat miles at 70% WHR
F   Rest day
S   18-mile run at 70% WHR

Week 13

S   Rest day
M   6-mile run at 60% WHR
T   10-mile run at 80% WHR
W   5-mile run at 70% WHR
T   Track: 5 repeat miles at 80% WHR

F   Rest day
S   13.1-mile time trial

Week 14

S   Rest day
M   6-mile run at 60% WHR
T   1-mile jog, 5 hill miles at 70% WHR, 1-mile jog
W   5-mile run at 70% WHR
T   Track: 5 repeat miles at 70% WHR
F   Rest day
S   20-mile run at 70% WHR

Week 15

S   Rest day
M   5-mile run at 60% WHR
T   6-mile run at 60% WHR
W   4-mile run at 70% WHR
T   Track: 2 repeat miles at 80% WHR
F   Rest day
S   10- to 12-mile run at 70% WHR

Week 16

S   Rest day
M   4-mile run at 60% WHR
T   2-mile run at 60% WHR
W   3-mile run at 70% WHR
T   Rest day
F   Rest day
S   Rest day or 2-mile jog
S   YOUR MARATHON!

The Twenty-Week Marathon-Training Program*
For a Forty-Minute-Plus 10K

Week 1

S Rest day
M 3-mile run at 60% WHR
T 1-mile jog, 1 hill mile at 70% WHR, 1-mile jog
W 3-mile run at 60% WHR
T Track: 2 repeat miles at 70% WHR
F Rest day
S 10K race

Week 2

S Rest day
M 3-mile run at 60% WHR
T 4-mile run at 70% WHR
W 3-mile run at 60% WHR
T Track: 2 repeat miles at 70% WHR
F Rest day
S 10-mile run at 70% WHR

Week 3

S Rest day
M 4-mile run at 60% WHR
T 1-mile jog, 1 hill mile at 80% WHR, 1-mile jog
W 4-mile run at 60% WHR
T Track: 2 repeat miles at 80% WHR
F Rest day
S 8-mile run at 70% WHR or 10K race

Week 4

S Rest day
M 3-mile run at 60% WHR
T 4-mile run at 70% WHR
W 3-mile run at 60% WHR
T Track: 1 repeat mile at 70% WHR
F Rest day
S 12-mile run at 70% WHR

Week 5

S Rest day
M 4-mile run at 60% WHR
T 1-mile jog, 2 hill miles at 70% WHR, 1-mile jog
W 3-mile run at 60% WHR
T Track: 3 repeat miles at 70% WHR
F Rest day
S 10K race plus 5K jog

Week 6

S Rest day
M 5-mile run at 60% WHR
T 1-mile jog, 2 hill miles at 80% WHR, 1-mile jog
W 3-mile run at 60% WHR
T Track: 3 repeat miles at 80% WHR
F Rest day
S 14-mile run at 70% WHR

Week 7

S Rest day
M 5-mile run at 60% WHR
T 1-mile jog, 3 hill miles at 70% WHR, 1-mile jog
W 3-mile run at 60% WHR
T Track: 4 repeat miles at 80% WHR

*See the notes on page 110.

F   Rest day
S   8- to 10-mile run at 80% WHR, or 10K race plus 5-mile jog

Week 8

S   Rest day
M   4-mile run at 60% WHR
T   1-mile jog, 2 hill miles at 70% WHR, 1-mile jog
W   3-mile run at 60% WHR
T   Track: 3 repeat miles at 70% WHR
F   Rest day
S   15-mile run at 70% WHR

Week 9

S   Rest day
M   5-mile run at 60% WHR
T   1-mile jog, 3 hill miles at 70% WHR, 1-mile jog
W   4-mile run at 60% WHR
T   Track: 4 repeat miles at 70% WHR
F   Rest day
S   10K race plus 5-mile jog

Week 10

S   Rest day
M   5-mile run at 60% WHR
T   1-mile jog, 3 hill miles at 80% WHR, 1-mile jog
W   4-mile run at 60% WHR
T   Track: 4 repeat miles at 80% WHR
F   Rest day
S   16-mile run at 70% WHR

Week 11

S   Rest day
M   5-mile run at 70% WHR
T   1-mile jog, 4 hill miles at 70% WHR, 1-mile jog
W   4-mile run at 60% WHR
T   Track: 5 repeat miles at 70% WHR
F   Rest day
S   10- to 12-mile run at 80% WHR, or 10K race plus 10K jog

Week 12

S   Rest day
M   4-mile run at 60% WHR
T   1-mile jog, 3 hill miles at 70% WHR, 1-mile jog
W   4-mile run at 60% WHR
T   Track: 4 repeat miles at 70% WHR
F   Rest day
S   18-mile run at 70% WHR

Week 13

S   Rest day
M   5-mile run at 60% WHR
T   8-mile run at 70% WHR
W   4-mile run at 60% WHR
T   Track: 5 repeat miles at 70% WHR
F   Rest day
S   10K race plus 10K jog

Week 14

S   Rest day
M   5-mile run at 70% WHR
T   1-mile jog, 4 hill miles at 80% WHR, 1-mile jog
W   4-mile run at 60% WHR
T   Track: 5 repeat miles at 70% WHR
F   Rest day

S   20-mile run at 70% WHR

Week 15

S   Rest day
M   6-mile run at 60% WHR
T   8-mile run at 70% WHR
W   4-mile run at 70% WHR
T   Track: 5 repeat miles at 80% WHR
F   Rest day
S   12- to 14-mile run at 80% WHR

Week 16

S   Rest day
M   5-mile run at 60% WHR
T   1-mile jog, 4 hill miles at 70% WHR, 1-mile jog
W   4-mile run at 60% WHR
T   Track: 4 repeat miles at 70% WHR
F   Rest day
S   21-mile run at 70% WHR

Week 17

S   Rest day
M   6-mile run at 60% WHR
T   10-mile run at 80% WHR
W   5-mile run at 70% WHR
T   Track: 5 repeat miles at 80% WHR
F   Rest day

S   13- to 15-mile run at 80% WHR, or 20K race, or 20K time trial

Week 18

S   Rest day
M   6-mile run at 60% WHR
T   1-mile jog, 5 hill miles at 70% WHR, 1-mile jog
W   5-mile run at 70% WHR
T   Track: 5 repeat miles at 70% WHR
F   Rest day
S   22-mile run at 70% WHR

Week 19

S   Rest day
M   5-mile run at 60% WHR
T   6-mile run at 60% WHR
W   4-mile run at 70% WHR
T   Track: 2 repeat miles at 80% WHR
F   Rest day
S   10- to 12-mile run at 70% WHR

Week 20

S   Rest day
M   4-mile run at 60% WHR
T   2-mile run at 60% WHR
W   3-mile run at 70% WHR
T   Rest day
F   Rest day
S   Rest day or 2-mile jog
S   YOUR MARATHON!

Notes on the Marathon-Training Programs

- All hill workouts should be done on a moderate grade (3 to 5 percent) and at a strong and steady but not exhausting pace. The ideal hill is a quarter mile to a half mile long. Stride out on the run downhill. The mileage listed for hill workouts combines both up _and_ down portions.
- All track workouts should be preceded by a 1- to 2-mile warm-up jog. Walk a lap between each repeat mile. And walk half a mile as a cool-down following your track workout.
- Unlike the Chapter 4 training schedule, these workouts are based upon _distance_ and WHR, and not upon _time_ and WHR.
- As with the training schedules in Chapter 4, a Saturday long run or race may be exchanged for a Sunday rest day in order to accommodate your personal schedule or to attend a local race that is held on a Sunday.

Your Potential Marathon Time

Use Table 7.1 to translate your best 10K race time of the past six months into a potential marathon time. The last column tells you the pace per mile recommended for your upcoming marathon.

Five Areas of Concentration

As you embark on the training schedule that's best suited for you, there are several areas to which you will want to pay special attention.

Injury Prevention

Any strenuous athletic endeavor opens the participant to the possibility of injury. Injuries associated with marathon training are typically injuries of overuse; the same body parts are

Table 7.1

10K Time	Marathon Time	Pace/Mile
34:00	2:45	6:18
35:00	2:50	6:30
36:00	2:55	6:40
37:00	3:00	6:51
38:00	3:10	7:16
39:00	3:20	7:39
40:00	3:30	8:00
41:00	3:35	8:09
42:00	3:42	8:29
43:00	3:49	8:48
44:00	3:54	8:58
45:00	4:00	9:10
46:00	4:06	9:23
47:00	4:13	9:40
48:00	4:18	9:50
49:00	4:23	10:00
50:00	4:30	10:18
51:00	4:35	10:30
52:00	4:42	10:45
53:00	4:49	11:05
54:00	4:55	11:20
55:00	5:01	11:30
56:00	5:08	11:42
57:00	5:15	12:01
58:00	5:22	12:15
59:00	5:30	12:35
1:00:00	5:36	12:41

used over and over in the same motion until the repetition breaks down a weak point and an injury results.

Some runners are more prone to injury than others. Certainly the more biomechanically sound a runner is, the less the chance of overuse injuries. The more weight the runner is carrying, the greater the chance of overuse injuries; the repeated impacts on the feet and legs are made more serious by the additional pounds being supported. Age and sex can also be a factor in dealing with running injuries. Older runners are more prone to injuries, since bones gradually become more brittle and the joints and connecting tissues less flexible. The wider pelvis of a woman causes a more radical angle of impact to the ground when running; as a result, women are more susceptible to certain leg and hip problems than men.

Here are some steps the marathoner can take to minimize overuse injuries:

1. Buy good running shoes and keep them in good repair. Alternate your running shoes: Do not use the same pair every day. Remember, a new pair of running shoes costs less than a visit to a podiatrist or orthopedist.

2. If you can possibly avoid it, do not run on concrete sidewalks. If you are running a course where you have a choice between concrete sidewalks and an asphalt bike path or roadside, always choose the asphalt. When you can manage it, do at least several of your workouts each week on dirt or gravel roads to give your legs a rest. Your weekly track workout will also provide a break from the typical concrete sidewalk bashing.

3. When your run is finished, walk for at least a quarter of a mile. When you complete a race, walk a quarter of a mile to half a mile for each 5 miles raced.

4. After your run, while the muscles of your legs are still warm, gently stretch them. If you have a particularly troublesome area (a weak left ankle, for instance), take a little extra time to work on that area. While you are reading or watching television in the evening, flex and unflex your legs and ankles at different angles in order to keep them flexible.

5. If you feel you are on the verge of an overuse injury (an Achilles tendon that becomes progressively more stiff, for example), take a day off and treat the potential injury. The rule of thumb is to apply ice for the first two to three days, and after that heat. The ice reduces the inflammation; the heat

increases the blood supply to the affected part and thereby speeds healing.

If you become injured to the point that it is painful to continue working out, stop immediately and give the injured area time to heal, then come back gently. Taking off the Monday workout, for example, gives you two days off in a row to allow a potential injury to heal.

Running Style

There is no such thing as an ideal running style, even among the elite athletes. Frank Shorter and Abebe Bikila had what we consider classic running styles, while Emil Zatopek's was once described as looking like "a man who has just been stabbed through the heart."

The perfect running style is one that accommodates that particular person's unique biomechanics. A person who is bowlegged will have a style radically different from a person who is not. A tall runner with long legs will have a different style from one with short legs.

In long-distance running, your style tends to deteriorate the farther into the run you get. When you are tired, your ideal style begins to fall apart.

The prime arena in which a distance runner can practice good style is at the track—one that is a perfectly measured flat course. There are no cars to dodge and no radically canted roadsides to work against you. Also, if you pick the right time of day, there are few disruptions at the track itself, since most runners avoid the track like the plague.

Practice as efficient a running style as you can while you do your track workouts. Your head should not bob or bounce, your legs should stride rhythmically, and you should make good use of your arms to maintain the rhythm of your legs. Many runners do not effectively incorporate their arm swing into their running style; women typically hold their arms high and tight to their chests, for instance. In fact, roughly 10 percent of your running efficiency comes from the proper use of the arms.

When you are running through a downtown area, glance at your reflection in store windows in order to check your style.

Run Relaxed

The most useful tool you can incorporate in your marathon-training program is one of the most difficult for the new runner to apprehend: relaxation.

The more relaxed you are, the more efficiently and the longer you will be able to run. The tense runner works against him- or herself because the tension causes stiffness, which in turn demands more work from the muscles.

The novice runner is typically prone to tension because he or she feels pressure to do everything right and is overwhelmed by this new activity. As the miles pass and fatigue ensues, neck and shoulders become tense as you almost begin to unconsciously guard against impending discomforts. Matters are made worse by the fact that most of us look up to and respect elite runners and we feel that there is such a wide gulf between their incredible talents and our meager ones. This typically causes us to work too hard. Too many runners do their running in a self-critical way, as though there is only one way to do it right.

Try to just let it happen. Go out and run your workout. Compare yourself only to yourself. Allow your body to have its way. It will gravitate toward the style that is right for it, and it will run better and longer the less tension you put in its way. It is usually easiest to find the kernel of relaxation in the middle portion of a noncrucial workout, such as the Monday recovery run. It comes once the body is warmed up and running more loosely. Key in on how it feels to run relaxed at those moments and attempt to allow that relaxation to happen with all your runs, even those at the track.

Racing and Your WHR

Most of the workouts in the marathon-training programs presented in this chapter are governed by your WHR (Working Heart Rate). As discussed, this is a universal method of gauging your body's effort based upon the number of times per minute your heart is required to beat.

There is no WHR listed next to the days when you are advised to run a race because a race situation calls for efforts beyond those called for in the average daily workout. Naturally, the longer the race, the lower the effort should be in order to be able to finish the race, recover, and continue your program without risking injury. Racing is typically done in the 75 to 90 percent WHR. If you were to run the mile, you'd put out an effort in the 90 percent area, while in a 20K race, you'd more likely be down around 80 percent.

When you run a 10K race, you'll want to put in a good, hard effort that pushes your body to the edge of its aerobic capacity and slightly into anaerobic. You should be breathing hard and fast but not gasping. You want to maintain your ability to process oxygen enough to supply your working muscles. This is a skill that comes with practice, which is why these training programs call for so many shorter races. Experience with racing will make you more comfortable with the process of racing.

When you go to a race, remember to arrive early enough to have time to warm up before the start. The longer the race, the shorter the warm-up. The warm-up loosens the major muscles of your legs, which helps you to go out smoother at the start and prevents injuries associated with racing. It also allows you to change your breathing over from anaerobic (which is where it is at the start of physical activity) to aerobic—therefore, you'll run more comfortably and process oxygen more efficiently.

For a 10K race, jog about a mile to get the legs warm and to change your breathing from anaerobic to aerobic. Then do a half-dozen sprints of about 40 yards each to stretch out the big muscles in the legs.

Based on your track workouts, have a minute-per-mile pace figured out for the race beforehand and line up in the starting field at a spot that seems as though it will match your effort for that day. If you are doing a track workout of four repeat miles at a 7:30 pace, you should be able to hold a 7:30- to 8:00-pace for the 10K. The last thing you want is to go through the first mile a minute-per-mile faster than you run at the track. You'll pay for the mistake before you reach 4 miles, and the final 2 miles will be torture. It is better to have something left over the last 2 miles so you can begin to pick it up a bit instead of dropping from seven-minute miles to ten-minute miles.

Once again, when the race is finished, jog or walk another half a mile to a mile to keep the stiffness out of the legs and to cool down safely. Don't cross the finish line and immediately stop! Keep moving until your breathing comes back to normal.

Nutrition

Despite a great deal of discussion in running circles about how nutrition can improve your running, you've got to practice running to run well. There is no nutritional secret that will ever replace good, solid training. You need only a few nutritional guidelines to succeed as a marathoner.

1. Carbohydrates provide the fuel on which a distance runner travels. Complex carbohydrates, such as fresh fruits and vegetables, are high-octane fuel. Eat at least one fresh garden salad and at least one apple and one carrot a day. Eat at least two slices daily of whole wheat bread.

2. Cut back on your fats and cholesterol, especially those in whole milk products and fatty meats.

3. When you do eat beef, make certain it's lean. When you eat chicken, remove the skin first. Substitute fresh fish for meat at least twice a week.

4. If you drink alcohol, do so in moderation. Don't drink more than two beers or two glasses of wine the night before

a race or before an important workout. Alcohol has been shown to interfere with the efficient transport of oxygen.

5. Drink enough water so that you are constantly well hydrated. As you move further into your marathon-training program, your body will need more and more water. If you live in a hot and/or dry part of the country, drink an enormous amount of fluid (a minimum of one gallon per day, two gallons if you can handle it). You can best judge your hydration by the color of your urine. It should be clear. If your urine is yellow, you aren't drinking enough.

6. For most marathoners, there is a curious phenomenon that occurs as the quality and quantity of their training increases. Their body begins to tell them what it needs, and there is usually a subtle but noticeable shift from the typical American diet to one more heavily grounded in complex carbohydrates. You'll find your tastes turning to salads, pasta dishes, and lighter cuisine.

8

Setting a Time Goal

> As a track athlete, I never had any problem finishing. In a dozen years I only had stepped off the track twice: once for good reason. But when I finally attempted the marathon in 1959 at age 27, I discovered I was a quitter. This character lapse on my part stunned me. But it happened because I did not want to run marathons; I wanted to race them.
>
> —HAL HIGDON, *On the Run from Dogs and People*

Some runners put the marathon distance off through most of their running careers, then come to it late—but they come armed with a formidable running background and racing experience.

For most of these runners, their intention in entering races is not so much to enjoy the camaraderie and the experience of the course as to seriously race the distance—against themselves, against the course, and often against long-running rivals in their age group. It is these ongoing age group rivalries that have served to push into the stratosphere physiologists' expectations of what the so-called aging body is capable of.

No spectator who has seen Sal Vasquez, John Campbell, or Ruth Anderson race thinks of these veterans as aging. Certainly not every veteran runner is able to keep up with them, but most are competitive and physically ready to go the distance. When hardy veterans like these approach their first marathon, they do so with a specific "hard" time goal in mind.

They presume that they will finish the marathon distance, and they are concerned only with how close they can get to their goals. They are willing to gamble with the matter of completion for the satisfaction of performance.

The same is true of younger runners who have run through high school and college, who never took on the marathon distance, but who suddenly take a shine to the idea.

These two tough groups of runners are capable of translating their years of experience in training for shorter distances to the more demanding workloads required for racing the marathon. Their muscles and tendons and ligaments are used to the necessary stress and strain, and psychologically they are hardened and able to assume the necessary discipline.

Consequently, a training schedule for these two groups of runners must be somewhat different and more demanding than it is for the relative newcomer. Therefore, I'm providing three sixteen-week schedules keyed for goals of 3:30, 3:15, and 3:00. (In marathon jargon, a 3:00 refers to a *sub*-three-hour time, just as in track running, a "four-minute mile" refers to a mile run in less than four minutes.)

These training schedules assume that the runner's years of experience at shorter distances will allow for greater volume and intensity of work—especially with track workouts, hill work, and long runs. Begin by determining a realistic first-marathon goal, using the chart on page 111.

Because most amateur long-distance runners work full-time jobs, none of the programs require more than 55 miles per week, and they stress quality over quantity.

Each schedule jumps off from a Base Week. While the concept is similar to the launching platform we used in Chapter 4 (where the runner was asked to run the foundation-level program for three months before embarking on the marathon-training program), the Base Week program is much more ambitious, and it should be attempted only if you have at least three years of regular training on your legs.

If the experienced runner can comfortably repeat the Base Week for four weeks, he or she can determine the marathon they wish to run, and then back up sixteen weeks to the start of the program that matches the time goal of 3:30, 3:15, or 3:00.

Unlike those in Chapter 7, these training schedules are based upon distance and performance—not WHR—goals.

Once you start one of these sixteen-week programs, racing should be curtailed. Track workouts and timed runs take the place of races, except where you can find a Saturday race of the length of the long run scheduled; the race should be run at 70 to 80 percent effort, or at the per-mile pace stipulated for the distance of that Saturday's long run. Do *not* exchange Saturday and Sunday workouts because of the severity of the Monday hill/fartlek schedule.

The training programs that follow continue into the week following the marathon. This involves an attempt to bring the runner through the experience and back onto a regular program as quickly and painlessly as possible (for more details, see Chapter 15).

Here's a key to the abbreviations used within these programs:

NE = Nonrunning Exercise. Activities such as bicycling, cross-country skiing, swimming, walking, or easy hiking—all done at a casual, easy pace.

R = Rest. This one may be difficult for the long-running athlete and may take some practice, but rest refers, literally, to doing nothing of a physical nature. Who says these training programs were all work?

E/R = Sundays call for *either* a bit of Exercise or Rest. If you are particularly tired, opt for the rest, considering the volume of work coming up on Monday.

F = Fartlek. This is a Swedish training method in which the workout is broken up by throwing in speed surges at regular intervals. An easy way to do this is to run on a road that is paralleled by utility poles. Throw in a surge between poles, then drop back to your regular pace between the next two poles; continue alternating throughout the workout. In fartlek workouts, as in hill workouts, the number of miles indicated *includes* a 1-mile warm-up jog and a 1-mile cool-down jog at the end. For example, if the schedule says Week 10 calls for "F: 6 miles," this means jog 1 mile, do fartlek for 4 miles, then jog 1 mile as a cool-down.

H = Hills. Like the fartlek workouts, the distance listed includes a 1-mile warm-up jog and a 1-mile cool-down jog. Hill workouts should be run on moderate hills—that is, never more than a 5 percent grade. The run up should be done with attention to style and strong use of the legs, but not at an exhausting or sprinting pace; the run down the hill should be done in a relaxed manner but with attention to striding out comfortably.

F/H = Fartlek with Hills. While most fartlek workouts are done on level or rolling terrain, this workout is done incorporating hills up which you can accelerate, recovering on the descent on the other side.

T = Track. Track miles are calculated differently from fartlek or hill miles in these programs. The mile you jog to warm up your legs does *not* count in the total listed for the workout; neither do the 1-lap jogs between timed miles and the half-mile cool-down following the workout.

16H-mile run. For the Saturday long run of the fourteenth week of all three programs, an H (Hill) is indicated behind the scheduled number of miles. This key workout should be done on a *relatively* hilly course (the hills should be rolling hills, not staggering mountains).

The Sixteen-Week Marathon-Training Program*
For a 3:30 Performance

Base Week
Do this for four consecutive
weeks.

S E/R
M F/H: 7 miles
T 3-mile gentle run
W T: 4 repeat miles at 8:00
T 3-mile gentle run
F R
S 14-mile run at 8:30

Week 1

S E/R
M H: 7 miles
T 3-mile gentle run
W T: 4 repeat miles at 8:00
T 3-mile gentle run
F R
S 15-mile run at 8:15

Week 2

S E/R
M H: 5 miles
T 3-mile gentle run
W T: 4 repeat miles at 7:50
T 3-mile gentle run
F R
S 12-mile run at 8:00

Week 3

S E/R
M H: 7 miles
T 3-mile gentle run
W T: 5 repeat miles at 7:50
T 4-mile gentle run
F R
S 16-mile run at 8:30

Week 4

S E/R
M H: 5 miles
T 3-mile gentle run
W T: 4 repeat miles at 7:40
T 3-mile gentle run
F R
S 13-mile run at 8:00

Week 5

S E/R
M H: 7 miles
T 3-mile gentle run
W T: 5 repeat miles at 7:40
T 3-mile gentle run
F R
S 17-mile run at 7:50

Week 6

S E/R
M H: 5 miles
T 4-mile gentle run
W T: 4 repeat miles at
   7:30
T 7- to 10-mile gentle run
F R
S 13-mile run at 8:00

Week 7

S E/R
M H: 7 miles
T 5-mile gentle run
W T: 5 repeat miles at
   7:30
T 7- to 10-mile gentle run
F R
S 18-mile run at 7:45

*A list of abbreviations appears on pages 120–21.

Week 8

S   E/R
M   H: 5 miles
T   7- to 10-mile gentle run
W   T: 4 repeat miles at 7:20
T   4-mile gentle run
F   R
S   13-mile run at 8:00

Week 9

S   E/R
M   H: 10 miles
T   4-mile gentle run
W   T: 5 repeat miles at 7:20
T   5-mile gentle run
F   R
S   19-mile run at 7:30

Week 10

S   E/R
M   F: 6 miles
T   3-mile gentle run
W   T: 4 repeat miles at 7:15
T   4-mile gentle run
F   R
S   14-mile run at 8:00

Week 11

S   E/R
M   H: 7 miles
T   3-mile gentle run
W   T: 5 repeat miles at 7:15
T   4-mile gentle run
F   R
S   20-mile run at 7:40

Week 12

S   E/R
M   F: 7 miles
T   4-mile gentle run
W   T: 4 repeat miles at 7:10

T   5-mile gentle run
F   R
S   13-mile run at 8:00

Week 13

S   E/R
M   H: 9 miles
T   3-mile gentle run
W   T: 5 repeat miles at 7:10
T   4-mile gentle run
F   R
S   21-mile run at 7:45 to 8:00

Week 14

S   E/R
M   F: 10 miles
T   3-mile gentle run
W   T: 4 repeat miles at 7:00
T   4-mile gentle run
F   R
S   16H-mile run at 8:00

Week 15

S   E/R
M   3-mile gentle run
T   7- to 10-mile gentle run
W   T: 2 repeat miles at 7:10
T   E
F   R
S   12-mile run at 7:50

Week 16

S   E/R
M   3-mile gentle run
T   R
W   3-mile gentle run
T   5-mile gentle run
F   R
S   R or 2-mile jog

Marathon Week

S   MARATHON
M   3-mile gentle run

T   R or 2-mile gentle
    run
W   E

T   5-mile gentle run
F   R
S   5-mile gentle run

*The Sixteen-Week Marathon-Training Program**
For a 3:15 Performance

Base Week
Do this for four consecutive
weeks.

S   E/R
M   F/H: 8 miles
T   3-mile gentle run
W   T: 4 repeat miles at 7:30
T   3-mile gentle run
F   R
S   15-mile run at 8:00

Week 1

S   E/R
M   H: 7 miles
T   3-mile gentle run
W   T: 4 repeat miles at 7:30
T   3-mile gentle run
F   R
S   16-mile run at 7:45

Week 2

S   E/R
M   H: 5 miles
T   3-mile gentle run
W   T: 4 repeat miles at 7:20
T   3-mile gentle run
F   R
S   13-mile run at 7:30

Week 3

S   E/R
M   H: 7 miles

T   3-mile gentle run
W   T: 5 repeat miles at 7:20
T   4-mile gentle run
F   R
S   17-mile run at 8:00

Week 4

S   E/R
M   H: 5 miles
T   3-mile gentle run
W   T: 4 repeat miles at 7:10
T   3-mile gentle run
F   R
S   14-mile run at 7:30

Week 5

S   E/R
M   H: 7 miles
T   3-mile gentle run
W   T: 5 repeat miles at 7:10
T   3-mile gentle run
F   R
S   18-mile run at 7:20

Week 6

S   E/R
M   H: 5 miles
T   4-mile gentle run
W   T: 4 repeat miles at 7:00
T   7- to 10-mile gentle run

*A list of abbreviations appears on pages 120–21.

F R
S 14-mile run at 7:30

Week 7

S E/R
M H: 7 miles
T 5-mile gentle run
W T: 5 repeat miles at 7:00
T 7- to 10-mile gentle run
F R
S 19-mile run at 7:10

Week 8

S E/R
M H: 5 miles
T 7- to 10-mile gentle run
W T: 4 repeat miles at 6:50
T 4-mile gentle run
F R
S 14-mile run at 7:30

Week 9

S E/R
M H: 10 miles
T 4-mile gentle run
W T: 5 repeat miles at 6:50
T 5-mile gentle run
F R
S 20-mile run at 7:00

Week 10

S E/R
M F: 6 miles
T 3-mile gentle run
W T: 4 repeat miles at 6:40
T 4-mile gentle run
F R
S 15-mile run at 7:30

Week 11

S E/R
M H: 7 miles

T 3-mile gentle run
W T: 5 repeat miles at 6:40
T 4-mile gentle run
F R
S 21-mile run at 7:10

Week 12

S E/R
M F: 7 miles
T 4-mile gentle run
W T: 4 repeat miles at 6:30
T 5-mile gentle run
F R
S 14-mile run at 7:30

Week 13

S E/R
M H: 9 miles
T 3-mile gentle run
W T: 5 repeat miles at 6:30
T 4-mile gentle run
F R
S 23-mile run at 7:15–7:30

Week 14

S E/R
M F: 10 miles
T 3-mile gentle run
W T: 4 repeat miles at 6:20
T 4-mile gentle run
F R
S 18H-mile run at 7:30

Week 15

S E/R
M 3-mile gentle run
T 7- to 10-mile gentle run
W T: 2 repeat miles at 6:30
T E
F 3-mile gentle run
S 13-mile run at 7:20

Week 16

S E/R
M 3-mile gentle run
T R
W 3-mile gentle run
T 5-mile gentle run
F R
S R or 2-mile jog

Marathon Week

S MARATHON!
M 3-mile gentle run
T 3-mile gentle run
W E
T 5-mile gentle run
F R
S 5-mile gentle run

The Sixteen-Week Marathon-Training Program*

For a 3:00 Performance

Base Week

Do this program for four
consecutive weeks.

S E/R
M F/H: 10 miles
T 3-mile gentle run
W T: 4 repeat miles at
   6:30–6:40
T 3-mile gentle run
F R
S 15-mile run at 7:30

Week 1

S E/R
M H: 8 miles
T 3-mile gentle run
W T: 4 repeat miles at 7:00
T 3-mile gentle run
F R
S 18-mile run at 7:15

Week 2

S E/R
M H: 6 miles
T 3-mile gentle run
W T: 4 repeat miles at 6:50

T 3-mile gentle run
F R
S 14-mile run at 7:00

Week 3

S E/R
M H: 8 miles
T 3-mile gentle run
W T: 5 repeat miles at 6:50
T 5-mile gentle run
F R
S 20-mile run at 7:00

Week 4

S E/R
M H: 6 miles
T 3-mile gentle run
W T: 4 repeat miles at 6:40
T 3-mile gentle run
F R
S 15-mile run at 7:00

Week 5

S E/R
M H: 8 miles
T 3-mile gentle run
W T: 5 repeat miles at 6:40

*A list of abbreviations appears on pages 120–21.

T   3-mile gentle run
F   R
S   19-mile run at 6:50

Week 6

S   E/R
M   H: 6 miles
T   5-mile gentle run
W   T: 4 repeat miles at 6:30
T   8- to 10-mile gentle run
F   R
S   15-mile run at 7:00

Week 7

S   E/R
M   H: 8 miles
T   6-mile gentle run
W   T: 5 repeat miles at 6:30
T   8- to 10-mile gentle run
F   R
S   20-mile run at 6:40

Week 8

S   E/R
M   F: 6 miles
T   8- to 10-mile gentle run
W   T: 4 repeat miles at 6:20
T   5-mile gentle run
F   R
S   15-mile run at 7:00

Week 9

S   E/R
M   H: 10 miles
T   5-mile gentle run
W   T: 5 repeat miles at 6:20
T   6-mile gentle run
F   R
S   21-mile run at 6:30

Week 10

S   E/R
M   F: 7 miles
T   3-mile gentle run
W   T: 4 repeat miles at 6:10
T   5-mile gentle run
F   R
S   16-mile run at 7:00

Week 11

S   E/R
M   H: 8 miles
T   3-mile gentle run
W   T: 5 repeat miles at 6:10
T   5-mile gentle run
F   R
S   23-mile run at 6:40

Week 12

S   E/R
M   F: 8 miles
T   5-mile gentle run
W   T: 4 repeat miles at 6:00
T   6-mile gentle run
F   R
S   15-mile run at 7:00

Week 13

S   E/R
M   H: 10 miles
T   3-mile gentle run
W   T: 5 repeat miles at 6:00
T   5-mile gentle run
F   R
S   25-mile run at 6:45–6:50

Week 14

S   E/R
M   F: 10 miles
T   3-mile gentle run

W   T: 4 repeat miles at 5:50
T   5-mile gentle run
F   R
S   19H-mile run at 7:00

Week 15

S   E/R
M   3-mile gentle run
T   8- to 10-mile gentle run
W   T: 2 repeat miles at 6:00
T   E
F   3-mile gentle run
S   13-mile run at 6:50

Week 16

S   E/R
M   3-mile gentle run

T   R
W   3-mile gentle run
T   6-mile gentle run
F   3-mile gentle run
S   R or 2-mile jog

Marathon Week

S   MARATHON!
M   3-mile gentle run
T   3-mile gentle run
W   E
T   6-mile gentle run
F   R
S   6-mile gentle run

Six Areas of Concentration

Now that you are about to embark on an intense sixteen-week program toward racing a marathon to a specific time goal, there are several areas of the training program that would benefit from some further elaboration, and several areas of training that, if mastered at this point, will complement and augment your training—and increase the good results of that training.

Upper-Body Workouts

Very few distance runners capitalize on an ongoing program of upper-body workouts. The strength of most distance runners is in their legs, lungs, and heart—the primary tools of the runner who typically competes in races beyond 5K. Long-distance runners think muscles in the upper body are for sprinters, and besides, they're extra weight.

The type of upper-body workouts to which I'm referring have little to do with those a sprinter such as Carl Lewis or Greg Foster uses. The last thing distance runners need is bulked-up muscles. What they *do* need, however, is all the strength and endurance they can beg, borrow, or buttress, even if it means carrying along an extra pound or two of muscle tissue.

By adopting a simple, modest routine of upper-body workouts, you can make major strides toward increasing endurance and strength with a minimal addition of weight. For best results, do these four exercises every other day; they can be incorporated into the cool-down process.

Sit-ups Limited range-of-motion sit-ups minimize the chance of lower-back pain yet strengthen and define your abdominal muscles. Since they are opposite the lower-back muscles, strong abdominals contribute to the prevention of lower-back pain. Strong abdominal muscles also help you maintain an erect posture even in the latter stages of a marathon. And good posture allows you to maintain an efficient running style while also keeping the chest open and unobstructed, which in turn assures continued full use of the lungs.

Push-ups Even a modest number of push-ups increases strength in the upper arms—remember that efficient use of the arms adds roughly 10 percent to running strength. Push-ups also expand and strengthen the chest muscles (thereby allowing full lung expansion) as well as the lower back.

Basic Arm Curls These build strength and endurance in the biceps, which is important for hill running, speed workouts, and sustained running rhythm. As long as the weight that you use is small enough, there is little if any muscle bulking. Bulking of muscles comes from moving large weights a few times; endurance comes from moving small weights many times.

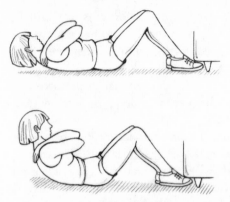

Sit-ups: To avoid lower back pain while doing sit-ups, do not raise yourself to a full 90 degrees from the floor, as there is a tendency to place too much strain on the back muscles instead of on the abdominal muscles to bring yourself to an upright position. Anchor your toes under a heavy piece of furniture and concentrate on doing the exercise slowly, precisely, and carefully. With your arms crossed over your chest and your knees bent, concentrate on using your abdominal muscles to raise your head and shoulders approximately 45 degrees off the floor for a moment. Pause in that position, then lower yourself gently back to the floor.

Chest Openers   By hefting a modest weight (I use the same piece of firewood for arm curls and chest openers) over your head, lowering it behind your neck, hefting it over your head again, and then returning it to its original position in front of you, the arms are strengthened and the chest cavity is expanded. This increases the area in which the lungs can expand when taxed. As you become stronger in the curls and the chest openers, you can always increase the size of your weight if you feel you need additional resistance.

How much is enough upper-body work for the ambitious marathoner? As with the yearly cycle of building mileage, racing, then backing off so that the body can rest, upper-body workouts should be increased as your running program expands toward a particular race, then decreased to a mainte-nance level over the winter months.

Push-ups: There are a number of ways to do push-ups. The standard form is to lie face-down on the floor. Place your hands palm-down on the floor approximately under your shoulders. Using your toes as the anchor, and keeping your back and legs straight, slowly raise yourself by using your arms. When your arms are fully extended, pause a count, then slowly lower yourself back to the floor. The standard push-up requires quite a bit of upper body strength. For those who are unable to effectively do the standard push-up at this point, a modified push-up will work. Instead of using the toes as the anchor point, use the knees. Proceed as you would with a standard push-up. Once you have progressed to the point where you can do 20 of the modified push-ups, promote yourself to the standard push-ups, but at a lower volume.

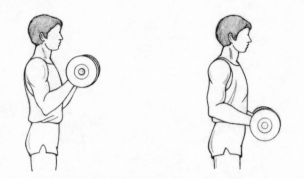

Arm Curls: Hold a weight of some kind (I use a hunk of firewood) at hip level, then curl it up to your chest, keeping your upper arms immobile. Hold for a single count, then lower it back to the original position.

Chest Opener: Begin as you would with the arm curl, holding the weight at hip level. But instead of holding your upper arms immobile, proceed right through the curl and raise the weight over your head, hold there for a count, then lower it behind your head. When the weight reaches its lowest possible point, hold again for one count, then again raise it above your head, hold for another count, then lower to starting position. This exercise stretches the front of the chest (thereby allowing for more lung expansion) while also building up the arms and shoulders.

If you haven't done an upper-body program before, start with the following:

Sit-ups	10
Push-ups	5
Arm curls	20
Chest openers	20 (using a two-count, which means counting one as you raise the weight over your head, and two when you bring it up again from behind your back, thereby doing 10 lifts in front and 10 in back)

Each week add one sit-up to your program and two arm curls and chest openers; add one additional push-up for each two additional sit-ups. When you reach 50 sit-ups, 25 push-ups, 100 arm curls, and 100 chest openers, hold at that level. You can count back on your marathon-training calendar so that you reach the maximum level of upper-body workouts two weeks before your marathon.

Training with a Partner(s)

The beauty of long-distance running is that it is an individual sport that can be done anywhere at any time. But for those runners who find they are less motivated to run, stick to a program, or run tough when the program calls for it, hooking up with one or more running partners may be advisable—*as long as the running partner is of similar abilities.* While running with someone who is a hair better than you are tends to encourage you to run a little better to keep up, running with someone who is markedly superior at this stage of the game can be frustrating and masochistic.

Actually, running with someone moderately slower than you is ideal on days that call for easy runs. Such a partner will tend to slow you down to an easy pace, something you may not easily do if you run solo.

Although you will run your marathon without help from anyone else, a partner can be a wonderful training adjunct, especially if he or she is also training for the same marathon.

Try to arrange to run at least two or three workouts a week together—particularly the long Saturday run, which almost always goes better if you are able to feed off a running partner.

Even if you have a good running partner, however, reserve several workouts each week for yourself—especially your track workout. There you need to get into the pacing and your running style, and a running partner can distract you from your primary objectives.

Do not be afraid to take on running partners even if they are not training for your marathon. By having one along for some of the more mundane workouts during the week, you can prevent the runs from becoming boring and monotonous.

How to Flow Up the Hills

Running hills well seems to be a specialty some runners are apparently born with and others spend their lives envying. Often, however, those who run hills well do so because they practice regularly and they have managed to convince themselves that they "like" hills.

Most people who run hills badly are scared of them and therefore "attack" rather than roll with them. When you attack you expend a great deal of energy and are likely to tire yourself long before the hill is behind you. Attacking a hill allows it to dictate your breathing pattern, which puts you behind in your breathing; you may therefore quickly go into anaerobic (breathless) breathing or gasping. Runners attacking hills also maintain a stride length that is much too aggressive for the pitch of the hill, which forces the legs to increase their workload in order to pull the body through the elongated stride.

Whether your weekly hill workouts, which are used to build thigh strength, lift, and endurance, are during a longer workout or during a race, here are some tips to keep in mind when you approach a hill.

- Picture yourself flowing up the hill well before you reach it; then make the picture reality.
- Approach the hill as though you are going to flow up it. Think of the hill merely as an extension of the terrain leading into it.
- Use your momentum from the terrain leading to the hill to begin your ascent.
- Begin increasing your breathing rate and depth as you approach the hill so that *you* control your breathing patterns, instead of their controlling you.
- Gear down your stride length in relation to the pitch of the hill, just as you would if you were riding a fifteen-speed mountain bike.

As you do your weekly hill workouts, work on maintaining breathing patterns that are under your control and that fit the pitch of the hill. At the same time, experiment with dropping your legs into various gears—that is, strides—for different pitches; always attempt to pick a shortened stride that is strong and determined but practical when it comes to maintaining it through the entire hill.

Positive psychological reworking can change your perception of hills. Regard the hill as a pleasant challenge on an otherwise featureless course. Convince yourself that if you can become a better hill runner, you will outstrip most other people in the races you run, because they will continue to be daunted by them. Play games with the hills you encounter, mentally flowing up the hill before you actually reach it.

Continue to control your breathing after topping out until it becomes easy again. Also, practice good downhill running; in a race, most people work so hard to reach the crest that once they top out, they forget to continue running efficiently when gravity again begins to work with them instead of against them.

Psychology and Running

When running exploded in the late 1970s it did so in large part because it was prepared to accommodate virtually anyone who wanted to strap on a pair of training flats to jog around the block. The running movement emerged from the grass roots, from a generation who wanted to head off the negative effects of aging. Because it was a populist movement, the raw material that entered the running movement was a varied lot. Many runners had little sports background, and certainly most had never been competitive runners.

Participants in the running revolution who managed to stay with it did so for the long haul because they gradually began to picture themselves as runners. It became a big part of their lives and helped to define these people in a world where physical endeavor was increasingly downplayed. Suddenly every office in America had one or two joggers or runners. These people who had seemed so normal six months before were now referred to, sometimes with a touch of derision, as "joggers." Little by little, those people began to see themselves not as joggers but as runners, as athletic animals instead of passive spectators in the human race. Once they accepted and then embraced that appellation, they moved to another plateau in their running. Running was no longer something they merely did; it helped define who they were.

In order to be successful at the marathon, the runner who intends to graduate to that plateau must begin to think in terms of _being_ a marathoner long before he or she toes the starting line. Once the runner begins to think like a marathoner, the goal of running the first one takes on a whole new dimension. Each workout becomes more important, more personal, more integrated with the runner's daily life and with the runner's long-term goals.

For some runners, the realization that they've taken that one very important step from thinking like a runner and a racer to thinking like a marathoner comes very early in the process, sometimes at the moment when the decision to go for the marathon is made. Others may be six weeks into their sixteen-week marathon-training program when suddenly, during the middle of a 6-mile run, the mental transition is made. And for still others, the transition comes at the last minute, as they lay out their running gear the night before the race or on the way to the starting line the next morning.

When, on a long run, with the legs warmed and the breathing regular and strong like a metronome, the hint of the idea that you are becoming a marathoner appears, allow it to infuse the rest of your run.

Mind Games

No sixteen-week-long training program is going to come easy every day. If it is, you probably aren't working hard enough at it. There will be some wonderful, unforgettable days when everything clicks, and there will be days when it takes a tremendous amount of willpower just to get out the door. But if you allow the workouts that are purely painful work to have their way, they will overshadow the truly wonderful days.

Don't be reluctant to insert your own fantasies and games into your workouts, especially those that start out as though they are a job you don't like. You will not be the first person who has gutted out a workout by pretending that Bill Rodgers or Grete Waitz is on your shoulder, going stride-for-stride with you, waiting for you to weaken.

There is nothing wrong with playing mental games to take your mind off the exertion of doing hill repeats. And there is certainly nothing wrong with making deals with yourself to get you through the dreaded track workouts: "If I can do my fifth and last mile repeat five seconds under a 7:00 pace, I'll stop on the way home and have a frozen yogurt cone."

The more you can turn your workouts, especially the tough ones, into a game, the more likely you will be to come back to the next scheduled workout refreshed and ready to kick ass. Your imagination can be one of your greatest tools toward keeping a tough sixteen-week marathon-training program on the right track. Make your running a creative act, not a chore.

Early in 1980, I interviewed Henry Rono, then the best distance runner in the world. In 1978, he set four world records (3,000 meters, 3,000-meter steeplechase, 5,000 meters, and 10,000 meters) in an eighty-day period. One point he made about training stood out.

Rono felt that "surging" (the act of breaking your competition in the latter stages of a race by unexpectedly picking up the pace) was something most runners didn't do well because they did not hold it long enough. A surge, Rono contended, should not be measured as a hundred-yard tool, but in half-mile, mile, or even mile-and-a-half segments. Hold a surge longer, he said, and you will truly break your competition; practice a longer surge in your workouts and you will break your own fear of pain.

Because I had dedicated 1980 to running a 3:00 marathon, Henry's talk of practicing extended surges struck home. I was certainly not going to be up in the lead pack where I'd need to throw in a surge to break my competition, but if I could surge for a mile or a mile and a half in practice runs (essentially overextending the principle of fartlek workouts to an extreme), perhaps in the latter stages of the race my legs would be strong enough to sustain a faster-than-usual pace. I began penciling in extended surges (I call them "burners," for reasons that will become clear to runners who try them) into my Arthur Lydiard–inspired sixteen-week training program, easily at first, but then with more vigor.

When I ran a 2:57:48 at the Humboldt Redwoods Marathon that October, I felt these burners were the ingredient I had needed to get the extra strength and speed in the latter stages of the race.

A burner is simply an increase in speed (fifteen to forty-five seconds per mile faster than scheduled) thrown into the long middle of a weekday workout or long run when your legs feel fresh enough to sustain the increase without jeopardizing your subsequent workouts. If your legs feel stale and dead, don't try it that day. If they feel springy and full of running after the initial fifteen to twenty minutes of warming up in the early miles, increase the per-mile pace for a mile, a mile and a half, or two miles and hold it there, easing back to the prescribed pace through the rest of the workout. This is in sharp contrast to the fartlek, which is a series of short surges at regular intervals. During the burner phase, however, you must be very conscious of how well your legs are behaving. At the first hint that they are straining toward injury or exhaustion, back off.

The use of burners is at the discretion of the runner. They are not required in the training programs outlined in this chapter. They should not be used by runners with less than three years of racing experience on their legs, because the extra effort can easily strain the various machinery of the legs of the runner who has not biomechanically built her- or himself up.

Even for the experienced runner, burners should not be used in more than two workouts a week. If your program is going especially well, however, it might be appropriate to throw a burner or two into your long weekend runs, but keep it to the mile or mile-and-a-half length. Used judiciously, the burner can be an effective tool to build race-day confidence as well as leg strength and speed.

_9_

The Fine Art of Pacing

> I could see myself whizzing around the track, shoulders
> and hips working in harmony with my legs. I'd looked like
> a real runner for the first time in my life.
>
> —JACK HEGGIE, _Running with the Whole Body_

In a world full of regulation and regimen, running can serve
as an escape from everyday concerns, a release valve for
built-up stress and tension. Running at whatever speed seems
right at the moment, in whatever direction, for whatever
distance, is both cathartic and enjoyable. At times, you return
home from one of these runs and cannot even remember the
course of the run. All you know and care about is that a
weight has been lifted. Some runners even run a marathon by
how they feel rather than according to a set plan—but even
if they finish the race, they almost never run to their potential.

In fact, a formal marathon-training program has little room
for this type of happy-go-lucky running. It's appropriate only
on recovery runs, such as on the Tuesday and Thursday runs
in the sixteen-week programs presented in Chapter 8.

The longer the race for which you train, the more important is the role of pacing. If you go out too fast in the
marathon, you flame out; if you go out too slowly, you have
too much left at the end and therefore have not raced to your
potential.

Pacing must be applied during the race; it's the single most
important skill a runner can learn during training.

Pacing is particularly vital during two segments of the

marathon: the first 5 miles and miles 7 through 16. The most common mistake for marathoners is going out too fast during the first 5 miles. The runner goes into the marathon at the peak of sixteen weeks of hard training and lines up at the starting line energized by a feeling of power and speed that wells up in the wake of two weeks of tapering. The runner is well rested, strong, nervous, and edgy, at the height of his or her running prowess. The electricity of the starting line is infectious. It is almost impossible to avoid being caught up in the crescendo that builds toward the countdown of the final twenty seconds until the start.

Too many well-trained, usually well-disciplined runners use this opportunity to throw away their sixteen weeks of training. When the gun goes off, so do they. Instead of running conservatively at their planned pace, they go out like a shot. It is coming so easy!

Of course it is. You are in the best shape of your life. You are prepared to run your first marathon or go for your best time. You go through the first mile and are startled to discover you are a minute faster than your planned per-mile pace. But it feels so good. "I feel I could hold this pace forever," you say to yourself. You go through the second mile at nearly the same pace (only five seconds slower), still feeling like a million bucks. What you forget is that there are still 24 miles left.

By the time you reach mile 5, possibly in personal record time, you've blown your marathon. This race requires a judicious parceling of energy, with an eye to saving more energy per mile for the last 8 miles than you used during the first 8—by that point, you'll be competing against your increasingly fatigued muscles. The extra energy you expended running a minute-per-mile faster in the first 5 miles is energy forever lost. You're now faced with the prospect of staggering and stumbling through the final 8 miles, well off your planned marathon time, possibly injured, if you finish at all.

The second scenario is somewhat more subtle, sneaking up on you around mile 7. You start the race exhibiting an admirable amount of restraint. You resist being sucked into the vacuum created by everyone else going out so fast at the starting gun. You hold to your planned pace and are amazed at how pedestrian the effort feels as you literally waltz through the first and second miles. It hardly seems like work. You feel the same at miles 3 and 4—in fact, the idea that you may be underrunning your ability and your training teases you for a moment, but you continue to exhibit restraint.

By mile 6 you begin to feel loose. The miles you've already put in have opened up the blood vessels, providing more than adequate amounts of oxygen to working muscles that have now warmed themselves through and through, all the way to the center of the thick thigh and calf muscles. You feel wonderful, like a running machine. It comes easily during the first miles; everything is incredibly smooth. The reserves of energy that came back during the final two weeks, when you tapered your mileage down, are enormous, and you feel as though you've hardly tapped that reservoir. You estimate where the 10K point is, check your watch as you go past, and realize that ten weeks ago this performance would have been a PR for the distance.

The 7-mile mark is just ahead. You're breathing regularly and quietly, your legs are like pistons in the well-tuned engine of a sports car. You've remembered to use your arms to set a comfortable rhythm and you check your watch. You're right on pace; in fact, you've got two seconds per mile in the bank.

This is like running in a dream! You think, "Perhaps I've underestimated my own training, my own talent. I've trained so well for those sixteen weeks that I've reached a new plateau, where I can run forever." You are exhilarated. You go through 8 miles without looking at your watch. Now this is really running! This is what it's all about! Without realizing it, by going with what it feels like, with how good it feels, with how strong you feel, you've picked up the pace by thirty seconds per mile. You've been passing some runners (obviously they haven't trained as well as you have). But there are others who seem to be feeling as good as you do. You hook up with one of them. You feel so good, so strong, that you begin chatting as you roll along. "Hey," you think to yourself, "the marathon *is* my event! I'm good at this!"

By the time you roll toward the 16-mile marker, however, you realize that you're concentrating more on your pace in order to keep it. And there's a bit of a tick on the outside of the right calf, as though you've developed a slight pull. It's a little more like work now, but by now it's supposed to be. Just for the heck of it, you check your watch against your planned pace. You say to yourself, "Either my math is getting faulty, or I'm five minutes ahead of where I'm supposed to be at this point! Five minutes ahead!" There's the 17-mile marker. "Yeah, yeah, I've been running thirty seconds a mile faster than I planned. Now I'm five and a half minutes ahead of my planned pace. That last mile felt a little too much like work. I'd better back off before I really blow it."

For many would-be marathoners who reach 17 miles and are five and a half minutes ahead of their planned time for that point, the next 9 miles will progressively become more hellish if they insist on trying to continue at their current pace. Those who trained to their potential but were conservative in their pacing plans may, by cutting back to the planned pace at this point, be able to end up close to their planned marathon time, perhaps even a minute or two under it. But invariably, 98 percent of them will slow noticeably with each subsequent mile. For none of them will it be the exhilarating experience it could have been had they stuck to their prerace pacing plan.

The reassurance of reaching each mile on schedule cannot be underestimated, especially as the runner reaches 18 miles and beyond. By maintaining your planned pace, you keep all resources from the psychological side of the arsenal on your side.

- You're on schedule.
- You're running a pace slower than you ran in your final long workouts.
- You're passing other runners who seem to be biting the big one.

• Yes, you are tiring, but you are still strong, still pulled by that wire that is your planned pace!

One of the most intelligent examples of proper, precise pacing was at the 1979 New York City Marathon, when Indian summer hit with a vengeance. Bill Rodgers, the favorite who'd won New York the last three years, was notorious for taking the lead in any race he ran but then crumpling in the heat. The field went out relatively fast for the day's temperature, and Kirk Pfeffer, a tall, lanky, talented but injury-prone runner from Colorado, set the pace. Considering the heat, it was an unusual strategy for winning the race; he was on pace to smash the course record. Bill Rodgers was nowhere to be seen.

By the time the race came down to the final miles, with the television-camera car rolling through the winding roads of Central Park, Pfeffer was running as though he were under water. The course-record pace had burned him out. Now he was hardly moving, having dropped from a sub-five-minute pace to a seven-minute pace. The camera occasionally picked up a speck of blue on the road far behind Pfeffer. Little by little the speck enlarged, taking on features. Viewers familiar with his unique running style began to realize that Bill Rodgers was overtaking Kirk Pfeffer. The figure began to become larger and larger, seeming to loom over the fading Pfeffer, even though Pfeffer was more than six inches taller. Rodgers pulled next to Pfeffer, talked to him briefly, and then moved on past, ultimately winning his fourth straight New York City Marathon.

Later that day, I talked briefly with the winner. "Your strategy was a little different today," I said.

"I know I don't run well in the heat," Bill said. "I knew what I could do under these conditions. . . . To be able to finish, I had to run my own race."

During the last week of July 1979, I spent a week in Boston with Bill as he went through his typical training routine building toward the New York race. It was the hottest week of the summer. Under those conditions he scaled down all of his workouts. He also rescheduled workouts for less punishing times of day.

On Thursday he went to a local track and did five repeat miles in the 4:27–4:35 range. Under the best of conditions, Rodgers was unable to do much better than a 4:20 mile at the track, yet his primary strength was that there was startlingly little margin between his current best mile time and the ability to hold a sub-five-minute pace for 26 consecutive miles. His greatest tool for monitoring his potential pace and for honing his pace was the once-a-week track workout.

The weekly track workout that so helped Bill Rodgers is an integral part of the training programs in this book. Repeat miles on the track at a prearranged pace are important for several reasons:

1. The track is precise, so the miles will be perfectly accurate. Unless you've taken the time to measure a mile segment of one of your road courses, rough estimates on road courses are useless. If you are as little as 50 yards off, over the length of a marathon you could be four to five minutes off, which is significant.

2. By doing repeat miles on the track, you can make adjustments in your pace to fit the scheduled per-mile pace for that day. (It is not unusual to be off a bit during your first timed mile of a track training session, but ten weeks into the program, you will be surprised at how close you can get to that prescribed first timed mile.)

3. Track workouts increase leg speed. You will ultimately be running faster at the track (and during the longer runs) than you will be in the actual race; this makes your race pace more comfortable and more possible.

4. Track workouts allow you to work on developing your running style to its maximum while honing your sense of pacing.

Knowing the lap splits for your scheduled pace may ensure accurate per-mile pacing for your track workout. Table 9.1

Table 9.1. Per Lap Targets for Repeat Miles at Track

Mile Pace	Lap 1	Lap 2	Lap 3
9:00	2:15	4:30	6:45
8:50	2:12	4:24	6:36
8:40	2:10	4:20	6:30
8:30	2:07	4:14	6:22
8:20	2:05	4:10	6:15
8:10	2:02	4:04	6:06
8:00	2:00	4:00	6:00
7:50	1:57	3:54	5:50
7:40	1:55	3:50	5:45
7:30	1:52	3:44	5:36
7:20	1:50	3:40	5:30
7:10	1:47	3:34	5:21
7:00	1:45	3:30	5:15
6:50	1:42	3:24	5:06
6:40	1:40	3:20	5:00
6:30	1:37	3:14	4:51
6:20	1:35	3:10	4:45
6:10	1:32	3:05	4:37
6:00	1:30	3:00	4:30
5:50	1:27	2:54	4:20
5:40	1:25	2:50	4:15
5:30	1:22	2:45	4:06
5:20	1:20	2:40	4:00
5:10	1:17	2:36	3:52
5:00	1:15	2:30	3:45

shows the per-lap paces for repeat miles of from nine to five minutes.

Table 9.2 will help you gauge your pace if you plan to run an evenly paced marathon.

Table 9.3 takes into consideration the fact that most runners become tired during the course of a marathon, and that their pace slows as the race progresses. Table 9.3 is not as good a pacing tool as Table 9.2 because your slowdown rate will vary.

Table 9.2. Even-Paced Running Chart for Major Marathon Splits

Mile	5 Miles	10K	10 Miles	15 Miles	20 Miles	Finish
4:50	24:10	30:02	48:20	1:12:30	1:36:40	2:07:44
5:00	25:00	31:04	50:00	1:15:00	1:40:00	2:11:06
5:10	25:50	32:06	51:40	1:17:30	1:43:20	2:15:28
5:20	26:40	33:08	53:20	1:20:00	1:46:40	2:19:50
5:30	27:30	34:10	55:00	1:22:30	1:50:00	2:24:12
5:40	28:20	35:12	56:40	1:25:00	1:53:20	2:28:34
5:50	29:10	36:14	58:20	1:27:30	1:56:40	2:32:56
6:00	30:00	37:17	1:00:00	1:30:00	2:00:00	2:37:19
6:10	30:50	38:19	1:01:40	1:32:30	2:03:20	2:41:41
6:20	31:40	39:22	1:03:20	1:35:00	2:06:40	2:46:03
6:30	32:30	40:24	1:05:00	1:37:30	2:10:00	2:50:25
6:40	33:20	41:26	1:06:40	1:40:00	2:13:20	2:54:47
6:50	34:10	42:28	1:08:20	1:42:30	2:16:40	2:59:09
7:00	35:00	43:30	1:10:00	1:45:00	2:20:00	3:03:33
7:10	35:50	44:32	1:11:40	1:47:30	2:23:20	3:07:55
7:20	36:40	45:34	1:13:20	1:50:00	2:26:40	3:12:17
7:30	37:30	46:36	1:15:00	1:52:30	2:30:00	3:16:39
7:40	38:20	47:38	1:16:40	1:55:00	2:33:20	3:21:01
7:50	39:10	48:40	1:18:20	1:57:30	2:36:40	3:25:23
8:00	40:00	49:42	1:20:00	2:00:00	2:40:00	3:29:45
8:10	40:50	50:44	1:21:40	2:02:30	2:43:20	3:34:07
8:20	41:40	51:46	1:23:20	2:05:00	2:46:40	3:38:29
8:30	42:30	52:48	1:25:00	2:07:30	2:50:00	3:42:51
8:40	43:20	53:50	1:26:40	2:10:00	2:53:20	3:47:13
8:50	44:10	54:52	1:28:20	2:12:30	2:56:40	3:51:35
9:00	45:00	55:54	1:30:00	2:15:00	3:00:00	3:56:00
9:10	45:50	56:56	1:31:40	2:17:30	3:03:20	4:00:22
9:20	46:40	57:58	1:33:20	2:20:00	3:06:40	4:04:44
9:30	47:30	59:00	1:35:00	2:20:30	3:10:00	4:09:06
9:40	48:20	1:00:02	1:36:40	2:25:00	3:13:20	4:13:28
9:50	49:10	1:01:04	1:38:20	2:27:30	3:16:40	4:17:50
10:00	50:00	1:02:06	1:40:00	2:30:00	3:20:00	4:22:13

Table 9.3. Effort-Adjusted Running Table for Major Marathon Splits

Mile	5 Miles	10 Miles	15 Miles	20 Miles	Finish
5:43	28:00	55:00	1:22:00	1:52:00	2:30:00
5:55	29:00	57:00	1:25:00	1:56:00	2:35:00
6:06	30:00	59:00	1:28:00	2:00:00	2:40:00
6:17	31:00	1:01:00	1:31:00	2:04:00	2:45:00
6:29	32:00	1:03:00	1:33:00	2:07:00	2:50:00
6:40	33:00	1:05:00	1:36:00	2:11:00	2:55:00
6:52	34:00	1:07:00	1:39:00	2:15:00	3:00:00
7:04	35:00	1:08:00	1:42:00	2:19:00	3:05:00
7:15	36:00	1:10:00	1:44:00	2:22:00	3:10:00
7:26	37:00	1:12:00	1:47:00	2:26:00	3:15:00
7:38	38:00	1:14:00	1:50:00	2:30:00	3:20:00
7:49	39:00	1:16:00	1:53:00	2:34:00	3:25:00
8:01	40:00	1:18:00	1:55:00	2:37:00	3:30:00
8:12	41:00	1:20:00	1:58:00	2:41:00	3:35:00
8:23	42:00	1:21:00	2:01:00	2:45:00	3:40:00
8:35	43:00	1:23:00	2:04:00	2:49:00	3:45:00
8:46	44:00	1:25:00	2:06:00	2:52:00	3:50:00
8:58	45:00	1:27:00	2:09:00	2:56:00	3:55:00
9:09	46:00	1:29:00	2:12:00	3:00:00	4:00:00
9:20	47:00	1:31:00	2:14:00	3:03:00	4:05:00
9:32	48:00	1:33:00	2:17:00	3:07:00	4:10:00
9:43	49:00	1:35:00	2:20:00	3:11:00	4:15:00
9:55	50:00	1:37:00	2:22:00	3:14:00	4:20:00

10

Twenty Questions:
Two Months and Counting

> The most important principle for the runner of the future is that one learns to run by running. All peripheral exercises recede in importance unless they have an immediate effect on running style and endurance.
>
> —ERNST VAN AAKEN, *The Van Aaken Method*

The farther into your marathon-training program you proceed, the more important each week of training becomes and the more significant each workout. When there are just two months to go until your marathon date, it's a good idea to review your understanding of the various integral elements of your training as well as your adaptation to the increased level of effort associated with your workouts.

The twenty questions in this chapter deal with everything from aches and pains (and how to tell the difference) to the racing clothes you'll need to select and try out well before the actual race.

What is the current condition of your running shoes?

As we've noted before, the single largest expense associated with the sport of running is the shoes.

From a biomechanical standpoint, there are some runners

who run so efficiently that they can run their shoes into the ground without fear of injuring themselves. But for most of us shoes are the single most important tool we have to prevent injuries. Our continued good running depends on well-maintained shoes.

With its increases in weekly mileage and in the severity of workouts, marathon training tends to wear out running shoes faster than mere fitness-maintenance running does. Therefore, it's important to regularly examine your running shoes to determine if they are providing proper protection. Unfortunately, one major problem—the amount of compression that has occurred in the mid-sole—is virtually impossible to check. Compressed mid-soles absorb less impact, feeding an increasing amount of the hard road up through your feet, ankles, legs, and knees. The only way to be able to detect compressed mid-soles is by feel: Have you gradually begun to feel a tenderness in your legs when you go out on a run? When you alternate between your several pairs of running shoes, do you notice more leg tenderness while wearing one pair?

If you suspect that the mid-soles of your running shoes have outlived their usefulness, retire the shoes and purchase a replacement pair immediately. The investment—and you should look at it as an investment—in a new pair of shoes will be much less expensive than the cost of a podiatrist or orthopedist to treat an injury.

You *can* visually check the wear on the outer soles of your shoes. If the outer soles or bottoms have worn down to the point that the mid-sole is showing through, but the mid-soles themselves are still absorbing shock, take the shoes to a shoe-repair store and have a new outer sole put on (most running-shoe stores can send the shoes out to such a repair shop for you). Or you can make your own repairs using a product such as Shoe-Goo, but such repairs are usually temporary, as the product wears off quickly.

Your shoes are your only protection against the impact of your ambitious training program. Make certain they are in good condition so they can do their job.

Have you developed any persistent aches or pains?

First of all, it's important to differentiate between an ache and a pain. An ache is a low-level discomfort associated with the exercise process; a pain is a sharp or intense discomfort that may suggest injury. An ache usually affects an area or region of the body while a pain is specific and can be pinpointed.

Aches are to be expected as you increase the quantity and the quality of your running toward your marathon goal. Because of the repetitive nature of the running motion, you can expect to suffer some achiness, and you can expect it to persist in certain areas of your body simply because you reuse that area five times a week. As long as the aches are not overwhelming or debilitating, they are usually nothing to worry about. In fact, they are an indication that your program is having a positive effect.

On the other hand, pains should be considered serious. Deal with them immediately, before they become injuries. Some pains in the feet, ankles, legs, or knees can be cured by changing shoes or by taking a day off. Others are not so easily treated.

And as opposed to the old days, when the typical advice a runner received from a doctor was "If it hurts while you're running, stop running," today there are sports-medicine specialists practicing throughout the country who may not agree with that prescription.

If you are experiencing a persistent pain associated with running, but it is not hobbling you, consult a reliable book that gives medical advice on running injuries. If this does not solve the problem, ask your running friends or your local running club about a good sports-medicine resource person in your area who can treat you.

Aches are to be expected when you engage in any type of sport, but a pain will seldom heal itself and should be treated as soon as possible before it progresses to the level of an injury.

What function does ice perform in the injury-prevention program of a marathoner?

All aerobic sports are characterized by repetitive movements of the same groups of muscles. Overuse injuries occur when a muscle, ligament, tendon, or bone can no longer sustain the repetitive load placed upon it.

Many overuse injuries can be avoided or at least delayed or minimized by immediate treatment of the affected area with the application of ice. Much of the "soft tissue" (muscles, tendons, ligaments) tenderness associated with a marathon-training program comes from inflammation and swelling of the affected area: a sore Achilles tendon, a strain in the huge thigh muscles, even a shin splint. Left untreated, these nagging aches can further weaken the area and can become an injury that seriously interrupts a training program.

Some runners tend to mask these problems by taking aspirin. The analgesic properties of aspirin will lessen the inflammation and swelling, but they will also mask the pain associated with the overuse. A better method of alleviating the inflammation and controlling the swelling is to apply ice as soon as possible after a workout. This brings down the swelling and inflammation and has no negative side effects. By keeping the swelling and inflammation down, the nagging aches that might otherwise interrupt your training can be minimized.

The response of some runners to a persistent ache in the Achilles tendon, for instance, is to apply heat, whether a heating pad or by jumping into a hot tub. Unfortunately, applying heat to a fresh ache is the worst thing you can do. The heat will increase the swelling and inflammation. The object for the first twenty-four to seventy-two hours is to minimize the swelling, not maximize it. Swelling will interfere with the smooth movement of the soft tissue around it and will make it a painful process to get out there and put in a worthwhile workout.

A simple rule of thumb is this: If the ache is new (as of the last seventy-two hours), use ice to reduce swelling and in-flammation. Once you have the inflammation under control, then apply heat to encourage healing through increased blood flow to and from the affected area.

The kind of ice to use depends on the site of the ache and on your ability to be comfortable applying the ice. If you are treating a shin splint, freeze water in a small paper cup and, after your workout, rub the ice up and down the affected area, tearing away more and more of the paper cup as the ice melts. If the affected area is the Achilles tendon, place a handful of ice cubes inside a sealable plastic bag, place a protective layer like a facecloth between the cold ice and your Achilles tendon, then secure the bag of ice in place with an elastic bandage.

Be careful that you don't burn your skin by placing ice directly against it. Never use dry ice.

Continue applying ice after every workout until the affected area heals. Apply the ice for as long as you can manage at each session. Some runners apply ice to an affected area for hours at a time; as it melts, it is replaced.

How does one determine recovery rate?

A hard quality workout is impossible if the body has not properly recovered from its previous quality workout. In such a case, the workout will be characterized by slower times, an abnormal amount of physical and mental effort, and possibly even by injury. Obviously, such a workout then sets the marathoner up for *another* inferior workout. It is therefore imperative to monitor your recovery rate, either through perceived rate of recovery or through monitoring of the resting pulse rate.

The more reliable of these two methods is the resting pulse rate.

If you have kept your training journal for any length of time, you can plot your resting pulse rate (taken first thing in the morning before getting out of bed). Do this with your past week of training. Compare the individual days to the workouts that occurred the day before. If you did a track workout Thursday and your pulse is elevated on Friday morning, your body is obviously attempting to recover. If your average pulse rate for the previous week was 60 and Friday's rate was 68, your body is working overtime to recover from the track workout. If on Saturday morning your rate is not down to within 5 to 7 beats of the previous week's average (baseline) of 60, you have not recovered sufficiently to embark on the hard workout called for on Sunday. Modify Sunday's effort downward so as to avoid injury and/or exhaustion.

If that's the case, you're obviously having trouble adapting to the increased workload. You may want to consider postponing your marathon date six to eight weeks; then drop your program back to that earlier (and easier) point on your schedule.

Or, if your personal life is interfering with your recovery (did you use your weekend "rest" day to paint the house?), try to put some of the household chores off until *after* your marathon.

Similarly, what happens at work often has a spillover effect on your training. Although your running may well be a release for built-up job stress, the stress from your job may also make it impossible for you to sufficiently recover from difficult workouts.

If the stress from your personal life or your job is washing over into your running, and your running is no longer able to relieve the stress, you may want to delay your marathon goal until your life is a bit more balanced.

If the stress that is making it impossible to recover properly appears to be temporary, take maximum advantage of your scheduled "rest" days (get as horizontal as you can and stay that way all day), or modify your race goals downward a bit and shift to one of the easier marathon-training programs in order to ensure better recovery.

What are the consequences of missed workouts?

The answer to this question depends on a number of clarifications, including: How often are you forced to miss workouts and which workouts are they?

If you occasionally (once in two weeks) miss one of the minor workouts (the easy runs), there should be little or no negative effect upon your marathon performance. If you miss one hill workout or one track workout, you will still likely perform well in the marathon.

However, the long weekend workouts form the backbone of any marathon-training program. If you miss one or more of them, you may well undermine your entire program.

If you miss one of the long workouts but can make it up the following day, do so. *But* if you are forced to make that adjustment to the schedule, you will need to schedule a rest or easy day the following day in order to allow for adequate recovery. Do not attempt to double up workouts or to make up missed workouts in addition to the scheduled workout! You must give your body time to recover after a hard workout. Skip the next hill workout on the schedule, and then get back on the scheduled workouts as soon as possible.

When you are forced to miss a hard workout, it's preferable that it be a hill or track workout rather than a long weekend run.

Again, if the rest of your life is regularly interfering with your workouts, you may be best served by rescheduling your marathon to a less stressful and less busy period in your life.

Have your sleep patterns changed since you embarked upon the marathon-training program?

An increase in aerobic activity levels can have two drastically different effects upon your sleeping patterns.

If you are at a fitness level that can accommodate the increased workload of the marathon-training program, the typical response to the increased training is an increase in both the quality and quantity of sleep.

However, if you are finding that the sixteen- or twenty-week marathon-training program is more than you were physically prepared for, your sleep patterns may be disrupted, especially in the wake of the hard workouts (long run, hills, track). This pattern, which is not uncommon when a runner pushes to new plateaus of training, usually comes in the wake of the every-other-weekend long run. It's a sign that you likely embarked upon a marathon-training program without the necessary foundation or that you've been training toward a goal that is beyond your current running potential.

If you embarked on the basic marathon-training program without the proper running background, merely reset your goals, back down your training, regroup, rebuild your foundation training, and begin again. If you have embarked on a time goal program that is beyond your current physical abilities, you can still salvage your marathon by dropping to the next time-goal training program—for example, change from the 3:15 marathon program to the 3:30 program.

How has your body adapted to the increased workloads?

If you are training for your first marathon, the increased workloads associated with the training program pushes your body into new physical territory. You can expect to go through periods of increased tiredness, leg achiness in the wake of a hard workout, lack of spring in the legs, and a general body stiffness and specific leg stiffness and heaviness, especially two days following the weekly long run.

While these signs may not be pleasant, unless they escalate radically, they merely indicate that your body is adapting to an ambitious workload. (If these characteristics are not apparent, you may have picked too easy a program.)

For instance, if the lack of spring in your legs following the weekly track workout is noticeable but does not get any worse from one week to the next, your body is obviously adapting because the workload the legs are accepting is increasing steadily each week.

If the stiffness in the legs gradually vanishes as you get into a workout and begin to warm up, your body is adapting appropriately to the increased physical stress and strain. No marathoner breezes through a sixteen-week training program. The stiffness and soreness should be expected; it is a sure sign that you are pushing your body to new fitness levels.

Naturally, the older you are, the more stiffness you are likely to experience, and the longer it will take to come back from a workout. (Again, this is why we incorporate rest days each week, and why two easy days generally follow one hard day.)

Also, regardless of age, people who are more flexible will experience less stiffness and tightness the day following a hard workout.

Neophyte marathoners with little or no experience in sports often assume that they have hurt themselves or are injuring themselves when they become stiff the day following a hard workout. This is because they are not used to feeling so tight and sore.

Training for a marathon is hard work. But at the same time, it is invigorating as the runner progresses week by week while the body gradually becomes increasingly capable of performances that two months before seemed unattainable.

As you force your body to adapt to higher and higher levels of performance, give yourself the reward of a sports massage every two to four weeks. An hour-long massage breaks up stiffness (and increases flexibility) while also preventing overuse injuries by loosening overworked and tight muscles in the legs, lower back, arms, and shoulders.

It is common to feel sore the day following a deep sports massage, which comes from the masseur or masseuse breaking loose stiff tissue, but by the second day following the massage, the body is usually more flexible and more able to adapt to the increasingly heavy workloads.

What does "carbohydrate-loading" mean?

Not so long ago, the dining tables of sports teams were heavily loaded with meat products; the theory was that athletes needed to fill themselves up with protein before a game or during periods of heavy training. However, when a 250-pound football player sits down to a steak before a big game, all he's doing is diverting blood flow to his stomach to digest the steak when the blood could be put to better use by his working muscles. Besides, a steak takes so long to digest that the game is long over before the body begins to convert it to usable protein.

What the athlete actually needs is carbohydrates, which are readily digested and serve as a ready fuel for athletic performance. In fact, carbohydrates are essential for marathoners.

There are two distinct types of carbohydrates: simple and complex. Simple carbohydrates are essentially sugars (e.g., a piece of butterscotch hard candy) while complex carbohydrates are most readily available in fresh fruits and vegetables. The marathoner needs to regularly consume complex carbohydrates, which are stored in the body for use as endurance fuels, and which fill the glycogen reserves in the muscles and liver. Simple carbohydrates become important *once the endurance activity is well under way.* Simple sugars serve as an excellent fuel source for the working muscles and the brain of the endurance athlete, since both muscles and brain work on simple sugars and since simple sugars are readily converted to energy by the exercising body.

Unfortunately, the human body is capable of storing only a limited amount of glycogen—a form of readily available stored carbohydrates. Other carbohydrates are converted by the body into glucose, which is then either stored in fat tissue or circulated in the bloodstream as free fatty acids. Glucose is not so readily available.

When we refer to carbohydrate-loading, we are referring to the process of increasing or maximizing those stores of glycogen in the liver and muscles. Physiologically, a runner carries enough glycogen for about two hours of running, one hour's worth stored in the muscles, the other in the liver. After two hours, the glycogen becomes depleted and, for fuel, the athlete turns to using stored energy in the form of fat. This is a very inefficient process and is part of what you're teaching your body to do more efficiently while on long runs. During the transition, if simple sugars are not available for quick conversion to energy, the runner "hits the wall," a very unpleasant process similar to the final throes of an automobile running out of gasoline.

Traditionally, the marathoner turns to carbohydrate-loading only in the final week of training. He or she begins the process by first going through the depletion phase. A week before the marathon, the runner goes on a long run and depletes the available glycogen. For the next few days, he or she eats a diet heavy in protein and very low in carbohydrates, thereby further depriving the muscles and liver of glycogen. Finally, the runner gorges on carbohydrates during the last several days before the race. Like a dried-out sponge plunged into water, the liver and muscles become supersaturated with glycogen.

However, the depletion phase itself causes problems. Just at the time when the runner should be building strength, depletion tears down the body, undermining a good bit of hard training. The high-protein, low-carbohydrate diet can cause nausea or headache, and generally make the runner feel miserable.

While some veterans still swear by the depletion phase of carbohydrate-loading, others consider it passé. There is a growing body of scientific evidence to suggest that a marathoner should carbohydrate-load constantly.

In 1981, a team led by W. M. Sherman measured muscle glycogen storage in three groups of trained athletes. Group A was put through the traditional seven-day carbohydrate-depletion/carbohydrate-loading regimen (15 percent carbohydrate diet for four days and then changed to 75 percent carbohydrate diet for three days); Group B was placed on a

50 percent carbohydrate diet for all seven days; and Group C was placed on a 50 percent carbohydrate diet for the first three days and then changed to a 75 percent carbohydrate diet. A typical American diet consists of 20 to 25 percent carbohydrates.

Groups A and C reached the same level of muscle glycogen saturation after seven days (nearly 40 grams per kilogram of wet muscle) while Group B reached only about 25 grams per kilogram.

The conclusion is simple: You can reach the same level of glycogen saturation by merely increasing your carbohydrate intake over the final three to four days of your marathon training as you can by incorporating the very unpleasant and sometimes dangerous depletion phase.

Have you gravitated more to carbohydrate-based foods?

The body is a very intelligent machine. Under an increased mileage load, it frequently sends out signals that it is running low on certain vitamins, minerals, and food fuels by creating a craving for foods that the runner may not typically be in the habit of eating. The foods for which the body develops an urge are usually in the carbohydrate family, especially complex carbohydrates such as those found in fresh vegetables, potatoes, and grain products.

The exercising body needs increasing amounts of carbohydrates to provide fuel for the exercising muscles and to keep the body's gas tank filled.

If you have paid attention to your eating habits during training, you may have seen a gradual and subtle shift away from high-fat meats to fish and chicken, from highly processed foods to more fresh foods.

If you are two months out from your marathon date and you still eat a typical American diet (one heavy in animal fats and cholesterol, bleached flour, and refined sugar), you can help your body adapt to the volume and intensity of training by making the shift to better-quality food fuels. Minor dietary changes will have a major effect on your ability to run farther faster and to recover more quickly.

- When eating chicken, first remove the skin—it contains half the fat (and cholesterol) in chicken.
- If you eat beef, trim off most of the fat and pick leaner cuts.
- When you eat green salads, the darker green the lettuce you use as the base the better (iceberg is the least nutritious lettuce).
- Eat at least one piece of fresh fruit per day.
- Eat fish at least once a week, twice if convenient.
- Avoid processed and prepared meats, such as bacon, hot dogs, or luncheon meats; these are high in fat, cholesterol, and nitrates.

You can't expect your increasingly sleek sports car of a body to perform well on low-octane fuel. Fill'er up with the good stuff.

Have you learned what brand of fluid replacement drinks your target marathon will serve? Have you begun practicing with the concoction during your workouts?

Marathons typically offer both water and one of the growing array of fluid and electrolyte replacement sports drinks at aid stations; and it's best to run your marathon by depending on the aid they provide. (Most marathons will set up a separate table at each aid station for special fluid concoctions runners provide for themselves before the race. Unfortunately, in the excitement there may be a mix-up and your fluid bottle may be picked up by someone else by mistake. It happens in Olympic marathons where only a few dozen runners compete, and it frequently happens at marathons with hundreds and thousands of runners.)

Some people (and race packets) still refer to aid by the

ubiquitous term *ERG* (Electrolyte Replacement Gookinaid), which was one of the first athletic drinks provided to runners back in the 1970s. ERG is difficult to find these days. If the race information you have from your marathon mentions that ERG will be supplied, it's worth your while to find out in advance exactly which drink they mean. The most common ERG-type drinks at marathons these days are Gatorade (or Gatorlode), from the Quaker Oats company, and Exceed, which is made by Ross Laboratories. A dozen or so minor brands have also entered the athletic-drink fray.

In addition, ask the race office which flavor they plan to provide (most drinks come in at least two flavors; there's no sense practicing with orange if they provide lemon-lime on race day), and what concentration they will use for the race. If you are unfamiliar with the specific drink, ask whether it is available for purchase in your area; if they don't know, ask for a phone number so that you can call the manufacturer yourself. You'll want to obtain some so you can practice with it.

Don't mix the drink as strong as the directions on the back of the packets suggest, because that will probably be hard to swallow. In fact, most race directors cut the suggested concentration in half. It is more palatable, it is processed more readily, and marathoners are going to be drinking so much fluid that they will easily ingest a sufficient amount of the nutrients in the mix.

Use the athletic drink not only on your long runs during the final two months, but also during and following your hill and track workouts, and carry some with you for weekday runs over 5 miles. If you are training in a warm or hot environment, take a bottle of replacement fluid along with you on all your runs and drink it during the first forty-five minutes of your workout.

Always drink the athletic drink well chilled. A chilled drink will be emptied from the stomach and processed much faster than will a warm one.

If you train in a hot environment, fill your bottle—not all

the way to the top, because fluids expand just before they freeze—the night before you run, and place it in the freezer overnight.

How have you responded to your upper-body workouts?

In the stressful, exhausting final miles of a marathon, when your energy level begins to fall and your biomechanics begin to deteriorate, strong abdominals, arms, chest, and shoulders can keep you on pace and can keep your running style efficient.

If you have regularly been doing your upper-body workouts, you will almost certainly have seen some alterations in your muscle definition, especially in the abdominals and the upper arms. You can safely continue your upper-body workouts through the final week of tapering.

Even the act of carrying a squeeze bottle filled with the marathon-day drink on your runs (or two, on the long workouts) can help increase your upper-body advantage. Alternate the hand in which you carry the bottle every mile. Most running shops sell straps that can be attached to the bottle, making it easier to carry.

Have you a running partner with whom you can do some of your long runs?

As discussed in Chapter 8, training with a partner has a multitude of advantages. The distraction provided by a partner can often make even the most formidable workout agreeable.

The ideal training partner is one of similar ability or one who is a slightly better runner than you are so that he or she can comfortably keep up with you on a longer run while also occasionally providing someone to key off of in an attempt to improve your own performance.

Many distance runners also band together to go to the

track one evening a week to do their speed workouts. The good company at the track can serve to outweigh any negative associations runners have with the concept of track workouts. Such groups typically retire to a local pizza parlor after the workout to socialize and wind down. However, many runners—myself included—prefer to do track workouts alone.

In some areas, groups who go out on long weekend runs together post notices on the bulletin board of the local running shop. If you want to join such a group, but their weekend long run is longer than your schedule currently calls for, you can always join the group for the first part of the run, then peel off and finish your workout alone. Such running groups are, of course, a valuable resource for all sorts of information.

If no notices are posted, ask the store manager whether he or she knows of any other runners looking to share the roads on longer workouts.

How have your long runs been going?

It bears repeating that the long run is the skeleton on which all other aspects of your marathon-training program are hung. The long run builds cardiovascular endurance while also progressively stressing the other essential body systems (muscles, tendons, ligaments, etc.). It also trains the mitochondria on the cellular level, teaching them to continue to yield energy without exhausting themselves.

It's essential to make the long runs quality workouts, especially if you are using a time-driven training schedule. Nevertheless, they should not be regarded as a grim duty. Long runs are an opportunity to bring together the good results of your specific weekday workouts, especially the hill and track workouts, to test your progress, to approximate a portion of the upcoming marathon, and to practice your mental toughness.

The long run should not be pushed through at any cost, however. If, well into a long run, instead of becoming smoother as your muscles warm, you feel yourself losing it (e.g., your concentration drops or you begin to go anaerobic), walk for a hundred steps, catch your breath, and then roll into an easy jog until everything comes back.

If, during a long run, you develop a specific and nagging pain, don't bravely push through the pain. You may end up injuring yourself. Instead, slow to a walk. If it vanishes while you are walking, walk for a little while and then gently begin running again. Or try running on the opposite side of the road; sometimes the angle of the road surface on the left (preferred) side of the road is the culprit and an occasional switch to the right side cures the problem. If the pain persists, end the run and have the potential injury evaluated by a professional.

A common way a long run turns sour is similar to what can happen at the actual race: You may tend to go out faster than you should, thereby using up too much energy in the first few miles, and having little left for the final miles. It is better to sacrifice a little on speed at the front end of your long run and make up for it at the far end, after your legs have warmed up and are moving more freely.

In addition, the first half of a long run frequently seems to be going bad only to come around within the final miles (some marathons go that way, too). If the workout begins badly, try to stay with it: It may not stay that way.

Never continue your long run beyond what is called for in the program, no matter how good you feel that day. Use restraint. If you feel extremely good and filled with running at the end of your long run, save it for your next workout. Running yourself to exhaustion in any workout invites staleness and injury.

And don't feel discouraged if you feel tighter and stiffer two mornings after the long run than you did the morning after it. The stiffness is caused by lactic acid accumulation, which peaks the second day after a hard workout. Once you get through the first mile or so of that day's workout, your legs will warm up, and the stiffness will lift.

How refined has your sense of pace become?

An evenly paced marathon is the most assured method of succeeding in your marathon effort.

The secret to successful marathoning is the careful metering out of energy along the way with an eye toward coming up dry only *after* crossing the finish line.

In this respect, marathoning resembles long-distance economy driving. Imagine you face a trip of 360 miles with a full tank of gasoline (twelve gallons) in a car that gets 30 miles to the gallon. If you drive the car conservatively, within its mileage abilities, you can arrive at your destination with a few drops of gasoline to spare. On the other hand, if you give into some bursts of enthusiasm along the way, you'll probably run out of gas with 20 miles to go.

As we've already discussed, the weekly track workouts provide the best opportunity to learn pacing. Once you become more adept at pacing on the track, it's time, now that the race is approaching, to apply that skill to your road workouts.

In rural and suburban areas, many roads have mileage markers at specific road structures (bridges, etc.) or at regular intervals. The latter kind of marker can be used in pacing yourself. Use the course between two such markers—preferably a mile apart—as a "speed trap." As you approach this segment of the run, estimate your per-mile speed, and then time yourself through the "speed trap." See how accurate you were in estimating your pace as you come out the other end (if your "speed trap" isn't a mile long, you'll have to convert the time to a per-mile one). Practice pacing on a road course will prove invaluable for your race.

In urban areas, this exercise is more difficult, but if your city has a street grid, call the city's engineer and ask for the exact lengths of the long and short sides of a city block. From that you can figure out the distance of running once around the block (two long and two short sides). During your weekday runs, throw in one such loop and see how accurately you can predict your pace.

If you run with a partner, turn the pacing exercises into a game. See which of you can more accurately predict your pace through the next mile or around the next city block.

How well have you adapted to hill workouts?

Whether you have picked a marathon whose course features hills or one that is flat as a board, hill workouts are important. As previously noted, hill workouts build leg strength, increase endurance in the quadriceps, and push back the anaerobic threshold.

However, hills go up *and* they go down. Grete Waitz, the queen of marathon running, learned the hard way how important it is to practice running well downhill. At her first Boston Marathon, she was forced to drop out in the final miles when her thighs began to cramp up from the many downhills on the course. "I practiced my uphill running," she said afterward, "but never thought to practice running downhill."

Running downhill provides an opportunity to practice proper style in running faster and to increase your stride length.

In a race, there is nothing to be gained by charging a hill. You never make up on the downside of a hill what you expend on the uphill side. Keep your rhythm, attempt to keep control of your breathing, and drop your stride length into a lower gear in order to smoothly flow up the hill as efficiently as possible. Once you've topped the hill, switch into overdrive: Increase your stride length while maintaining your rhythm, and continue to control your breathing until it stabilizes. By regularly practicing running uphills and maximizing your efficiency running downhills, you can come as close as humanly possible to equalizing the effort put out climbing as you gain rolling down the other side.

Have your weekly track workouts improved your leg speed?

If you plan to run your first marathon at a nine-minute pace (3:56), you won't be able to accomplish your goal if all of your workouts are at a pace of nine or ten minutes per mile. You must practice regularly at a pace faster than that. In fact, in order to be capable of stringing together twenty-six nine-minute miles, you must be capable of comfortably running four or five 7:30 or eight-minute miles at the track or of inserting an eight-minute mile or two in the middle of your weekday runs.

As already discussed, the track is where you hone your ability to run fast. The surface is so smooth that you can work on perfecting your running style as you increase your leg speed.

Taping your track workouts can increase the fun quotient and the effectiveness of the workout itself. If you have access to a camcorder and a tripod, ask a friend who knows how to operate the camcorder to set them up in the middle of the playing field. As you do your repeat miles, have your friend frame you in the camcorder viewfinder and then, using the tripod to keep the camcorder steady, follow you through your entire mile. (If the camcorder has a clock function, which most of the current models do, make certain it's turned on.)

When you get home after your track workout, you can study your style by popping the tape in your VCR.

- Are your shoulders drooping during the final lap as you tire?
- Are you able to keep your leg turnover the same during all four laps?
- Does your head stay perfectly parallel to the ground throughout the mile?
- Are you using your arms properly to provide the necessary rhythm and the additional power? Are you exaggerating

your arm swing in the final lap in an attempt to keep your pace as you tire?
- Does your running style change as the repeat miles pile up?

If you record later track workouts on the same tape, you can follow your progress as you work on your running style. The improvements should become quite pronounced if you watch the most recent workout and then rewind to your first video track session.

You can do much the same thing by having a friend video-tape you during your hill workouts, especially if the video camera has a good telephoto lens.

Have you perfected surging during your fartlek-compatible workouts?

Fartlek, as discussed, is the exercise of picking up your speed in the midst of a road workout by surging between landmarks (every two telephone poles, for example). This should not be used when you are still recovering from a hard workout a day or two before. (If in doubt, your legs will tell you if they are capable of picking up the pace and if they feel up to one surge or a half-dozen). And remember that surging does not mean sprinting—it means picking up the pace smoothly by fifteen to thirty seconds per mile.

Do not begin fartleks until you have been running long enough to warm up the leg muscles—at least fifteen minutes. The technique can effectively be used in the middle of any workout, from a 5-mile recovery run to the weekend long run.

Are you adapting well enough to your intensive training program to throw in a "burner" or two each week?

A "burner" is an extended surge and can be an effective tool if you are one of those runners who is adapting extremely well to the marathon-training program. Burners should never be used by runners who are running on the verge of an injury, whose legs are tired or dead when they go out on easy recovery runs, or who find that it takes two easy days to come back from one hard day.

A burner provides an opportunity for the well-adapting runner to get in an additional sub-maximal speed workout or two each week, depending on the rate of recovery. A burner should always be placed in the middle of a road workout, and should never begin until the legs have had at least 2 miles to warm up. The burner is a smooth increase to a pace fifteen to forty-five seconds faster than the speed called for on that day's run, and the burn should be extinguished at least one mile from the end of that day's scheduled run. If Thursday's schedule calls for a "5-mile gentle run" and gentle has been a 7:30 pace, a burner would involve running the first and second miles at 7:30, the third and fourth miles at 6:45–7:15, and the final mile at 7:30.

While an occasional surge during a weekend long run is acceptable if your legs feel good, a burner should not be used during any hard workout.

If you begin a burner and your legs begin to feel it, back off immediately. Burners are meant as additional training tools and not as substitutes for the good, more gentle workout that the schedule calls for.

Have you been able to recover well from scheduled time trials and races?

In the time-oriented marathon-training schedules, racing shorter distances is deemphasized in favor of time trials. The runner who is using one of these programs already has a brace of recent 10K race times from which to gauge his or her marathon pace potential. Time trials are preferable to races for these runners for several reasons.

- In races there is too great a tendency to race instead of using the race as a test.
- The time required to travel to and from the race would be

better used in resting before and after a time trial of similar length.

- You and your watch are in total control of a time trial. You can make appropriate adjustments to the pace and the effort without the distraction of a race setting.
- You can do your time trial at the point in the day that's most convenient, instead of being forced to run at the race starting time.

Nevertheless, runners who have not run a marathon before or who have not run one in many years will derive value from using races as time trials.

- You will gain valuable experience in fitting yourself into a race situation, which is important as you approach your marathon.
- The race environment will typically encourage a novice marathoner to run faster than he or she might while solo, thereby bringing out the best possible performance (some people theorize that a race situation is good for a fifteen-second-per-mile increase in speed).
- The camaraderie of a race situation helps further initiate the first-time marathoner into the world of road racing.

Where a time trial is called for, treat it as though it were a race situation. In order to maximize your performance, first jog for a mile or so in order to loosen up your legs and to switch from anaerobic to aerobic breathing, and do a few wind sprints to stretch out the legs.

Have you chosen your wardrobe for your marathon?

Two months before the marathon date is not too early to begin picking the clothes you'll wear on the big day.

There have been instances where well-meaning friends of first-time marathoners have presented them with brand-new running outfits a day before the marathon; feeling obliged to wear the outfit, the novice marathoner runs the race with chafed underarms or bleeding inner thighs because he or she had not had time to do trial long runs in the clothes.

When you selected your marathon, the weather was a key determinant (see pages 93–94). If you picked an autumn marathon (New York, Humboldt, Portland, etc.), you will want to practice in gear that is relatively warm and that you can wear in layers. This way, even if the day is chilly, you can remove a layer or two as your body warms up; then either discard the top layer or tie it around your waist for the remainder of the race. If the race is typically chilly, practice long runs wearing a polypropylene turtleneck and a hat. Half the heat produced by the exercising body is lost through the head, so under chilly conditions, you'll want to hold in as much heat as you can.

If your intended marathon is typically warm, practice in a singlet and a light-colored hat to keep the radiant heat of the sun off your head. And consider sunglasses designed for running (i.e., of light construction that won't injure the bridge of your nose or slip down repeatedly during a run).

With the way weather patterns have been changing over the past few years, practice in and take along with you clothes that will accommodate temperatures opposite to those expected at the race. (In 1991, the Western States 100 on June 30 suffered its first ever chilly, snowy running; it is usually marked by canyons where the temperatures go well above 100 degrees. For the first time in nine years, it didn't rain once during the 1991 Leadville Trail 100 in Colorado, thereby catching some runners unprepared.)

Be prepared for anything as far as weather goes. Practice in everything you are likely to wear, especially during your long runs. You won't know whether some running clothes will chafe until you have perspired sufficient amounts of salt between your legs (around 18 miles).

The synthetic materials now available are a boon to the modern marathoner.

Here's a list of clothing that you should take on shakedown long runs and that you should pack to take to your marathon:

Light hat of a light color, with brim
Woolen or polypro hat
Polypro turtleneck
Racing singlet
Short-sleeve T-shirt (to wear as a possible discard layer over
turtleneck)
2 pairs of running shorts—one loose-fitting for hot weather
marathon, the other more snug-fitting for cold weather
Polypro tights
Ankle racing socks in the Thor-Lo range to provide blister
protection
Gore-Tex warm-up/cool-down pants and jacket for before
and after race—or, if conditions are atrocious, during
the race
Lightweight sunglasses
Running bra

If you find that you need to make adjustments in the way
you are doing your workouts in the wake of discussions in
this chapter, you still have two months to go—sufficient
time to make adjustments without negatively affecting your
performance.

11

The Ideal Long Run

> If one trains hard and pushes human courage and endurance to the utmost you come out on the summit.
>
> —RUDY FAHL, in his foreword to John R. Rose's *Foster Sons of Pikes Peak*

The long run is the centerpiece of any marathon-training program. In fact, it is possible for an experienced runner to successfully run a marathon with minimum training during the week if he or she faithfully does the long run each weekend. (Of course, I don't recommend such a one-sided program.) Let's review why the long run is so important.

- By progressively increasing the distance of the long run, the body's capacity for work is increased. This increased endurance is essential for successfully completing the marathon distance.
- The long run gradually pushes back the anaerobic threshold as endurance is increased.
- The increased time on the legs gradually strengthens the muscles, ligaments, and tendons of the legs, ankles, and feet, thereby adapting them to marathon distances.
- The increasing length of the long runs builds confidence. As the runner is able to go farther and farther as the long runs progress, the distance between the runner's current ability and the marathon distance shrinks.
- The increases in the body's capacity for aerobic work have

a spillover effect on the weekday workouts, making them easier and reducing recovery time.

The long run should, as much as possible, approximate the course on which you will run your marathon. If the marathon you've entered is an urban one, at least half of your long runs should be done on urban courses so that your body can become used to and familiar with the challenges of urban running, especially the uneven and interrupted running surface. If your marathon is an out-and-back course, try to use such a course for most of your long runs.

If your marathon is run in hot weather, do your long runs at a time of the day when the temperature approximates the weather you'll face on race day. If running at midday is still not hot enough, wear dark-colored clothing and a thick hat. And anyone running a warm-weather marathon must teach the body how to process at least two quarts of fluid an hour.

You don't need to do every long run on a course that approximates the marathon course. In fact, an occasional long run on a course that is totally opposite your upcoming marathon course will provide a much-appreciated break from routine. But attempting to run at least half of your long runs on a course similar to the one you will face on race day will be of great benefit.

Because the length of your long run increases every two weeks, it is not always possible to retain the same course. You may have a perfect 12-mile course but you may need to go to a different course once your scheduled long runs jump to 14 and 16 and 18 miles. You can modify your current 12-mile long-run course by using it as an out-and-back course; by adding a 2-mile loop at some point along the 12 miles to extend it to 14 (and beyond), you can repeat portions of the course to add extra mileage as needed, and you can run the course backward on alternating weekends in order to keep it fresh.

What *is* very important with your long-run course is that

you measure it as accurately as possible. Although car odometers are not especially accurate, they are better than merely making an estimate. Modern electronic bicycle cyclometers, if installed correctly, are fairly accurate tools. As you measure your course with a bicycle cyclometer, also mark off mile-long segments within the course for use as speed traps during your run. Of course, the first mile is the most important for establishing pace, and the first mile of your course should also be the most convenient on which to establish a measured mile.

Factors to Consider in Designing a Long-Run Course

Availability of Fluids

You can carry your fluids with you in a squeeze bottle (remember to use the same fluids that will be available during the actual marathon), you can plant them along the course the night before, or, if your course includes grocery stores or water fountains where you can replenish your fluid supply, you can stop your chronograph long enough to refill your bottles.

Accessibility

Although it is a pleasant change of pace to make a road trip to a new long-run course occasionally, training for a marathon is very time-consuming. Therefore, the best long-run course is one that is close to home, so that you need to travel only a minimal distance to get to it.

Availability of an "Out"

Because long runs occasionally turn sour—you might twist an ankle or a thunderstorm may roll in—the well-designed long run has a reasonable emergency exit. Perhaps the course parallels a city bus line, so you can hop a bus to return home, or is designed as a loop course, so you can cut across the loop to get home if something goes wrong. Or there are phone booths along the way, so you can call home to have someone pick you up.

Always carry some money with you in the pocket of your running shorts, whether for bus fare, to buy some extra fluid, or to make a telephone call. The ideal long-run situation from a course and fluid standpoint is to have a friend in a car or on a bicycle meet you every few miles with fluid and with a way to get you home should problems develop. However, not everyone is fortunate enough to have a friend who is willing to dedicate several hours each Saturday morning to look after you. Most of us become better marathoners by learning to rely on ourselves as much as possible.

Proximity of Shelter Near the End

The ideal long-run course allows you to finish your run at a point approximately one mile from your home; from there you can at least walk the mile as a cool-down, walk in your front door, and proceed directly to the shower. (Ideally, try to cool down by walking ¼ mile per 5 miles run.)

It is important to have some shelter available in the wake of your long run. Your metabolism is stoked to a very high level and your body is throwing off a tremendous amount of heat. For fifteen minutes following your long run, your body is similar to a raging furnace. It is temporarily impervious to the cold around it. But that envelope of protection gradually dissipates after you stop. You need to stay warm if the day is cold; at the other extreme, you need to get into a cool place if the day was hot, so that you do not further break yourself down and open yourself to germs that under other conditions would be turned back by your body's natural resistance.

When your long run is finished, take care of yourself as soon as possible. If you drove to your long-run course, attempt to end your run within a mile of your car. Make certain that you've brought along dry clothes into which you can change.

Your body doesn't need to be stressed any more. The long run is designed to carefully break down your body so that it bounces back and becomes stronger—it is not designed as an opportunity to open you to sickness.

Aesthetics of the Course

The long-run course should be as pleasant as you can make it so that you look forward to and enjoy the experience. Some runners will tell you that they like to do their long runs on courses that they pick specifically for their ugliness because completing such a course makes them mentally tougher; but that isn't an advisable technique if you are just beginning or restarting your marathon lifestyle. Make your long-run course as pleasant as possible without making it totally different from the marathon course you will run on race day. The pleasanter you can make the long-run experience, the more you will anticipate the run next weekend and the weekend after that.

Comfort Considerations

Your long run approximates many of the conditions you will face while actually running your marathon race, and there are a number of contingencies for which you should prepare in advance.

It is advisable to carry a dozen or so sheets of toilet paper folded neatly and slipped into a Ziploc baggie that you can then hang over the waistband of your running shorts. You never know when you might need it. On race day, you would not be the first runner to wait in line at the portable outhouses only to find when it's your turn that the toilet paper is gone.

If it's cold, wear light gloves or slip a pair of socks over your hands to keep them warm. If and when you warm up, slip the gloves or socks into the waistband of your running shorts.

As your runs become longer and longer, you may find that various body parts begin to chafe. Your inner thighs may rub together when you run. Your underarms may become chafed from roughly one thousand swings per mile. Chafing of body parts is usually aggravated if you perspire, since although the water from the sweat evaporates, it leaves the salt behind, which gradually builds up and works like sandpaper. Chafing may also occur at places where your running clothing is too tight or where there is too much excess material, which is why it is essential to take several long runs in the clothes you anticipate wearing on race day.

Generously spread petroleum jelly on any areas of your body that have a tendency to become chafed. Some runners also like to spread a thin film of petroleum jelly on areas of their feet that tend to rub inside their running shoes. If you are running in weather that is particularly hot, use lanolin instead—petroleum jelly may eventually be broken down by your perspiration. When purchasing either product, buy it in a tube; in hot weather, it will not leak out around the cap.

Some men have a tendency to suffer bleeding nipples when they run long distances—this is caused, in large part, by salt crystals forming as perspiration evaporates. The salt crystals eventually build up enough to cause severe chafing. This problem can usually be rectified by putting tape over the nipples before a long run or before the race.

Most women find that running long distances is much more comfortable while wearing a sports bra, and there are a number of them on the market, the most common being Jog Bra. If you plan to wear a specific bra for the marathon, wear it on your long runs. Some women find that their sports bra works well for 15 to 18 miles but then begins to chafe at various pressure points. You may wish to experiment with several different designs until you find one that works well over the long run.

Also, there is no medical evidence that the female runner need reschedule a run because of her menstrual cycle. A variety of fanny packs are on the market, any one of which can be used to carry products you may need on a long run. Fanny packs weigh almost nothing and provide a measure of confidence at being completely prepared for any eventuality while putting in your miles.

Some runners also find that they increase the comfort factor on a long run by carrying along some hard candy, which they lodge in their cheek out beyond 15 miles or so; this provides a steady drip of simple carbohydrates to the working muscles. If you find that this helps on your long run, be certain to practice in order to prevent accidentally swallowing it while running.

Some older runners begin to feel their age out beyond 18 miles, and carry a few aspirin or aspirin substitutes to take along the way to head off inflammation of the joints. However, a danger associated with such products is that they tend to mask symptoms that may be pointing to a potential injury. The latter stages of a long run or a marathon are difficult because the fatigue combined with the overuse of the muscles and joints can lead to increasingly sloppy biomechanics in our running styles. This deterioration of style can aggravate or instigate overuse injuries. Aspirin and aspirin substitutes may blind the runner to an increasingly serious situation as his or her style goes bad. The use of aspirin and aspirin substitutes, then, is something you should consider very carefully based upon your needs and the advice of your physician.

The Use of Caffeine to Stimulate Free Fatty Acid Use

Your increasing level of endurance over the sixteen- to twenty-week program will, among other things, teach your body to make a subtle shift to rely more on the free fatty acids that are available in your bloodstream as an energy source instead of almost exclusively on the glycogen stored in the muscles and liver. There is an almost limitless supply of free fatty acids, but it is much more difficult for the body to convert them to energy than it is to use the limited supply of glycogen. It has been found that caffeine can jump-start the free fatty acid use sequence, which is why before a long run or a marathon some runners drink a cup or two of strong coffee. (The other side effect is that the caffeine helps stimulate the intestines, facilitating an early-morning bowel movement.) Some people, however, do not perform well after drinking coffee because it upsets an already nervous stomach. The use or avoidance of caffeine is something with which you may want to experiment on your longer runs.

12

T Minus Two Weeks

> ... There is a bond that links the 4:15 marathoner with the "god" who finishes more than two hours earlier. They share a common energy that frightens them and makes them brothers under the sweatband.
>
> —ERICH SEGAL, in his introduction to Richard Benyo's *Masters of the Marathon*

To complete an ambitious marathon-training schedule is to walk a high wire where one slip or miscue can bring you and your dreams tumbling down. It seems something of a paradox, then, that the final two weeks of training, in which you taper off on the volume and intensity of your training, is absolutely, positively, definitely the most dangerous period of the entire program.

A number of very positive things can happen during the final two weeks:

- Your long-running commitment to faithfully training is rewarded as the training regimen is gradually diminished leading up to race day.
- Microscopic tears and near-injuries have time to heal.
- No longer expended on training, your stores of physical energy come back, possibly in more volume than ever before in your life.
- Your psychological energy, which has been expended on a

nearly daily basis to stay current on and to push through your training program, now pours into your reserve tanks as you roll toward your marathon date.

You are fit, you are filled with energy, you are healing and becoming whole, you are strong, you begin to feel you could leap tall buildings with a single bound—and therein lies the danger.

Fourteen or eighteen weeks of hard work to build to this point can be thrown away in fifteen minutes by giving in to what are essentially the baser instincts. The more earthy way to put it is, Don't let your ass overrule your head.

The inflow of energy and strength in the wake of tapering off on your heavy exercising load tends to infuse the would-be marathoner with a royal cockiness. After weeks of putting out great amounts of mental energy to drag the tired body through the last miles of a workout, that poor body that seemed as though it was too often on its last legs now seems capable of anything.

The tendency is to take advantage of the tanks filled with energy and power, to go out and do benchmark workouts, to blow out some of the carbon. You feel that you deserve a few good runs after all the work you've put in to earn this sense of power. This feeling usually comes in the middle of one of your workouts during the final week, when you are moving like a mist over the ground, your legs so strong and smooth they seem to be doing no work at all, your breathing slow and even, your arm rhythm perfectly in sync with the rhythm of the spheres. You feel as though you could run forever—or even longer. It is at that moment when your judgment is least fit to the task of holding you back. At that point you are a running animal, not a thinking, rational human being.

You're scheduled to do a 5-miler but this run feels so damned good you don't ever want it to end—so you allow it to continue, you indulge yourself. You run 7, 8, 9 miles, and it still feels wonderful. You continue on to 10, and perhaps beyond.

And what you've just done is steal good miles from your upcoming marathon.

The tapering period is the culmination of your entire program, when all the miles are in the bank, and when you are looking for every little bit of energy you can hoard for the big day.

There is no such thing as going into a marathon with *too much* energy or *too much* rest. The more energy you take into it, the better the final miles will go. It is no failing in arithmetic when Frank Shorter says, "The marathon is only half over when you reach 20 miles."

There are five things you should do during the final two weeks of your program leading up to your marathon, and three of them is to rest. The fourth is to eat meals that are very high in complex carbohydrates and drink plenty of fluids. The fifth is to carefully and faithfully follow the workouts as outlined in your program.

Oh, yes, there is one other thing you can do: You can wallow in your newfound power. You've reached a point where you are in better aerobic condition than 99.9 percent of the people in the world.

There are some things you *should not* do in addition to not running one step more than your program calls for. For instance, don't use these two weeks and this newfound energy to do any projects around the house that require a great deal of physical energy or strength, even if you've been putting them off for three months. Save every ounce of your energy for race day.

13

The Last Supper

The translation from saying to doing will demand an effort
I can't even imagine. How can I, without ever having tried
such a thing?

—JAMES E. SHAPIRO, *Meditations from the*
Breakdown Lane: Running Across America

The final two weeks of a marathon-training program are
critical to allow the months of training to come together while
the body and mind energize themselves in anticipation of the
big day. The final two days are hypercritical.

By overdoing it during the final two weeks, you can undo
all of your training. By losing your focus during the critical
final two days, you can undermine your effort. By allowing a
last-minute lapse in the discipline that made it possible to get
to the starting line, you can affect how you'll arrive at the
finish line.

Throughout the final weeks, days, and minutes before the
race, there is a multitude of temptations that will conspire to
undo your hard work. Run too far or too hard a week before
the race, and you use precious energy and strength that you'll
need on race day. Spend too much time on your feet the day
before the race, and it will most certainly affect your ability
to continue running well in the final miles of the marathon.

The best single bit of advice you could receive concerning
the two days before the race is this: Don't get caught up in the
hype surrounding the race.

Before deciding to do anything during the final days, simply ask yourself, How will what I'm about to do affect the outcome of my marathon?

Travel to the Marathon

As recommended earlier, the first-time marathoner would do best to enter a race close to home. This allows for a short trip by air, bus, or automobile that usually doesn't involve a time-zone readjustment. If you can take Friday afternoon off from work, the ideal scenario is to leave directly from work and get to your lodging as early as you possibly can. Once you're there, wind down a bit, get off your feet, eat a meal high in carbohydrates very early, and get a good night's sleep. Have a glass of wine or a bottle of beer if you ordinarily do or if you think by doing so you'll be more likely to get to sleep.

You should also be hydrating constantly during the final days, so that your body is supersaturated with fluids. If you are driving, carry a squeeze bottle along with you filled with water, fruit juice, or carbohydrate replacement fluid. If you are flying, do the same thing, especially since the air inside an airplane is pressurized to an altitude near 10,000 feet, where the dehydration effects are considerable. Drink with dinner, drink more before you go to bed. (If you drink too much, your body will process it and urinate it out.) The more fluid you can take in during the final days, especially while you are traveling to your race and are out of your normal element, the better your body systems will function on the day of the race.

If you are traveling to a race that is several thousand miles away, review the hints on pages 41–44 about making the trip easier for you.

Most runners traveling to their first marathon are inclined to stay at the official race headquarters hotel. Unfortunately, that hotel is full of other runners who are just as nervous and wired as you are. And many of them will attempt to ease stored-up energy by pacing up and down the halls most of the night. (I was kept awake one night by a looney who felt it was appropriate to get in some last-minute wind sprints up and down the hotel corridor.) No matter what motel or hotel you stay at, when you make your reservation, ask for a quiet room. Insist that it be *away* from the ice machine; runners have a tendency to carry their fluids with them in ice chests and find it necessary to refill them at the most ungodly hours.

Nevertheless, if the official hotel or motel is the site from which the buses leave for the starting line on race morning, it is worth some of the potential disturbances to be able to sleep an extra forty-five minutes.

Two Days Before the Race

As the race approaches, here are some items to keep in mind. (Since most races are on Sunday, we'll refer to the last day before the race as Saturday.)

Hydrate   Drink at least eight glasses of water, juice, or replacement fluid during the course of the day. Sipping smaller amounts regularly is preferable—if you drink intermittent large volumes, you'll urinate more fluid out. Don't be concerned if you find yourself gaining a few pounds. Your increase in carbohydrate consumption during this final week in order to supersaturate yourself with glycogen is responsible; carbohydrate molecules make water molecules bind to them. Think of yourself as a camel storing water for a long journey. And remember that the cells that make up the human body function best when bathed in fluid.

The Course   You will have researched the course description before ever planning to run your marathon, but seeing a course profile and reading a course description aren't the same as actually riding the course. Some runners like to know exactly what the course is going to throw at them; others don't. You may want to go out with a runner who knows the course or get a group of runners together to chip in for a taxi ride along the course. Be certain to carry along a map of the course, so you don't get lost. Some marathons offer organized bus tours of the course for those who are interested. Personally, I'd rather spend the day resting and be pleasantly surprised on race day. Knowing the course isn't going to change the topography one iota.

Eat a Dinner Very High in Carbohydrates, and Eat It Early   Every meal during this final week should be high in complex carbohydrates. Whether it's pancakes at breakfast or pasta for dinner, you want to add to the glycogen. A beer or two or a glass of wine is fine, as long as you don't overindulge—too much alcohol may interfere with a good night's sleep. For the same reason, avoid caffeine before you go to bed; this includes coffee, tea, chocolate, and most soft drinks. Caffeine is also a diuretic, which can cause you to lose precious fluid you've worked so hard to store.

You also need to get to bed early Friday night. The more sleep you can get Friday night, the better off you'll be, because most runners don't sleep well the eve of the race. Some people find that they sleep better if they bring their own pillow from home. It's not a bad idea, because some hotel pillows are so thick they give you a crick in the neck, while others are so thin they're useless. Do not set an alarm unless there's a mandatory meeting on Saturday morning.

The Day Before the Race

Here are some hints for the day before the race (typically, a Saturday).

Sleep In   Indulge yourself. Every extra minute in bed is a minute you're staying off your feet. In fact, if you like coffee in the morning, why not take a thermos with you, fill it Friday evening before you go to bed, and have your coffee in bed? After all the months of training that you've put in, you deserve it.

Hydrate   Begin hydrating from the time you get up until you go to bed. In fact, keep a glass of water by your bedside when you go to sleep that night.

To Jog or Not to Jog   All the training schedules in this book provide for an optional jog on the day before the race. By this time, you will have listened to your body well enough to know whether it runs better with a little jog the day before a race or long workout or whether staying off your feet as much as possible the day before is more effective. Personally, I like to use the light 2-mile jog as an outlet for pent-up energy, and I like to remind my legs how to run. Just a light, little jog serves as a pressure-release valve. If you exercise this option, don't run fast and certainly don't run long. As soon as your run is finished, shower and change into warm clothes.

Continue Hydrating   Drink fluids regularly. Remember that even if the race is held on a cold day, you still need to process a great deal of fluids. For instance, the 1991 Napa Valley Marathon was unusually windy and cold, but runners were still taken to the hospital suffering from dehydration.

Stay Horizontal   The more you can stay off your feet the day before the race, the better off you are. There will be a tremendous temptation to get involved in all the hoopla surrounding the race, especially when many of the major races require you to come by the runners' expo to pick up your number.

Check the Weather Forecast   Ideally do this midway through the afternoon, in order to gauge which clothes you should lay out. Keep your alternate clothes handy in case conditions change by the next morning.

Lay Out Your Racing Clothes   Before you go to eat your last supper, put out everything you are going to wear to the starting line tomorrow. You don't want to bump around in the dark in the morning trying to find things at the last minute. Check what you think you need against this list:

Running shorts
Running top(s), plus bra if appropriate
Socks and shoes
Hat (if appropriate for sun or rain)
Sunglasses (as needed)
Gloves (or a pair of socks) to keep your hands warm
Race number with pins attached to the holes
Some hard candy wrapped in cellophane, if you want to
    guarantee yourself extra sugar in the final miles
Warm-up outfit
Bag in which to send your warm-ups back
Fluid bottle (so you can continue sipping on the way to the
    start)
Pacing card, if you need one; attach it upside down to your
    race number
Petroleum jelly
Ziploc bag containing toilet paper
A ten- or twenty-dollar bill

Eat Early   Eat your high-carbohydrate meal about 5 or 6 P.M.
so you can begin digesting it early.

Hydrate Some More   Drink more fluids with dinner. A beer or
two is fine; but no more. Stay away from wine tonight—it
tends to dehydrate the body and you need to be superhy-
drated.

Set Your Alarm Early Enough   You want to get to the starting
area at least thirty minutes before the start, so you can jog a
mile or so to warm up and do a few sprints to stretch the legs.
Backtrack from the starting gun of tomorrow's race to give
yourself plenty of time to wake up, have a bowel movement,
shower, and dress.

Go to Bed Early   If you can't sleep, at least get into bed so you
are horizontal (and off your feet), and do whatever works to
become drowsy, short of taking sleeping pills. Do not drink

coffee, tea, or soft drinks before bed, as most contain caffeine, and don't eat chocolates, even if the hotel management puts some on your pillow. Save them for after the race.

Sleep Well   If you've been following your program faithfully and to the best of your ability all these months, you have done everything you can to be prepared for your marathon. Now get some well-deserved sleep and dream pleasant dreams of how everything tomorrow is going to go just as you planned!

Review Checklist for the Last Two Days

Traveling to the race:
[ ] Hydrate.
[ ] Arrive early.
[ ] Take direct flight.
[ ] Stay at hotel that will allow peace and quiet.
[ ] Eat early.
[ ] Sleep late.

Friday:
[ ] Hydrate.
[ ] Tour course?
[ ] Stay horizontal as much as possible.
[ ] Eat high-carbohydrate dinner.
[ ] Get to bed early.

Saturday
[ ] Sleep in.
[ ] Hydrate.
[ ] Jog or don't.
[ ] Hydrate.
[ ] Stay horizontal as much as possible.
[ ] Check weather forecast.
[ ] Lay out your racing clothes and accessories.
[ ] Eat early.

[ ] Hydrate.
[ ] Set alarm to give yourself plenty of time; don't rush on race morning.
[ ] Go to bed early.
[ ] Sleep well.

III

How to Finesse Your Race

14

The Race: From
Start to Finish

> Bad races are the result of giving in to natural urges:
> running fast when you feel fresh and slowing down when
> you start to hurt.
>
> —JOE HENDERSON, *Think Fast*

Getting Up

When the alarm wakes you on race morning, calmly lie in bed
and check your pulse rate. Although your natural anxiety
about the upcoming race may cause it to be five to ten beats
above the last several days, that's nothing to worry about. Its
strength and regularity should reassure you that you are ready
for your marathon.

Before you leave for the starting line, calmly go about a
routine that will allow you to have a bowel movement, to
shower, and to dress properly for the weather you will encounter during the race.

It's okay to enjoy a cup of coffee first thing in the morning.
You'll recall that back in Chapter 11 we briefly discussed the
effect caffeine can have on the increased use of free fatty acids.
If you've found that strong coffee the morning of a long run
does not disrupt your stomach and seems to have a positive
effect on beginning the conversion to more free fatty acid use
in the fatty acid/glycogen proportion, you can follow the

same procedure this morning. The coffee should be drunk less than two hours before the race starts. In any event, don't drink more than two cups of coffee.

If you need to eat something to absorb stomach acid due to apprehension or to keep your stomach settled, eat a small portion of something bland, such as a piece of dry toast or a very bland muffin. Do not eat anything sugary at this point. To do so will precipitate an insulin reaction, a phenomenon that will lower your blood sugar to the point where you will feel weak and in need of energy at a time when you need to feel strong and ready to produce energy.

In the wake of your bowel movement, take a shower. It will help wake you up, and it will begin to loosen up your muscles in preparation for the race.

Before dressing, look out the window to see if you need to adjust your race wardrobe. Next apply petroleum jelly (or lanolin) as needed: a thin layer to the feet if you're prone to blisters; liberally to any friction or chafing points; and, for men, to the nipples (followed by tape).

Now dress slowly and carefully in your racing clothes. Make certain your socks are not creased.

Once you have your racing shirt or singlet on, pin your race number over your abdomen. (Don't pin it up higher, because it can restrict your chest expansion.) Pin the top of the number first, then pin the bottom. If you were given a ticket for the bus ride to the start, pin it to your number.

When you lace your shoes, apply double knots so that you are not forced to stop during the race to retie them. Also, don't make your laces too tight; halfway through the race your feet will begin to swell, and they'll need space inside the shoes in which to expand.

If the weather is going to be sunny or hot, wear your light-colored hat; if the weather will be cold, take your warm hat to prevent heat loss.

Dress in layers and dress as comfortably as possible. You want to be pleasantly warm on your way to the starting area, and then discard outer clothing (warm-ups and such) just before the start.

Don't forget to secure a Ziploc bag containing some toilet paper in the waistband of your running shorts.

Take a last rundown of your list of clothing to make certain you have everything with you. Place a ten- or twenty-dollar bill in the pocket of your shorts—just in case you run into trouble along the way.

Off to the Starting Line

If you are catching a bus to the starting line, aim for one of the later buses. If you arrive at the starting area thirty minutes before the start, you'll have plenty of time to warm up and get ready without getting tight and wasting precious energy standing around.

If you are driving to the start, leave earlier than you feel is necessary. Parking can be a problem near the starting line of a race, and you don't want to have to walk too far. If you arrive early and can park close enough, stay inside your car until thirty minutes before the race. (If you drive to the start by yourself, take your car key off your key chain and tie the single key to your shoelaces—do not hide it on a tire or under the bumper of your car.)

At most races, if the weather is inclement, the buses will remain near the starting line to provide shelter for the runners until nearly race time.

Keep your warm-ups on as long as is practical. Then find the sweats buses that will transport your warm-up clothing back to the finish line (they're usually located near the start). Make certain you have clearly marked the bag in which your sweats are placed and that it is securely knotted.

The Final Thirty Minutes

Your efforts during the thirty minutes leading up to the start should be as follows:

Fifteen to Thirty Minutes Before　Gently jog a mile at a shuffling pace (ten to twelve minutes per mile). This will begin to loosen up the big muscles of the legs, and it will gradually shift your breathing from its initial anaerobic to aerobic, making the initial miles of the race more comfortable.

Ten to Fifteen Minutes Before   Shed your outer clothing and either secure it in your car (if it's an out-and-back or loop course) or bag it and stow it on the sweats bus.

Five to Ten Minutes Before   Do a half-dozen 40-yard pickups (sprints); begin gently and then, as your legs respond, increase the speed and power; jog fifteen seconds between each.

Five Minutes Before   Find your place in the starting field. Many marathons have standards on the side of the starting field indicating the pace that segment of the field hopes to maintain throughout the race. At other races, the start announcer will give directions for lining up in an appropriate place in the field. Unless you are able to run 26 five-minute miles in a row, do not place yourself near the front of the field. If you are unsure as to where to line up, ask one of the other runners.

The ability to get rolling at the start is, naturally, a much bigger problem at marathons like New York, Marine Corps, or Los Angeles than at the marathons that feature a thousand runners or fewer. At a big marathon, it will take a while before you even see the starting line, while in a smaller marathon you'll likely cross it in thirty seconds or less.

While you are waiting for the starting signal, shake some of the tightness out of your arms and shoulders; gently lift your legs, one at a time, to your chest (this gently stretches the muscles and tendons); blow the air out of your lungs and take a few deep breaths, filling your lungs with oxygen.

The Start!

At most marathons, a countdown from the starting area is chanted by the assembled runners, so you will have a good sense of when the race is about to begin. Be prepared to punch your chronograph at the signal of the start even though you will not immediately move; your finishing time is based upon the time elapsed from the starting signal. (At some large, sophisticated marathons where runners are corralled by qualifying times, such as Boston, adjustments are fed into the computer to more accurately reflect the time the specific groups of runners crossed the starting line.)

However, if it takes more than three minutes to reach the starting line, reset your chronograph to zero and restart it when you cross the starting line (see page 201).

In a large field you'll hardly move at all at first. Then a shuffling begins with some forward movement and periodic stops as the front of the pack moves away down the course, opening space for runners coming from behind to fill in. Don't panic. Move as the opportunity permits. Shuffle forward smoothly. Even when you begin to move somewhat regularly, try to walk fast initially, saving your running muscles.

Once the field moves forward enough to allow you to roll into a shuffling jog, do so, but don't push too hard. If an opening is in front of you, move into it. If an opening is ahead and to one side, check to see if anyone else is coming up to fill it. If no one is, move gently into the opening. Take pains to make all moves smoothly and well planned so as not to run into or trip other runners, or be stepped on yourself. The first mile of any marathon can be rather confusing and also somewhat frustrating; you don't want to waste all your pent-up energy by immediately trying to get into a running rhythm. In reality, the close quarters during the first mile tend to save more marathons for runners than ruin them. The tightly packed field makes it hard to get pulled out too quickly. If you are shuffling along on the side of the field and it is clear for 20 yards ahead, roll into the opening, *don't sprint into it.*

Gradually, as the runners in front move farther ahead, more and more space will be available for you to maneuver in. Again, avoid make abrupt movements or dashes to the right or left, so you don't catch another runner's trailing leg, which could deposit both of you in a tangled mass on the ground. You will gradually be able to increase your pace. Do not attempt to make up within the first mile the time you may have lost at the start!

Mile 1

When you reach the first mile, check your time. If you are several minutes slower than you had hoped to be, don't panic, and don't attempt to make up the difference over the next mile. The idea is to get back on your pace over the first 5 miles if the field is not too congested, or over the first 10 miles if it is. Readjust your time goals if it took you an unreasonable amount of time to reach the start.

Think of the marathon as four consecutive races: a 10-miler in which you get into your rhythm by gradually warming up, a 5-miler in which you flow smoothly and strongly, a 5-miler in which you concentrate on staying on pace and setting yourself up for the final segment, and a 10K in which you dig down inside to consummate the race.

If you planned to run the marathon at an eight-minute pace, and you reach the one-mile mark in ten minutes, plan to run between 7:45 and 7:50 for the next 9 miles. This will put you back on an eight-minute pace by mile 10. *Do not attempt to make up the difference in the first several miles.* (I cannot repeat this admonition too often.)

If the field is small, and you get out smoothly, immediately try to get into an easy rhythm. It's better during the first mile to be on the slow side rather than the fast. Considering the tremendous physical conditioning you are in at this point, the first mile may very well seem incredibly pedestrian, but don't give in to the urge to pick up the pace. At 20 miles, your eight-minute pace will not seem so pedestrian and it may even be a struggle to hold it.

If you reach the first mile a bit on the fast side, immediately slow yourself to what you feel is the proper pace. Don't attempt to slow below your planned pace in order to average out your first 2 miles to equal your planned pace. Just put the few extra seconds in the bank and forget about them.

For instance, if you ran a 7:45 first mile and planned to run an eight-minute-per-mile pace, plan to reach mile 2 at 15:45.

To recap, if you're behind your schedule after one mile, work your way back onto schedule _gradually;_ if you're ahead of schedule, get back onto your proper schedule immediately.

If it took more than three minutes to get to the starting line and you reset your chronograph to zero as you crossed the starting line, run the race according to _your_ chronograph and not according to the official time. Your first goal, after all, is to safely complete the marathon.

If you had also set a specific time goal that now seems impossible because it took so long to reach the starting line, you have two options. Accept that you cannot regain the lost time and run on your own watch, ignoring the official clock. Then you can still strive to achieve your time goal. Although the published results won't reflect it, you'll know what you did. The second option is to try, if you are feeling good when you reach the final 10K, to regain some of the lost time.

It's not worth jeopardizing your race by attempting to make up more than three minutes within the first 10 miles. This inability to get to the starting line quickly in a mega-marathon is a prime drawback for the first-time marathoner.

Miles 2 Through 10

Late in the race, it becomes almost impossible for many marathoners to do even the most simple math. This is not the case during the initial 10 miles, so take advantage of the segment by settling in, finding your breathing and running rhythm, and do the necessary math and pace adjustments you need to get back onto your planned pace.

You'll find yourself running the same pace as many of the runners around you. If you are shooting for a popular time goal, there will be whole clumps of runners rolling along together. They are attempting to feed off one another and to stay on pace to reach their goals.

If you want to join such a group mirroring your target pace during the first 10 miles, that's fine. If you do join them, run at the edge of the group. Its leaders will typically change periodically. As a new marathoner, you do not want to lead, and you do not want to be absorbed to the point where you feel hemmed in or where you become lulled by the group mind. If you are sensitive to it, and if the group you are with is an experienced one, you can literally feel the energy feeding back and forth. It is always easier running the initial 10 miles with one or more other runners than it is alone, especially if headwinds prevail.

However, there is a tendency to allow the group to dictate your pace, thereby seemingly relieving you of the responsibility of staying on top of your planned race. Continue to monitor your own pace at each mile marker. If the group begins dropping behind or getting ahead of your planned pace, gradually leave them and get back into your own groove.

Some groups converse as they roll along, but don't you participate. Save your breath for later in the race. If someone addresses a question specifically to you, answer as simply and precisely as possible. It's fine to add, "This is my first marathon so I want to listen and learn," but don't become engaged in a conversation.

You want to stay on top of all of your body systems, so monitor your physical condition from head to foot at least once a mile: How's my breathing? Can I hear my footsteps or are they silent? Am I drinking enough? Could I urinate right now if I wanted to? Am I too hot or too cold? Should I remove a layer of clothing now that I'm warmed up so I don't overheat? Am I using my arms as I practiced at the track? Is that a twinge I feel at the outside of my left knee? Is it a passing twinge or have I experienced it before? If I move to the other side of the road will the different slant of the road alleviate the twinge? Dozens of systems need to be checked each mile. Stay current on your condition.

Begin taking fluids from the very first aid station onward. When you approach aid stations, slow down, take your fluids, and walk briskly through the aid station area as you drink them. Do not attempt to drink on the run; fluid splashed on your T-shirt won't do you any good. By walking, you temporarily give your running muscles a break, and, more important, you remain hydrated. Drink, then flow out the other side and roll back into a run. Eventually you'll catch back up with your group or get back onto your pace. (If you are running in a group, make sure that you're not too hemmed in as you approach an aid station—you don't want to miss your chance to grab a cup.)

If it's a cold day, drink one cup of water at the first aid station. If it's hot, drink two cups at the first aid station. You want to begin taking fluid immediately, since it takes about forty-five minutes for even plain water to be emptied from the stomach and properly processed through the body where it will do some good. Even if it's cool, your working muscles are using a tremendous amount of fluid to keep themselves cool. Don't be lulled into dehydration just because you are enjoying cool weather. You are still perspiring. You need fluid during a marathon no matter what the temperature.

Don't use electrolyte replacement fluids during the first 10 miles—take only water. You don't need other fluids yet, and if you take them too early, the sugar in them could interfere with your body's switch to using a greater proportion of fatty acids from the bloodstream.

Once you get beyond 10 miles, your body will be lusting after sugar in as simple-to-process a form as possible, both to fuel the working muscles and to keep the brain, which requires tremendous amounts of sugar to function properly, stable. Now is the time to start taking the electrolyte replacement fluid. You can drink it alone or, if the ERG is too concentrated for you, use a cup of water from the aid table to dilute it in your stomach.

By the time you reach 10 miles, your muscles should be warmed through and through, even to the middle of your dense thigh and calf muscles. Between miles 4 and 15 you should enjoy some of the smoothest, most effortless running of your life. It is during this period, however, that you must be careful not to succumb to an urge to run the way you feel, which is typically running too fast because it feels good.

Miles 10 Through 15

This is a dangerous segment of the race because you are running like a well-oiled machine. The muscles are thoroughly warmed up, you are in excellent physical condition, you have dropped into a smooth rhythm, and you are still fresh. The pitfall of this segment of the race is one of perceived effort. If you maintain the same level of perceived effort during mile 12 as you did in mile 4, you are going to run mile 12 faster than you did mile 4 simply because a well-oiled machine produces more work with seemingly the same or less effort.

It is imperative that between mile 7 (the point at which most of your body systems become smooth by warming fully) and mile 17 (when your energy reserves are no longer filled to overflowing) you run not by feel but by your chronograph.

Mile 10 is also where you should consider leaving the company of any group. At this point the group will either move too fast (because it feels so good and everyone is feeding off one another) or slower than they think they are (because they've become complacent). For instance, in one race I hooked up with a fairly large group of runners who were planning to break three hours. By the time we reached 12 miles it became apparent that they were becoming complacent, losing a few seconds per mile. The charismatic leaders among the group were blasé: "Don't worry. We'll make them up later." On hearing this, two of us broke from the group; at the speed we were going, this was at first an almost imperceptible break. Little by little we moved ahead. One other runner in the group wanted to break and go with us, but the leader assured him and the others that we were going to burn ourselves out. At the turnaround at 13.1 miles, the two of us were thirty-five seconds ahead of the others. At the finish line, the two of us crossed in 2:57:48; the rest came in between 3:00:12 and 3:10:00.

Run your own race at this point. If the group is going too fast, drop back. It's likely they won't even notice. If the group is going too slow (even if it is only five seconds per mile too slowly, five seconds multiplied by 26 miles is two minutes and ten seconds) and you feel uncomfortable moving away from them in plain sight, move over to the opposite side of the road and slowly begin to pull away.

Think of a group you've been running with as the first stage of a multistage rocket. You've been with them for 10 miles, they've served their purpose, but now it's time to peel off and take control of your own race. Move away and concentrate on your pace per mile. Enjoy the fact that these miles are coming easily and well, because once you reach mile 15 you'll be brought back to earth fairly quickly.

At the half-marathon point, revel in the fact that you've covered half the distance. With each step forward, you have less distance to cover than you've already done. You're on your way home.

Remember that if and when you are about to encounter hills, increase your breathing rhythm before you physically reach the hill so that you can stay ahead on your oxygen needs. Don't hyperventilate, but do gradually increase the rate and volume of your breathing as you approach the hills. Also, visualize yourself rolling up the hill, not attacking it. Cut back on the length of your stride but keep up the same leg rhythm. Use your arms. Remember that what you expend going up a hill always outweighs what you will save going down a hill; do not charge the hills—flow up them. As you go over the top, shake out a bit of the tension in your arm and shoulder muscles, continue to control your breathing, and flow smoothly down the other side as your breathing returns to normal.

Keep your impulse to run wild under control during this all-important segment of the race. You'll have plenty of occasion to use some of the energy you save during the final 10K segment.

Miles 15 Through 20

It is the rare runner who goes through these critical miles without experiencing a profound change in perceived effort. For virtually everyone—from the world-class marathoner to the first-timer—mile 15 to mile 20 is a segment of transition. If mile 10 to mile 15 went smoothly, there will be some point during the following 5 miles where the runner notices that he or she needs to work harder to cover a mile and needs to pay more attention to stay on pace.

Mile 18 is usually cited as the point at which the race becomes real work. It is nonetheless imperative that you maintain the prescribed pace. Continue to treat each mile as a separate entity. Do the simple math on your chronograph for each mile. If you are maintaining a nine-minute mile as planned and are approaching mile 17, add nine minutes to the time you reach mile 17 as a target for when you should reach mile 18.

It is from mile 15 to mile 20 that you truly become a distance racer, and from mile 20 to mile 26.2 that you become a marathoner. Work to keep your pace. Each mile will probably feel as though it is more work than the previous one, but it should not be so different than it was during your long weekend workouts. Stay as relaxed as you can—if you allow yourself to become tense, it will drain much-needed energy. Continue to monitor your body parts and their functions. Some parts will be getting stiff and tired, but that's normal.

If you use aspirin or some other analgesic to reduce swelling on longer runs, as some of us old coots do, hold off until you push yourself through several of the increasingly tougher miles. Never give in immediately, because to persevere at this point will set you up for getting through the rough spots during the final 10K. Make a deal with yourself. If you are beginning to really work at mile 18 and you typically use aspirin or if you brought along some hard candy to suck for the sugar through the final stages of a long run, put it off for another mile or two, or at least until the next aid station. Besides building your perseverance and mental toughness, this also serves as a reward for real work done.

Continue the routine of walking briskly through each aid station, taking at least one cup of ERG on a cold day or two cups of ERG or one cup of ERG and one of water on a hot day. If you stay hydrated, the final miles will come much easier, and the point of glycogen depletion ("hitting the wall") will be delayed.

As you work more for each mile, treat the process as though you were studying it from afar. Your body may be tiring, but it is all part of the process. Hold your pace as well as you can. Don't consider how many miles you have left to go; instead, deal with the mile you are on. This allows you to focus your attention and helps alleviate negative thoughts about the miles remaining.

(Occasionally, a runner will bring to his or her first marathon certain genetic abilities and a solid training program that conspire to hold off the hard miles of the marathon until near the end. If this is the case as you near 20 miles, glory in the feeling. Most of us experience this mastery of the race once out of twenty marathons—if ever.)

Again, concentrate on confronting one mile at a time. Monitor your body functions and make improvements where necessary. Are you still using your arms properly? This is where you can capitalize on all of those upper-body workouts you did. Use those arms to keep the rhythm of the legs and to keep the power going to the ground. Remember all of those hill workouts? Your thighs are tiring, but they are tiring more slowly than they would have if you had skipped the hill workouts. Remember all that time you spent at the track paying attention to developing and maintaining an efficient running style? Now's the time to reap the payoff as you maintain that style and keep your pace smooth. If you allow yourself to become biomechanically sloppy at this point, each step you take will cost you more energy than it needs to and you will open yourself to overuse injuries. Run smoothly and efficiently, using as little energy as possible.

As the 20-mile point nears, relish every step that brings you closer to the final 10K—to the race within the race.

Mile 20 to the Finish Line

All of the tough workouts you pushed yourself through, all of the mental toughness you built up over your long training program, has come down to this: a 10K race.

If you have faithfully followed your training program and carefully followed your planned pace, you will reach 20 miles tired and a bit stiff but still moving with power and purpose. Your head and your body will probably be playing games— your body will tell you it is tired and wants to take a rest, while your mind attempts to convince it that it is not as tired as it thinks, and that all of this will be over much sooner if you keep going as you are.

As much as you can, suppress the feelings of discomfort that come with running this hard for this long. Continue to monitor your body systems, but most important, monitor your pace. As each mile arrives and is conquered, the next will seem even more formidable. The minutes will feel elongated; the miles will seem stretched out in some evil way—even if the course is an out and back and you distinctly remember that the miles were accurate enough when you came this way back when you were fresh and new.

These are the miles that forever separate the mere distance runner from the marathoner. Your mind will be working against a body that seems to be working against itself. Each stride may be an individual effort instead of one small piece of the whole cloth of the run, as it was a mere 5 miles ago.

You may find it shocking now to remember how good you felt a mere 5 miles ago in comparison to how you feel now. You'll wonder when or if it will ever be over. Can you hold on that long? Does completing the marathon distance really matter? These final miles may rank as the most difficult thing you have ever done in your life—but also as the most satisfying.

If you have trained faithfully and paced yourself carefully, be assured that you are capable of pushing through these final miles. Do not consider how far you have run to this point; think in terms of how few miles you have yet to run. If you are 4 miles from the finish, visualize the 4-mile course you used for your Monday recovery runs at home while you were fulfilling your marathon-training program to help push through the final miles. If, toward the end of a particularly difficult workout, you ever imagined Bill Rodgers or Grete Waitz running stride-for-stride with you as you pushed for the finish, visualize that again as you hold your pace steady.

If you have maintained your pace throughout the race, you have been regularly passing those runners who have fallen off theirs or who have been reduced to walking when they attempted to outrun their current training level.

Forget about your total time. As you reach each mile, add your planned per-mile time to the tally thus far to get the time when you should reach the next mile marker.

Continue to drink at each aid table; concentrate on drinking the electrolyte replacement fluid. The more sugar you can get at this point, the better your head will hold together. If you have an extra piece of hard candy with you, place it in your cheek and allow it to melt slowly. Don't chew it all at once.

Do not be surprised or distressed if your breathing has increased noticeably—this is normal. You are pushing into new territory. Make every attempt to keep the breathing under *your* control. Keep your breathing just ahead of your body's needs. Make it regular and forceful, filling your lungs with each inhalation.

Work on maintaining your perfect running style. Keep

your back straight and use your arms. Make certain you are not leaning forward, thereby closing off some of your lung capacity—at this point you need all of the oxygen your lungs can process.

Make whatever deals you need to with your body to make it to the end. Promise it ice cream or pizza or a vacation—whatever it wants. At this point it may seem as if it is a completely separate entity as it cries out for mercy. As long as you are not experiencing sharp, specific pains—but only a general and all-encompassing discomfort—your body is still sound. The discomfort may be something unlike anything you've ever before experienced. It will hurt to run and may hurt even more to walk, but remember that it is *merely* discomfort, and when the race is finished, it will pass. *Everything* will pass.

Narrow your focus to your pace and to the finish line. That is all you need concern yourself with. Tell yourself if you can just keep putting one foot in front of the other you will reach the finish line! Each step gets you that much closer to the finish, and to your goal.

If the effort you are expending is simply overwhelming, if your breathing has become so labored that you feel you cannot go on, that you must stop here and give it up, *don't!*

If you feel that you cannot go on, that you cannot possibly take another step—if you know that your marathon itself is in jeopardy—there is a technique to salvage the race. Roll into a brisk walk for a hundred steps, counting your steps by twos using your left leg. Walk a hundred steps and regain control of your breathing; then roll gently back into a run for five hundred steps. Go back to a brisk walk for a hundred steps, and run for five hundred more.

Do *not* drop into a walk and stay there. If you must walk, use the walking as an extension of your pacing. You can cover a fair amount of ground by briskly walking a hundred steps and then running five hundred. When you roll into the five hundred running steps, don't sprint and don't try to pick up the pace above what you had planned to run at this point. Your priority, remember, is to successfully finish this marathon.

As you approach the final mile, concentrate on expanding your mental focus. For the last several miles you have narrowed your focus to your style, stride, and pacing. Now allow your body to continue its work at the pace you have set, while gradually expanding your focus to take in the final mile of your race. Look out at the course as it passes under your still-moving legs, regard the spectators, take in the other runners you are approaching and passing. Too many marathoners cross the finish line and for the life of them cannot recall the final miles. This final mile is one you have never before experienced; grab it and stow it in your memory and hold it there. It is something for which you have worked for months, perhaps for a whole lifetime.

As the finish line comes into sight, do not radically increase your pace: to do so at this point, while your body is so fragile, could cause injury. If you are within seconds of your goal, increase your pace smoothly, but do not sprint.

As you approach the finish line, absorb the sights, sounds, spectators, the goal after which you have lusted. Pull yourself together with all the energy you have left and put on your best running style. Meter out all the energy you have left to approach and cross the finish line with authority, with power, with the sharp resolve you have used to get yourself to this point.

Do not leap across the finish line, even if you happen to have that much energy left. Such a move is asking for injury. Your Achilles tendons are as taut as violin strings, your glycogen reserves like a desiccated sponge.

Run toward the finish line smoothly and with confidence. Punch the button on your chronograph as you cross under the finishing banner. Congratulations! *You are a marathoner!*

15

Quick Recovery

The marathon is the ultimate endurance test. Oh sure,
people sometimes go longer than that. But 26 miles 385
yards is where racing ends and where ludicrous extremes
begin.

—JOE HENDERSON, *Jog, Run, Race*

As you cross the finish line, glory in your accomplishment, in
the fact that your exquisite ordeal is now an intimate and
integral part of you. Move through the finishing chutes, absorbing as much of the moment as you can manage. Volunteers will help steer you along the chutes and remove your
coded race information from your number. Continue walking
through the chute as briskly as the jamming up will allow. Do
not pass other runners, or allow other runners to pass you.
Correct finishing places are important to the timing and
scoring apparatus, and to the results.

Do not, under any circumstances, give in to your weariness.
Do not stop moving, and definitely do not sit down or allow
yourself to fall down. If you stop at this point, you'll regret
it for the next several days, and you could conceivably put
your heart at risk. When you emerge from the far end of the
chute, continue walking.

If it has been a cool day, your intense body heat will create
an envelope of comfort around you that will last for several
minutes. Proceed to the sweats area and retrieve your warm-
ups. Your legs will be stiff and sore and will not bend very

easily, so you will need support as you struggle into them. Family and friends can help you into the warm clothes, or one of the volunteers will be happy to do so. Remember to keep moving.

If the race was warm, before going for your sweats, make a pass by the fluids table that will be set up near the finish line. Drink two cups of water or fluids. Even though you have stopped running and the race is over, your body's metabolism is still stoking like crazy. In fact, you'll need to replace your body fluids for the next several days in order to satisfy your needs and to help your body recover. By drinking some of the fluid used in the race, you will immediately start your body on the road to glycogen recovery.

The Importance of Walking

The next thing to do is merely to continue walking. There are several reasons that walking, even if you end up quite a way beyond the finish line, is vital after a marathon.

You must bring your body back from its strenuous exercising mode to a calm mode *gradually,* so that your heart can make the necessary adjustments. You do not want to shock your heart with an abrupt change from intense effort to dead calm, especially if you're over thirty. By walking, you will allow the heart to gradually adjust its output downward, assuring a safe recovery. You want to avoid ischemia at all costs. You don't want the flow of blood through your body to slow faster than the beating heart or it will come up dry and will begin to grate like a water pump that runs out of water.

You want to massage the growing stiffness out of your muscles, flushing out some of the lactic acid that has accumulated. By walking 1½ or 2 miles following your marathon, you'll begin the recovery process immediately after finishing the race, thereby putting yourself nearly two weeks up on your recovery. The few days following your marathon will still be marked by stiffness in the muscles, but the stiffness will be milder than if you had simply stopped dead after you crossed the finish line; nor will the stiffness last as long. The hour following your finish is the point at which you embark on the marathon lifestyle, and its hallmark is quick recovery from the effort expended in order to more quickly clear you for additional efforts.

There's one other, more psychological reason to walk. Like many marathoners, you may want to spend a few minutes alone with your own thoughts. You've been surrounded by hundreds or thousands of other runners as you've competed in what is basically a solo event. Taking a walk gives you the chance to meet your new self and face the enormity of the challenge you've just accomplished. That accomplishment is yours and yours alone. You have just gone the distance under your own power. You have climaxed a sixteen- or twenty-week intensive training program. You have climbed to a very special plateau in the world of sports. These moments following the finish are very special, and they will never occur again. You will never again run your first marathon. You entered this race hours ago as a marathon virgin; you emerged at the pinnacle of distance running—a marathoner. You've earned the right to wallow in the celebration, or to wander off and meet your new self for a few solitary minutes, a part of yourself that most people will never encounter in themselves.

Once you've walked a mile or two, wander back through the carnival-like atmosphere at the finish line. Accept congratulations from other runners and offer congratulations to those you meet. The finish-line area at a marathon is much like a rescue station processing survivors from a shipwreck: No matter how diverse the survivors, they all have something very special in common; they all have a story to tell. Tell bits of your story and listen to the stories of the others. Drink more fluid. Absorb the moment.

Carbohydrate Reloading

You probably want to get back to your room, take a shower or bath, put on your race T-shirt, and bravely hobble through the various race-related events that evening.

Don't spend too much time in hot water, because the heat will aggravate any swelling or discomfort from inflammation. Hot tubs at this time are not the order of the day. Shower or bathe quickly, then run down a checklist of your condition. You might want to take an anti-inflammatory to minimize any swelling in your joints. If you have any spots that are particularly painful or sore, apply ice to reduce the swelling and to start that spot toward recovery.

If you want to go out and mix with your fellow marathoners despite your soreness, put some ice into a Ziploc bag and attach it to your tender spot(s) with an elastic bandage, then wear baggy sweat pants to cover it. Take care of any blisters after you bathe and before going back out; be sure to use an antiseptic cream on the treated blisters in order to avoid infection. You'll also want to wear flip-flops or a larger than normal pair of shoes, in order to go easy on your feet. Elevate your feet and legs when possible.

Most races hold an awards ceremony several hours after the race. Attend the ceremony if you can, if for no other reasons than to mix with your fellow marathoners and to again relive the common experience.

It is not unusual to experience upset stomach following a marathon, especially if the day was warm. Your stomach has been hard at work processing quite a bit of fluid and pumping out stomach acids. The best thing you can do for your stomach is to eat a dry roll and sip some soup or drink a glass of milk (if you can manage to get them down).

Many races offer soup and rolls following the race, as well as bananas, orange wedges, cookies, chips, yogurt, and ice cream. These foods start you on your way to replacing your depleted glycogen stores; it's important that you replenish glycogen as soon as possible following your successful marathon. Your first full meal following the marathon should be the same kind of a meal you were eating for the days leading up to the race, one heavy in carbohydrates. You will thus speed your recovery enormously, and you will take on fuel to accommodate your recovery runs over the next month. Your body at this point is crying out for carbohydrates; indulge it for the next three to four days.

In the wake of your marathon, you may have one of two extreme reactions when it comes to sleep. You will either crash early, the victim of a wonderful weariness, both from the physical expenditures of running the distance and from the fact that you probably didn't sleep well the night before the race. Or you may be so wired that you find it impossible to fall asleep (or you may initially fall soundly asleep but after only several hours find yourself wide awake). In either instance, simply go with whatever your body dictates; it will let you know when it is tired enough to pass out.

The First Workout of Your Marathon Lifestyle

The last thing a person feels like doing the day following a marathon is to get out and put in a run. However, a gentle run—or even a walk—the day after is the best thing you can do for yourself, provided you are not nursing an injury (stiff and unyielding muscles do not count). The massaging action of the moving muscles will help flush accumulated waste products from your tissues, thereby hastening recovery. Ironically, the way to get rid of the aches, which are due primarily to a lactic acid buildup in your muscles, is to immediately go back into *gentle* training.

Having put in the requisite months of training for your marathon, you don't want to begin to lose all of the fitness advantages you've gained for yourself. You want to begin moving into the benefits of the marathon lifestyle immediately, and the way to do that is to get rid of all the aches that set in following your race effort.

Those runners who trained for 3:30, 3:15, or 3:00 goals

should refer back to their training schedules (pages 122–28) for the week's worth of training following the race. If this was your first marathon (or if you used the twenty-week training schedule), take a 3-mile walk the following day.

Even though you walked some 2 miles immediately following your effort yesterday, you will still be stiff in the legs. But trust me—if you hadn't walked those 2 miles, today you would feel as if someone had poured concrete inside your legs.

The first mile of your recovery walk or run is always the most difficult. You may feel like the Tin Man in _The Wizard of Oz,_ with all his rusted joints. Begin your walk or run _very gently._ It is normal to have sore spots following your marathon. But if you gently roll into your walk or run, you'll be astonished how after the first mile things begin to warm up, and your movements begin to smooth themselves.

If you feel acute pain, cut your walk or run short, head home, and apply ice. Aches, however, don't count—they're part of the package, your badge of courage.

As you slowly warm up, the aches will diminish. They won't vanish entirely, but they will moderate. By the third mile, you may actually begin to feel good and loose. If you feel the urge to keep going, however, resist it! Stop after 3 miles, go home, put ice on any spots that continue to bother you, and stay as horizontal as you can.

For the next several days, plan meals heavy in carbohydrates and drink plenty of fluids to replace the fluids your body continues to use up.

Plus One Week

The week following your marathon should be marked by _easy_ workouts, rest, and heavy carbohydrate-loading.

If this was your first marathon, here's a schedule for the entire post-marathon week:

M   3-mile gentle walk
T   Rest or 2-mile gentle walk

W   Exercise gently by bicycling, swimming, or walking for
20–30 minutes

T   3-mile gentle run

F   Rest

S   4-mile gentle run

S   Rest

(Again, those who followed the sixteen-week training schedules should follow the routine in Chapter 8.)

For the second week following your marathon, repeat the same workout as the first week. Continue to go heavy on the carbohydrates, especially fresh fruits and vegetables; have pasta several times; and remember to drink plenty of fluids, including the sport replacement fluids. Reinstitute your upper-body workouts at a level half what you reached two weeks before the race.

For the third week, add a mile to each run or walk, continuing the rest and alternative exercise days. Again, ingest plenty of carbohydrates and fluid, and continue the upper-body exercise routine at the same level as the previous week. At this point you want to build toward a maintenance level that will provide a springboard from which you can launch your next marathon effort—or at which you can hold your fitness level indefinitely.

For the fourth week, drop back to the level of running called for in the first week following your marathon. By this point, aches and pains should have thoroughly faded, and you should be recovering well. Do not plan any races, even 5Ks, until this week is behind you.

Starting with the fifth week following your marathon, use the following maintenance program in a twelve-week cycle. This is a training cycle based upon the basic training program (see Chapter 4), but it's beefed up to take advantage of your new level of fitness. The hard/easy is built into the day-to-day program, and also into the week-to-week aspects of the program's four-week cycle. Remember that you can exchange Saturday and Sunday on this program, so if there is a race you want to run Sunday, rest on Saturday instead.

Weeks 1, 5, and 9

S   Rest day
M   30-minute run at 60% WHR
T   40-minute run at 70% WHR
W   40-minute run at 60% WHR
T   T: 3 repeat miles at 70% WHR
F   Rest day
S   Long run: 75 minutes at 60% WHR or a 10K race at 70 to 80% WHR

Week 3, 7, and 11

S   Rest day
M   40-minute run at 60% WHR
T   45-minute run at 70% WHR
W   35-minute run at 60% WHR
T   T: 4 repeat miles at 70% WHR
F   Rest day
S   Long run: 90 minutes at 60% WHR, or a 10K race at 70 to 80% WHR, or a 15K or 20K race at 70% WHR

Weeks 2, 6, and 10

S   Rest day
M   35-minute run at 60% WHR
T   40-minute run at 70% WHR
W   35-minute run at 60% WHR
T   T: 3 repeat miles at 70% WHR
F   Rest day
S   Long run: 60 minutes at 60% WHR

Weeks 4, 8, and 12

S   Rest day
M   35-minute run at 60% WHR
T   40-minute run at 60% WHR
W   35-minute run at 60% WHR
T   T: 3 repeat miles at 70% WHR
F   Rest day
S   Long run: 60 minutes at 60% WHR

Congratulations on becoming a marathoner! In a world increasingly sedentary, you are the exception, the person at the top of the pyramid, the more complete human animal.

IV

Subsequent Goals

16

How to Construct
Your Best Marathon

> Yet here, perhaps more than in any other event, runners
> need competition to draw out the best from themselves.
> They need to lose themselves in the pace of the field to find
> what they can do. They need others to show them that the
> "impossible" can happen.
>
> —JOE HENDERSON, in the introduction to
> *The Complete Marathoner*

Even experienced marathoners have crossed the finish line
promising that it will be a cold day in hell before he or she
does another one of these insane things. The commitment to
training for four months in order to run a race that can last
less than four hours suddenly seems unworthy of the effort.

This post-race annoyance with the idea of ever again running 26.2 miles, which is often accompanied by post-race
depression, discourages some from ever again contemplating
running—much less training for another god-awful marathon.

But the runner who is, at heart, a true marathoner, emerges
from the other side of this post-race phase with a different
attitude. Hitting the road the day immediately following the
marathon serves to somewhat short-circuit the post-race depression. Having adopted the marathon lifestyle, the runner
has a goal: to continue running for as long as one is able.

The true marathoner regards the race just past as a stepping-stone, one rung in a ladder that vanishes into the clouds, climbing to who knows what. Often the post-race reaction includes a series of questions about how he or she would have done an even better marathon if . . .

- If I'd gone out just a little slower in the first five miles, would I have had more strength and endurance left for the final 5 miles?
- If I'd paid a little more attention to pace when I hooked up with that group running my planned pace, would I have left them behind a bit earlier and perhaps knocked two minutes off my time?
- If I'd been faithful to the track workouts instead of skipping two or three of them over the four months of training, would I have been able to stay more in control during the final miles?
- If I'd been able to keep running during the final 2 miles instead of dropping into an alternatingly running/walking survival mode, would I have been able to reach my goal?

Questions like these occur to the true marathoner even if he or she managed to meet the stated goal for the marathon (whether that was "merely" to complete the race or to do so within a specific time goal). Marathoners are notorious for being harder on themselves than anyone else could possibly be, so there *is* an inclination to analyze the hell out of the race. The true marathoner, having just finished a first marathon, invariably wants to run the next marathon better.

If, in the warm glow of post-race accomplishment, you resolve to run another marathon soon, you have two choices: (1) To work toward progressively better marathons, building up experience and putting miles and years on your legs gradually in order to increase the body's capacity toward doing your best possible marathon, or (2) to jump right into a program that will allow you to push toward your best marathon in the shortest amount of time possible.

I would strongly advise against the second choice, especially if you have just recently come to running or if you are more than thirty years of age.

Your running body is capable of adapting to a tremendous amount of marathon training toward your best marathon, but the adaptation of the heart and lungs occurs much faster than does that of the joints, ligaments, and tendons. The longer you've been away from a regular exercise program and the older you are, the longer your body needs to bring these very vital biomechanical systems around. To go into a strenuous, high-intensity program to run your best marathon with some of your body systems unprepared is to court disaster and disappointment.

The more logical approach to running your best marathon is to set up a long-term program that gradually stresses your body toward better and better marathon performances over a matter of years.

Evaluate Your Body's Response to Your First Marathon Training

Once you feel sufficiently healed in the wake of your recent marathon and the recovery training program, it's time to compete in several 10K races. Then evaluate your four-month training program and your recovery from the marathon.

How easily did the long runs in your program go for you? Did you literally sail through them or were they quite a bit of work? Did you find that you recovered rapidly from the long runs, or did you find yourself battling against a dead, stale, tired feeling in the legs for several days?

How comfortable were your repeat miles at the track? Did you feel you could have done the repeat miles significantly faster than the speeds called for in the program? Did you finish the track workouts with plenty left, or did they leave your legs tired and weak?

If you managed to stay on pace for your first marathon, did you find that you had plenty left during the final miles?

Or were you holding on tenaciously by your teeth just to finish it?

How quickly did you recover from your marathon? Did you feel the aches gradually vanish and your reservoir of energy refill itself fairly rapidly, or did you still feel the physical effects of the marathon a month or six weeks afterward?

How well did you recover from the marathon psychologically? Were you psyched to go out on the 3-miler the day following your marathon, seeing the workout as an ongoing extension of your marathon training, or did you have to force yourself to take every step of that first run? Did the marathon leave a bad taste in your mouth? Do you look forward to going out on a workout now, or must you still force yourself as a sort of obligation?

Have you seen any improvements in your 10K performance in the wake of your marathon?

If your long runs in training for your marathon went extremely well *and* if your track workouts were much less work than you expected, *and* you recovered from both of those key weekly workouts with little or any negative effects, you obviously have plenty of potential you can call upon to move you to the next level of marathoning. If you did not readily recover from your long runs and if your track workouts were much more work than pleasure, your body is pretty much working at capacity right now. You need some careful pampering in order to get your body ready for the next hard workout, and any improvements are going to have to be planned slowly and worked at faithfully.

If you had plenty of running left in your legs as you crossed the finish line of your first marathon, there's the potential for a better next marathon in the near future. If you did not cross the finish line with plenty left, you were running near to capacity or at capacity—your push to the next level must be made carefully and one step at a time.

• • • •

As we've discussed, the older you are or the newer you are to the sport, the slower your recovery will be. If you give your body the time it asks for to recover, you will find that your progress toward faster marathons will come more quickly. While two marathons a year—one in the spring and the other in the fall—is ideal, some marathoners would do better to run only one a year, allowing their bodies to recuperate fully. In any event, it's not advisable to run more than three marathons a year.

If, in the month following your marathon, you have followed the recovery running program, but your head is still not into it, don't force yourself to set up another marathon date. Extend the recovery program for as long as it takes for your head to come back around, for your legs to be filled with running, for the hunger to run to return.

Once you are back running, once it has again become something to which you look forward (and *no*, this feeling does not have to be in evidence every single run!) you are ready to begin thinking about your next marathon goal: to run a second marathon with a solid time goal attached.

As stated before, your performance in a 10K race is a good indicator of your marathoning abilities. Once you have at least a month of recovery running behind you, a few 10Ks per month will keep your edge but not excessively exhaust you or take a great deal of time from your schedule.

If you are still feeling a bit sluggish and your 10K time is not what you feel it *can* be, give yourself more time to gradually recover from your marathon. If your 10K times generally get better and you feel as though you are racing with more confidence and power, you may wish to begin thinking in terms of planning your next marathon four to six months down the road. If your 10Ks are lackluster, you have trouble recovering from them, and your running still feels heavy and tired, continue training at the maintenance level—but on the occasional day when you *do* feel extra life in your legs, let them have their way.

Once you're having three to four decent runs per week,

consider your next marathon date. It doesn't have to be exactly sixteen weeks away either. You may want to plan it six months away, and then gently build back into the new training schedule at the next level up.

In summary, *listen to your body!* You'd be surprised at how many veteran and experienced runners *and* marathoners think they listen to their bodies but actually do not. Your body will give you a plain indication of what it is or is not ready for. Don't force it to do something for which it is not ready.

When the three of you—you, your body, and your head—are ready for the next marathon training program and the next goal, the vote will be unanimous.

How to Customize Your Next Training Program

If, for your next marathon, you wish to set a goal of breaking 3:30, 3:15, or 3:00, use the programs in Chapter 8.

If you failed to break four hours in your first marathon, use one of the programs in Chapter 7 but add an additional 5 miles per week, as follows:

Monday   Add 1 extra mile to your easy run

Tuesday   Add 1 extra hill mile

Thursday   Add 1 extra repeat track mile

Saturday   Add 2 extra miles to your weekend run; if a 10K race is called for, jog 2 extra miles after crossing the finish line

This revised training schedule will still keep you under 60 miles per week, and the emphasis will remain on using quality miles to improve your abilities.

If you want to shoot for one of the more difficult time goals (3:30, 3:15, 3:00) and you also pick a more difficult marathon course, use the appropriate training schedule in Chapter 8 but add an additional 5 miles per week to the program in the following manner:

Monday   Add 1 mile

Tuesday   Add 1 mile

Wednesday   Add 1 repeat mile

Saturday   Add 2 miles to your long run

These additional miles will help give you the edge in strength and endurance you need to take on the added challenge presented by a more difficult marathon course.

Even if the course of your next marathon is not especially challenging, you may want to consider adding the 5 miles to your selected week's program in order to increase your capacity to handle the distance. This strategy is especially beneficial for those runners who made it through their first marathon with something left or who felt that their initial training program did not fully tax them.

If you feel you will be working fairly hard just to keep on the 3:30, 3:15, or 3:00 program, don't tack on the additional miles. In your case, the rest you will receive from not doing the extra 5 miles will be more beneficial than the benefits the additional miles might bring.

17

Lessons from the Great Marathoners

The winners ran at speeds equaled or surpassed by no more than a handful of runners ever in the world. As important for me was the fact that more than fifteen thousand people from sixty-eight countries completed our race.

—FRED LEBOW with RICHARD WOODLEY,
Inside the World of Big-Time Marathoning

As major marathons near, friends who know I've dabbled a bit in marathons begin to ask questions about who I think will win Los Angeles or Boston or San Francisco or Marine Corps or New York City. My typical response is "I don't know. Who's running?" Although not marathoners themselves, these friends frequently know more about the elite runners who will compete than I do. I'm more interested in what my fellow dabblers will do than in who will win $75,000 and a German high-performance car.

When I do watch network marathon coverage, I become frustrated that it never stays on long enough for the commentators to report on how the "human interest" stories turned out. I want to know about the finishes of the extraordinary regular folks the network has used in a short feature—people like the Jenkins family of Hoboken, New Jersey (all seven of them); Ben Speckt, the fireman who by running fought his way back from injuries suffered in the big Club Zong fire of 1988; Gail Prescott from Tucson, the mother of triplets, who trained every day by pushing her trio in a customized Baby-Jogger; Rita Plumm from Des Moines, the seventy-nine-year-old great-grandmother who was going for an age-group mark; and Dr. George Sheehan, the medical guru of my generation of runners. Did Sheehan have any memorable quotes or did he just snort and wander off like a prophet in the wilderness? Or how about Amby Burfoot or Joe Henderson? They were there. How'd they do?

I just can't seem to get worked up about who finished first as much as I can about who finished. Marathoning is one of the only sports in the world that is truly open. You and I can line up at the starting line, run the same course, and cross the same finish line in the same race with the best long-distance runners in the world. But most of us would line up at that starting line whether there was anyone in the race capable of doing it under 2:45 or not. In fact, some long-running marathoners studiously seek out races where there is a deemphasis of elite and an emphasis on everyone else.

Joe Henderson, editor of *Runner's World* from 1970 to 1977, and the author of many of the seminal books in the category I like to think of as "running for the rest of us," put the importance of the marathon for the average person in perspective in his 1991 book, *Think Fast*:

> The marathon takes more runners farther into areas normally left unexplored than any other race. That's the main reason most people run this distance. They don't come to marathons to win prize money or divisional awards, or for the chance to start with the stars. They come for the chance to take chances, to make some unknowns known, to win without having to finish first.
>
> Among running events, the marathon beats all others as a natural attraction because it is more than just a race. The 10K is a race, a speed test. But for most runners, the marathon is a *survival* test where native speed and skill count for less than

careful preparation and dogged persistence. Getting to and through a marathon is an experience never to be forgotten.

Indeed, if the 10K is the senior prom, the marathon is life.

It could be argued that today's marathoners who make a living at road racing do so because they ride on the shoulders of the also-rans, who, by their very number and their prized demographics, bring sponsors and entry fees to the sport. Nonetheless, those of us who line up well behind the stars can learn something from them. Ironically, we can learn lessons from the heroes and heroines of marathoning that they, in their heyday, were unable to intuit and learn from themselves.

The lessons I find most profound are the ones that underline truths rather than illuminate them. Of the marathoners I use for inspiration and to teach and reteach me how simple marathon training really is, two are dead and two are no longer competing; only one is still racing competitively. Which means that I tend to revere those who have gone before or who have broken new ground rather than those who are merely fast.

In this chapter you'll meet the five marathoners I learn from; these runners have shaped the sport and have lessons to teach that are still very much applicable today: Clarence De Mar, Emil Zatopek, Abebe Bikila, Derek Clayton, and Grete Waitz.

A Good and Faithful Scout: Clarence DeMar

Stanley Provost, a retired shipyard worker who lives in Hough's Neck across the bay from Boston, remembers the first Boston Marathon he attended: "I was six or seven. There were a lot of people standing against police barriers and I squirmed my way between some of them and ducked under one of the barricades and this big Irish cop saw me. He started walking over toward me, to chase me back into the crowd, I guess, when there was a commotion down the street and some cars were coming along. Instead of chasing me away, the cop stood me in front of the barricade and pointed with his nightstick down the road. 'Here he comes,' the cop said to me, pointing. 'Here comes Clarence DeMar!' I looked down the street and there was this fellow wearing baggy shorts and black shoes running up the street. People began calling his name and applauding. Even the cop put his nightstick under his arm so he'd have his hands free to applaud."

For most of the history of American marathoning, Clarence DeMar defined the public idea of the marathoner: small (five feet, eight inches), slim (127 pounds at his first Boston win in 1911), soft-spoken, a hard-worker, introverted. The bigger-than-normal, beefy, loudmouthed, and outgoing marathoner who came along once in a while was merely an aberration. Marathoners were supposed to be like Clarence DeMar—*demure.*

During his lengthy marathon career, Clarence DeMar won the Boston Marathon an unrivaled seven times, and would have likely won several more if he hadn't, at the prime of his career, taken more than five years off from competing. He was three times an American Olympian and an inspiration for several generations of marathoners and marathon fans. "To many of us back in those days," Stanley Provost says, "Clarence DeMar *was* the Boston Marathon."

By his own admission, Clarence DeMar wasn't much of a runner in his youth. His wins at Boston were the result of putting in the necessary mileage and stumbling upon what was then an advanced training routine. The school he started attending at age seven was a mile away; he ran to and from it. When his father died, he made money to help his mother and five younger brothers and sisters survive by selling pins, needles, thread, and soap; his sales trips involved walking 10 to 20 miles a day.

At age ten, Clarence badly injured his ankle while skating over some crusted snow, his ankle became infected, and he nearly lost his foot.

Even though his fatherless family had free use of a house in Warwick that belonged to relatives, the DeMars could not make ends meet—they were forced to break up the family. Clarence, not yet a teenager, was placed in a home called The Farm School on Thompson Island in Boston Harbor.

DeMar attacked his loneliness by reading and studying. When he graduated from The Farm School at sixteen, he secured a job with a fruit farmer in South Hero, Vermont; he earned less than twenty dollars a month there, some of which he sent to his mother. While working, he continued his studies at the Maple Lawn Academy.

He eventually entered the University of Vermont. His time was filled with studying and working at anything he could find (from beating rugs to slopping hogs at the experimental farm) to finance his education. He continued to run between classes and his jobs. He even managed to convince his gym instructors that he needn't take gym, that he was getting enough exercise running all over the place.

While he had been on Thompson Island, Clarence had read vague reports of long-distance races held in foreign countries. He had always harbored the dream of excelling in some sort of sport, although the sports he tried never seemed to work out for him. "One morning the thought came to me," he wrote years later in his autobiography, "that I could run a marathon, and perhaps go abroad to represent my country."

DeMar continued his incessant running between classes and jobs, intent on staying in shape, but as yet with his dream only half focused. In his junior year, Clarence went out for the cross-country team. The coach attempted to change his low-slung, efficient, ground-eating style of running. "Run on your toes, on your toes!" the team captain admonished him. Clarence tried, but found that his own method served him best.

In his first meet (a 4-miler) he placed fourth. The next week at a meet at Union College, he again came in fourth, ahead of the team captain.

DeMar's college career ended in 1909, when he turned twenty-one. At that age he was legally able to help support his mother, so he went to live with her in Melrose, where he remained for twenty years, while he worked as a printer in Boston.

Clarence continued his habit of running to work, carrying a dry shirt, which he could change into when he arrived at the printer's. During Christmas vacation in 1909, Clarence decided that it was about time to see what he could do at longer distances. The longest he'd run at one time was 10 miles. He ran through Reading to a section of Andover; a road sign there indicated that Boston was 20 miles away. He ran into Boston, then turned around and came back out to Melrose, covering roughly 26 miles in three hours. On February 22, 1910, he entered a 10-mile handicapped race from Boston to Chestnut Hill and back. He won.

He felt confident enough to set his sights on the April 19 Boston Marathon. In those days the race started in Ashland and the course was about 24 miles. The day was hot and Clarence decided to conserve himself in hopes that the other runners would run themselves into trouble. Clarence ran steadily about seven minutes behind the leaders. As the race progressed, Clarence passed more and more runners sprawled on the grass beside the road.

Coming down Commonwealth Avenue, he caught sight of the leader, Nova Scotia's Freddy Cameron. Clarence picked up the pace but could not catch Cameron, finishing one minute behind the winner's 2:28:52.

During the next several months, Clarence raced often and did well. But in midsummer he made a terrible mistake, going against his own beliefs when he allowed two athletic trainers to coach him for a return match against Cameron later that summer. As part of their strategy, they took Clarence to an over-the-hill doctor in Roxbury to have him examined. The doctor declared that Clarence had a heart murmur and for his own safety should give up running within the next year or two if he valued his life.

Clarence's two trainers managed to change his training just enough to allow him to place dismally in his next several races, so Clarence used the bad showings as a reason to go back to his own self-coached methods. In the fall he placed third at the Brockton Fair Marathon.

In preparation for the 1911 Boston Marathon, he fell into

a training pattern of doing about 100 miles a week, with one run of at least 20 miles and with much of his weekday training broken into two sessions. This is the regimen that many modern world-class marathoners swear by.

At the prerace check-up before Boston, the doctor who examined Clarence confirmed that he did have a heart murmur. The doctor advised him to make this his last race and said that if he got tired, he should drop out of the race. Clarence shrugged his shoulders. He wasn't sure how you could get through *any* marathon without getting tired.

Clarence's training paid off. He ran a textbook-perfect race, took the lead at 19 miles, and won by a half-mile in course record time of 2:21:39. He continued to race regularly through August, winning every race he entered. He also went on to win the Brockton Fair Marathon that fall. For 1911 he was ten for ten.

After conferring with A.A.U. officials about his chances of making the 1912 Olympic team, Clarence DeMar cut back radically on his racing so as not to exhaust himself. He watched the 1912 Boston Marathon from a press car as Mike Ryan won the race, breaking Clarence's record by 21 seconds. On the strength of his 1911 performances and a 10-mile exhibition run, Clarence was selected, along with eleven others runners, to make up the U.S. marathon team at the Olympic Games in Stockholm.

On the boat to Sweden, coaches set rigid schedules for training routines for all athletes—schedules that in many cases undermined what was potentially the most remarkable track and field team America would assemble until 1936.

The problem was aggravated when Mike Ryan, based upon his Boston win, decided to take a domineering role among his fellow marathoners, and when the marathon coach, Johnny Hayes, demanded that all marathoners train together, including days of 20-mile workouts when the ship put in at Antwerp for a layover. Clarence began to go stale and then ruptured a blood vessel and began to go lame.

Marathon day dawned hot. Near the halfway point, Mike

Ryan dropped out. A Portuguese runner collapsed from the heat and died the next day. For one of only two times in the sixty-five marathons Clarence would run in his career, he broke stride and walked nearly a mile. Several of the marathoners, among them Clarence, had to use canes to limp back onto the ship for their return to the United States.

The experience left a very bad taste in his mouth.

Although he ran a few races in the fall, he didn't defend his title at the Brockton Fair Marathon and ultimatly gave up the sport for the next five years—prime years in the life of a runner.

The perception was that he stopped running races on advice of the doctors, but Clarence claimed that was only one-third of the reason. As a member of the Baptist church, Clarence had begun thinking that his running was vainglorious; before and after church services his fellow parishoners, instead of asking him about the condition of his immortal soul, would ask after the condition of his legs. The third factor was simply one of time. He was working full time as a typographer and taking extension courses at Harvard and Boston universities. Clarence did not like to do anything halfheartedly and he knew that under those time constraints, his training was going to have to be halfhearted.

Clarence did not give up running entirely. He still ran the mile to and from work, doing it in about six minutes, through traffic, wearing street clothes, and he ran a few races for fun. During this period he received his A.A. degree from Harvard and became a scoutmaster in Melrose.

After five years off the running circuit, Clarence DeMar decided to return. He went into training for the 1917 Boston, but ran only three times a week in training. He placed third. In the fall he took a day off from work to run Brockton Fair, which he won, breaking his old record. But then he was drafted into the army for World War I. He was sent to England and France and didn't get much time to run.

Back in the United States in 1920, he skipped the Boston Marathon on April 19, instead taking his Scout troop on a canoeing trip on the Shawsheen River. Clarence didn't attempt to make the 1920 Olympic team (which was just as well, since Mike Ryan was now the marathon coach). On the day of the 1921 Boston race DeMar was up at the Boy Scout cabin in North Reading making repairs.

Between the 1912 Olympics and 1922, Clarence had essentially dropped out of running, coming back to run Boston only once (in 1917, when he'd taken third). Between his health and religious considerations (1912–17) and World War I and his Scouts (1917–22), DeMar had abdicated the Boston Marathon when he should have been at the peak of his career.

His retirement, however, was about to end. A co-worker at a new print shop, Bob Campbell, convinced him to go back into training for the 1922 Boston; Campbell volunteered to be his handler while riding a bicycle (the accepted mobile aid station in those days). Only Campbell and DeMar's Boy Scouts believed he could do it. He began to gently settle back into training, running the 4½ miles to and from his new work location. On race day, Clarence finished off his rivals in the Newton Hills and rolled across the finish line in 2:18:10, a new course record.

Clarence got a late start on training for the 1923 race, when he was forced to spend ten days in bed suffering from erysipelas (the result of a blow to the lip from a dog owner whose dog Clarence had kicked when it had lunged at him on a training run). In spite of that, a bout with the flu, and a hot day, Clarence won the 1923 race. In 1924, he came back and again won, this time with little opposition over the final miles.

Clarence was picked for the 1924 Olympic team, which consisted of six runners and an alternate. This time he laid out his training ground rules to Coach Mike Ryan before he agreed to go. (The 1924 Paris Olympics was the setting of the film *Chariots of Fire,* which concerned itself with the shorter track events.) As usual with the Olympic marathon, the temperature was high. Clarence paced himself well and took third place. The highest an American who had trained under Ryan's coaching could manage was sixteenth.

In 1925, Clarence placed second at Boston and in 1926 took third. He then went off on a tear, winning his next five marathons: Baltimore in May 1926, the Sesqui-Centennial in Philadelphia in June, Port Chester in October, Baltimore again in March 1927, and Boston in April. Boston was another hot day, and Clarence described it wonderfully: "It was hot, so hot that the tar was like flypaper." He led from the start; course-record holder and defending champion Johnny Miles attempted to hold to Clarence's early lead pace, but was forced to drop out at 6 miles.

Again, Clarence began to spend more of his time on church activities and with his Scouts. But he still managed to win a 44-mile race from Providence to Boston in the spring of 1928. That year DeMar married and changed jobs; he became the printing teacher at the Keene Normal School. He won his last Boston Marathon in 1930 at the age of forty-one.

He continued to run Boston during the 1930s (eighth in 1933, sixteenth in 1934, eighteenth in 1935, and sixteenth in 1936), but his education and career took more of his time. He had received his master's degree from Boston University in 1934 by taking courses on weekends and at nights.

DeMar died on July 10, 1958, four days after his seventieth birthday. Pathologists who examined his heart found it to be larger than normal, not from disease but from a surfeit of health.

Johnny Kelley, who won Boston in 1935 and 1945 and who *still* runs Boston annually, and has become an institution in the race, summed up Clarence DeMar best: "He was a very determined person. Brought up on hardships, a man of high moral standards."

The Lovable Beast: Emil Zatopek

Like Clarence DeMar, Emil Zatopek arrived at his astonishing athletic accomplishments more from hard work applied logically and well than from boundless genetic ability. The most famous Czechoslovakian athlete in history and the world's greatest distance runner was also the possessor of the ugliest running style in the history of world-class running: His arms flailed as though he were in the climax of an epileptic fit, while his head would be cocked back and to one side, his face distorted in pain. One journalist described him as "like a man who has just been stabbed through the heart." The famed American sportswriter Red Smith, after seeing Zatopek for the first time along with thousands of other track fans at the 1948 London Olympics, had this to say about the memory of the experience: "Witnesses who had long since forgotten the other events still wake up screaming in the dark when Emil the Terrible goes writhing through their dreams, gasping, groaning, clawing at his abdomen in horrible extremities of pain."

What were Zatopek's contributions to the world of marathoning? Certainly not a string of marathon victories. He ran only two marathons in his life.

What Zatopek did was perfect speed workouts to effectively complement the strength and endurance of the typical distance runner. He remains the only athlete to win gold medals in the 5,000 meters, 10,000 meters, and the marathon in the same Olympic Games. Incredibly, it was his first marathon and he broke the Olympic marathon record in the process.

Like Clarence DeMar, Emil Zatopek, the son of a carpenter, was born into poverty in Koprinivince, Czechoslovakia. He moved to Zlin at sixteen, where he worked at a shoe factory and went to school in the evenings. He was filled with ambition and good humor and was described throughout his life as "a tireless worker."

In 1941, the shoe company sponsored a race through the streets of the town, and all employees were required to take part. Emil finished second.

Emil ran a few more races and, despite his awkward running style, was singled out by several trainers and coaches as a prospect. Emil's first big race was a 3,000-meter contest in which he finished only three seconds behind his trainer. The local newspaper had this to say: "A good performance by Zatopek." That single sentence sparked his ambitions to be the best he could be. He carried the clipping with him for years, reading it over and over (although it had long been committed to memory).

Emil's training and strategy were always based upon his own view of where he was going—and how fast. Instead of seeking out races he knew he could win, he signed up for the races with the toughest competition, determined that the only way to improve was to be pushed to his best.

Emil also became an ardent student of training methods. He studied every scrap of information he could find, discarding that which he found unworkable and customizing what he found workable. His studies and their applications to his own training earned him the reputation as the father of interval training: Endurance + Speed = Performance.

"When I was young, I was too slow," Emil said in a 1979 interview. "I thought, 'I must learn to run fast by practicing to run fast.' So I ran 100 meters very fast. Then I came back, slow, slow, slow. People said, 'Emil, you are crazy. You are practicing to be a sprinter. You have no chance.' I said, 'Yes, but if I run 100 meters twenty times, that is 2 kilometers and that is no longer a sprint.' "

Other distance runners at that time were training strictly for endurance and stamina. Emil's reaction? "Why should I practice running slow? I already know how to run slow. I want to learn how to run fast."

Although credited with developing the interval training method, Emil claims he merely modified methods then being used by his hero, Finland's Paavo Nurmi. Coaches, trainers, and track enthusiasts watching him train thought him a fool. But they'd felt the same about Nurmi.

When the Soviets drove the Germans out of Zlin, Emil joined the army but continued training by running in place in his combat boots while on sentry duty.

After the war, he signed up for officers' training and continued running. In his first international competition, in 1946, he ran the 5,000 meters in the European Championships in Oslo. Although he did not win, his 14:25.8 was a Czech record. Encouraged, he marched off a quarter-mile straightaway in the woods at the army base and began doing daily sprints up and down the runway, still wearing his heavy military boots, running through mud and snow and against cruel winds; at night he ran with a flashlight.

In 1947, he ran 5,000 meters in 14:08.2, beating Finland's Heino, one of the top runners in the world, by one yard. When officers' training was finished he received a month's vacation, which he used to accept every track invitation he could fit in. He went unbeaten in the 5,000 in 1947 and was ranked first in the world.

Because of his unorthodox running style, because of the gesticulating arms, the eyes rolling into the back of his head, and the look of extreme pain, track journalists loved him. They came up with a litany of nicknames: The Beast of Prague, Emil the Terrible, and the Czech Locomotive; the last was based upon the pistonlike movement of his legs, which is the center from which Emil won races. ("Don't watch his arms," astute coaches said, "watch his legs.") But the press loved Emil Zatopek most because of his obvious love of running, his good humor, and his almost naive enthusiasm at winning or participating in a good race. His was an un-ashamed animal-like joy of movement.

Although well known behind what was to become the Iron Curtain, Emil was not known on the international circuit. Track enthusiasts had of course heard of his domination of the 5,000 meters in 1947, and he was in fact favored to win that event at the 1948 London Olympic Games, the first Olympic Games after World War II. The English had never seen Emil run, and when they did, they unanimously agreed that he was the worst runner they'd ever had the misfortune to watch.

He wore a faded red Czechoslovakian shirt, and although he was young, his corn-colored hair was thinning, his tongue hung limply out of his mouth, he made noises that sounded like tortured huffs and wheezes, and his face contorted into such a panted grimace that people in the stands winced to see him. When the 10,000-meter race began, Emil ran at the back of the pack; he looked exhausted. Spectators felt that he had been allowed onto the course only to fill out the field and to appease the Eastern Bloc.

After the eighth lap, however, at a signal from a Czech cohort in the stands who held up a red vest to indicate that the pace had dropped below seventy-one seconds per lap, Emil seemed to limp into fifth place. The fans took Emil to their hearts, although they were certain that against the great Heino, the world-record holder, he had no chance. They were unaware that the previous month, in only his second 10,000, Emil had come within 1.6 seconds of Heino's record.

Czech fans began chanting: "Za-to-pek, Za-to-pek, Za-to-pek!" Emil closed on Heino, then passed him, with 6,000 meters to go. The rest of the crowd took up the chant. "Za-to-pek, Za-to-pek, Za-to-pek!" Heino again took the lead. Emil's timer in the stands again held up the red vest. Emil again went into a sprint, something unheard of in the *middle* of a 10,000-meter race. The stands erupted: "Za-to-pek, Za-to-pek, Za-to-pek!"

The day, which was hot and humid, began to add a note of confusion to the proceedings. Secretly shooting for 29:35, Emil concentrated on the red vest. The Czech fan, caught up in the excitement of the moment, kept waving the vest. Emil became confused. "Where's Heino?" he called to an official on one lap.

"Heino is out," the official said.

Emil shook his head and continued, crossed the finish line in seeming triumph, only to learn that the official who had been counting laps had miscounted. He had to run one more lap. Emil rolled into his awkward gait and circled the track again, picking up his pace until it turned into an awesome sprint. He finished in 29:59.6, a new Olympic record.

The next day the crowd was again with him as he ran his qualifying race for inclusion in the 5,000 meters. He won by thirty seconds, a bit of excess for which he would later pay.

The 5,000-meter final two days later was held in the middle of a downpour. Emil led the first eight laps, knocking off machinelike laps of sixty-eight or sixty-nine seconds. But he began to tire. At 3,500 meters, Gaston Reiff of Belgium took the lead and, seeing that Reiff's move had worked, Willi Slykhuis of Holland followed. Emil fell 65 yards behind the leader. But with a lap to go, Zatopek dug down to his soul and began a sprint. On the backstretch, he blasted past Slykhuis as though he didn't exist. He closed on Reiff. The crowd went wild. Emil ran madly, wildly. On the homestretch, Reiff was still 20 yards ahead, exhausted, zoned out; he attempted to go into his own sprint. Reiff suddenly heard the chant of the crowd: "Za-to-pek, Za-to-pek, Za-to-pek!" Reiff turned his head and what he saw scared him enough to push him forward. Reiff won by 2 yards. The stands erupted. Never again would a track fan ask: "Who's this Zatopek fellow?"

In October of that year Emil married Dana Ingrova, a Czech Olympian who had placed seventh in the javelin. She was a true soul mate for Emil: She shared his enthusiasm for life, his high spirits, his love of movement. They were born on the same day (September 19, 1922); Emil was six hours older. On the day of their wedding, legend has it that they were kissing while riding bicycles and crashed, which made them late for their own wedding. In a 1991 interview, Emil claimed that Dana was knocked off her bike by a forest ranger's dog. Her scraped knees made it difficult for her to kneel at the very formal and solemn wedding ceremony, much to the consternation of the presiding cleric. In spite of the skinned knee, Emil and Dana danced until dawn.

Married life agreed with Emil. During 1949, he lost only one race: at 1,500 meters.

On August 2, 1950, Emil ran his fastest 5,000 meters: 14:06.2. Two days later, with Heino in the stands watching him and cheering him on, he broke the world record in the 10,000 by eighteen seconds, finishing at 29:02.6.

Later that year he developed food poisoning when he ate a tainted goose. Doctors pumped his stomach and advised him to drop out of the upcoming European Championships. Emil ignored them, and during the following month ran two of the best 10,000 meters in history to that point, and the second, third, and fourth fastest 5,000s. In 1950, he was never beaten.

Compared to 1949 and 1950, 1951 was somewhat disappointing. Breaking from tradition, Emil did indoor exercises, using weight training and riding a stationary bicycle with 4½-pound weights on each foot. This was revolutionary at the time. But it wasn't the switch to this new form of endurance training that did Emil in. It was his tremendous enthusiasm for sports. He injured his leg skiing and had one leg in a cast until April.

On the comeback trail, Emil lost a 3,000-meter race. He managed to win all his 5,000-meter races, but in what he considered mediocre times. He also remained unbeaten in the 10,000 meters, but again with what he considered inferior times. Toward the end of the year, he decided to try longer races. At the Czech military championships, he decided to go after Heino's one-hour track record, a now seldom-run event in which a runner attempts to run as far as possible around a track in the space of one hour. Emil did 19,558 meters (12 miles, 268 yards). He continued to run through 20,000 meters in a time of 1:01:16. Heino's reaction? "Believe me, Zatopek could run 20 kilometers in one hour." That was heady talk, since only six men in the world (Zatopek and Heino among them) had ever run 10 kilometers in under thirty minutes. To run 20 kilometers in under sixty minutes would require two back-to-back world-class 10,000-meter performances. Two weeks later Zatopek went to a beautiful track in a forest setting and did just that: He ran 20 kilometers in 59:51.8, breaking the world record for 10 miles along the way with a 48:12 split. "After running for an hour on a track at a military base, to be in such a beautiful forest to run, it was very inspiring," he recalled in the 1991 interview.

Over the winter, Emil rested, went ice-skating, and did runs in knee-deep snow. He had rung up four of the five fastest 5,000s in history and six of the seven fastest 10,000s.

Emil suffered a bout with the flu that actually put him into bed, and when he came back, he felt his performances were lackluster. By the time of the Olympics in Helsinki, he felt confident in taking on the 10,000 meters but shaky about anything else.

There were thirty-two runners in the 10,000 meters. Emil started conservatively, but by lap six began to take control. He ran every lap in the sixty-eight- to seventy-two-second range, gradually wearing down everyone else with his dogged pace. He uncorked a sixty-four-second final lap to win by 90 yards, setting an Olympic record of 29:17.0 (his third-best 10,000).

Two days later in the 5,000-meter qualifying heat, Emil ran back and forth between runners he wanted to make the final, urging them on, speaking to the runners in their own language. "Sasha, come on, we must get a move on," he said in Russian to his friend Aleksandr Anufriev of the Soviet Union. "Hurry up, Stone, or you'll miss the bus," he admonished Curt Stone of the United States.

In the final that came two days later, Herbert Schade of West Germany, the fastest qualifier, took the field out quickly, hoping to burn off the competition. Emil held back in sixth place. At the halfway point, Emil made a move on Schade but Schade had enough strength to hold him off. Emil tried again and again to pass Schade, but failed. Finally Emil passed Schade and took a moment to reassess the field. But in that moment, three other runners (Chataway, Reiff, and Mimoun) blasted past him. Suddenly Emil was fourth and Schade was fifth. Emil and Schade tucked in behind the freight train and hung on.

For the next several laps the lead changed frequently. With two laps left, the race could go to any of the five.

But with 500 meters to go, Reiff stepped off the track; he had quit. Four runners went into the final lap together.

Emil squirted out of the tight group but was soon passed by Chataway, then by Schade, and then by Mimoun on the backstretch. Within seconds, Zatopek was in fourth place, 6 yards back, and looking exhausted.

But it was in such situations that Zatopek—the Zatopek of courage unbounded, strength incarnate—came to the fore. With 200 meters to go, he metamorphosed into his alter ego of "the running beast," his head back, his shoulders hunched, a look of near-terror on his face, his stride awkward and seemingly painful—but enormously effective. The crowd became hysterical.

Emil moved out into the third lane, giving up yards in the turn, but setting himself up for the final straight.

Emil went past Schade and moved up on Chataway and Mimoun, but Mimoun was moving around Chataway at the time and bumped into Emil, who seemed not to notice. Chataway, although not touched, tripped and fell to the inside of the track. Mimoun, the earliest disciple of Emil Zatopek's revolutionary training methods, tried to hold on but Emil was just too fast. The crowd had fallen silent as Emil had made his move. And even after he crossed the finish line in first, the crowd remained strangely silent, as though they were as exhausted as he was.

Emil stumbled back to the Olympic Village and as a result failed to see the finals of the women's javelin, where his wife took the gold. When he heard the news, he claimed the score in the Zatopek household was getting too close for comfort—two golds to one—so he'd have to run the marathon to open a commanding lead. Actually, he had decided several days before to attempt the marathon for the first time in his life. It was scheduled three days hence.

For two years the marathon had been dominated by Jim Peters of England. Zatopek wanted to race Peters, but he was no fool. His strategy was twofold: to follow Peters, the reigning expert at the marathon, and to exhibit some patience, since the marathon was run at a pace much slower than he was used to in his racing.

Peters, however, was not feeling very well. He had been transported to Helsinki in an old, drafty, cramped surplus World War II plane and he was feeling less than top-flight. Like the competitor he was, though, he went out quickly.

Emil was taken by surprise; the pace for the marathon was much faster than he had anticipated. It took him 10 miles to catch Peters. The two of them, running side by side, were a study in atrocious running styles. Emil ran like a man stabbed through the heart, and Jim's style was so rolling that he seemed to be constantly flopping from side to side, always on the verge of tipping over.

Emil moved up beside the Englishman. "Jim, the pace—it is too fast?" Emil asked. Peters, hoping to psych out the seemingly naive Zatopek, replied, "Emil, the pace—it is too slow." Emil was shocked.

"You say 'too slow'?" Emil said. "Are you sure the pace is too slow?"

"Yes," Peters said.

Emil shook his head in disbelief and picked up the pace. "Come with us," he said to Peters, "it's much easier when there are three together." (The third runner was Gustaf Jansson of Sweden, who had followed Emil through the pack.)

At the turnaround, Emil was surprised to see Peters dropping back. When they turned, it was into a headwind, something Emil was used to in his repeat quarter-mile workouts.

By 25 kilometers, Jansson had fallen five seconds back. Emil charged up the hills between 25 and 30 kilometers as they presented themselves, effectively breaking Jansson. At the top, he looked back to assess his competition, then rolled along, chatting with the cyclists and spectators as he went. He began concentrating to fight his growing weariness. He went through 30 kilometers some twelve seconds under world-record pace.

Now he began to see that the marathon was something not to be taken lightly. He began to feel overwhelming pain and discomfort, he was developing blisters, he gasped for air, and the crowd noise was giving him a headache. But at ten minutes from the finish, he had a 150-second lead.

His exhaustion was beginning to drain his face as he approached the stadium. His scarlet racing singlet hung limply over his bony shoulders, and he moved with an old man's shuffle. The marathon distance had done something to him that no other race and no other competitor had ever been able to do: It had nearly done him in.

The stadium crowd had been kept abreast of the marathon's progress and they were electrified with the prospect of seeing Olympic history made: a sweep of the distance events. As he approached the stadium Emil began to hear the chant: "Za-to-pek, Za-to-pek, Za-to-pek!" He smiled weakly—he loved the crowds to love him.

He reached the tape, raised his arms in victory, limped to the side of the track, sat down, removed his shoes, examined his bloodied feet, and breathed a profound sigh of relief. The announcement of his time came: 2:23:03.2, a new Olympic marathon record, and a world record for an out-and-back course.

He rose, put on his sweats, and limped to the finish line, where he ate an apple and handed out orange slices to other finishers.

The clean sweep of the distance events, which remains unique in Olympic competition, set him on a rampage of breaking world records. He took the 30-kilometer track record on October 26 during a rainstorm. He now held every world record from 10,000 meters to the marathon.

During the next four years, the young lions all began to train as Emil did. In hopes of defending his marathon gold at the 1956 Olympic Games in Melbourne, he decided he needed to train harder, since he felt he was deficient as far as innate talent went. He began running with his wife on his shoulders, hoping that this would give him additional strength in his aging legs. Instead, it gave him a hernia. He continued to train—badly—with the hernia, until late in the summer when he had it surgically repaired. Incredibly, still recuperating from the operation, he _did_ run the marathon, placing sixth. Alain Mimoun of Algeria (who was running for France), who had on three occasions in Olympic competition placed second to Emil and who was one of his earliest training disciples, won the race, then waved press and photographers away while, out of respect, he waited for Emil. When Emil crossed the line, the two embraced warmly.

By 1957, at the age of thirty-five, Emil decided to retire. He stepped back into the daily life of Czechoslovakia. But he embodied a sort of paradox. His country hailed and revered him as its hero, yet he personally stood for individuality. "I am not Czechoslovakia. I am me," he said in a 1979 interview. "I always liked the American athletes because they owed nothing to the state. In Russia, athletes have everything handed to them, much more so than here [in America], but they are expected to win. In my country, the same. Before Helsinki, I said, 'I think I can win the 10,000 again.' They said, 'Only one gold medal?' It is not good that way. Better to be given nothing by the state and owe nothing in return. Sports should be a free activity."

When Alexander Dubček rose among the Czechs, preaching personal rights and freedoms for his people, Emil was right beside him. When Russian tanks rolled into Prague in the summer of 1968, Zatopek donned his colonel's uniform, walked into Wenceslas Square, and faced the oncoming Russians. "Why are you invading our country?" he demanded to know.

If it had been anyone but Zatopek, he would have been shot on the spot.

In an attempt to belittle him, the Russians shipped him and Dana to a trailer deep in the woods, where he was required to dig wells and mine for uranium. But instead of being belittled, Emil Zatopek's dedication to his new job enshrined him even more in the eyes of his countrymen.

Neither was he forgotten by the rest of the world. West Germany requested his presence as a guest of honor at the 1972 Munich Olympics; there were invitations to the Scandinavian countries; and as the running revolution took off in the United States, he was invited there. Unable to break Emil Zatopek's spirit and eager to use him in the West as a propaganda weapon, the Communist party declared him rehabilitated.

He is now retired and travels regularly to the West at the invitation of admirers and race directors.

The Totally Perfect Tragedy: Abebe Bikila

Arguably the most graceful distance runner to ever stride a step—and arguably the world's greatest male marathoner—Abebe Bikila did not begin running seriously until he was twenty-four years old. And then the Ethiopian star's brightness would not have shone throughout the world were it not for a fortuitous circumstance: Following World War II, Onni Niskanen of Sweden accepted an appointment in Ethiopia to train Haile Selassie's Imperial Body Guards at a camp situated at 6,000 feet altitude.

Niskanen's idea of physical education included cross-country running, often 20 miles at a time, and 1,500-meter repeats. It was into that environment that the Ethiopian army sent Private Abebe Bikila. Like many of his countrymen, Bikila had grown up with running as a basic form of transportation. And, like many of his countrymen, he did much of his running barefoot.

Then, like now, Ethiopia was essentially a closed society. Very little information filtered out of it. So at the Rome Olympics in 1960, when Ethiopia sent its distance runners, they were an unknown quantity.

Unknown to the spectators, the barefooted, skinny, frightened-looking Bikila was not a novice to marathoning. In order to pick its team for the 1960 Games, marathon trials had been held in both July and August at the Ethiopian capital of Addis Ababa, which sits on a plateau at more than 5,000 feet altitude. Bikila had run both qualifying marathons, the July race in 2:39:50 and the August event in 2:21:23, a remarkable performance considering the altitude and the African heat.

The Rome Olympics were unique in several ways. It was the first time in the modern Olympic Games that the marathon race neither started nor finished at the stadium where the other running events were held. And in consideration of the September heat, the race was to begin at 5:30 P.M. and continue into the darkness. To celebrate the fabled city of Rome, the course was laid out to run by and through various Roman landmarks.

The race began near Capitoline Hill. Within a few miles, spectators saw that they were in for a unique contest. A group of four runners had moved to the front, taking control of the pace. One was Arthur Keily of Britain, who had been the first Englishman since Jim Peters to break the 2:20 barrier, a feat he'd managed in April. Another of the leaders was Aurele Vandendriessche of Belgium, who'd been that country's marathon champion for five consecutive years. The third and fourth members of the front-running group were Africans, neither of whom was well known outside his native continent: Rhadi ben Abdesselem of Morocco, who'd placed fourteenth in the 10,000 meters two days earlier; and the nut-brown, barefooted runner who had tried shoes but found that they caused blisters and pinched his feet—Abebe Bikila, twenty-eight years old.

The group went through 10 kilometers in 31:07. At that point Brian Kilby of Britain caught up with them, as did Allal Saoudi, another Moroccan. Keily and Vandendriessche dominated the pace, while the rest seemed content to sit back and wait. Also in the field, but back by more than thirty seconds, was the world-record holder, Sergey Popov of the Soviet Union, running in a group of five.

Between 15 and 20 kilometers, a dramatic change took place. The Europeans began wilting while the Africans began putting on a surge. Bikila and Rhadi went through 20 kilometers in 1:02:39; Vandendriessche was nearly thirty seconds back, while Keily was fifteen seconds behind him.

While the Africans kept up their relentless pace, there were changes taking place behind them. New Zealander Barry Magee and Popov had moved out of their pack of five and worked their way together into third place, running step for step, but they were more than three minutes behind Rhadi and Bikila.

At the 30-kilometer point, the course turned onto the

Appian Way. Magee and Popov were closing the gap, and then Magee started pulling away, closing to within less than ninety seconds of the leaders by the 40-kilometer mark. It was at that point that the Africans consummated their duel. Running up a tunnel of light engendered by the thousands of torches and lights, Rhadi made his move, but Bikila fought back and threw in his own surge, pulling away by twenty-five seconds in the final 2 kilometers and winning in 2:15:16.2. Bikila had broken Popov's world record by less than a second.

Abebe Bikila's victory, run over the cobblestones of Rome barefooted, served notice that in the 1960s the world of marathoning would belong to Africa.

Bikila returned to Ethiopia for some rest and recuperation, and then embarked on a marathoning spree around the world.

On May 7, 1961, Bikila ran the fourth annual International Classic Marathon, which went from the Plains of Marathon to Athens over a very hilly, very hot course. He won in 2:23:44.6.

On July 25, he traveled to Osaka for the Mainichi Marathon, a race contested before 700,000 spectators. The day was hot and humid. Forty-six elite marathoners began the race; only fifteen finished. Bikila won in 2:29:27, while countryman Wami Biratu took second, some ten minutes back.

On October 12, Bikila ran the invitational Kosice Marathon in Czechoslovakia. He led from 20 kilometers on after breaking local favorite Vaclav Chudomel, and went on to win in 2:20:22.

Bikila didn't race internationally for eighteen months. During that period, on February 17, 1963, one of the most impressive marathon races in history took place at Beppu, Japan. Toru Terasawa ran an amazing 2:15:15.8, breaking Bikila's world record by less than half a second. But even more amazing was the fact that the top ten finishers were all under 2:20!

It was time for Bikila to reemerge. It was announced that he would run in the famed Boston Marathon. The 1963 Patriots' Day race featured one of the strongest fields ever: Eino

Oksanen of Finland was back to defend his title, Brian Kilby and Aurele Vandendriessche were there, as was America's extremely consistent John J. Kelley of Connecticut. Abebe Bikila would attempt to break the hex that hovered over Olympic marathon gold medalists: none had ever won Boston. (Not until 1990 would that hex be broken, when Italy's Gelindo Bordin, the gold medalist at the 1988 Seoul Games, won Boston.) Bikila was accompanied by his countryman Mamo Wolde.

The weather was perfect for a Boston Marathon: temperatures in the fifties and a slight crosswind. The Ethiopians went out fast. Bikila and Wolde were on record pace, but they were not used to running in the cold and soon began cramping up. Going up the Newton Hills, Wolde began to cramp badly and Bikila caught up to him, but the hills only aggravated *his* cramping.

At Coolidge Corner, Vandendriessche caught and passed Bikila. Then John Kelley, Brian Kilby, and Eino Oksanen also passed him. Vandendriessche won in 2:18:58.2, a new course record.

Marathon observers felt that Bikila's brilliant career was over, that he'd had his time in the sun and was finished. Again, he returned to Ethiopia and vanished from sight. But as the time approached for the 1964 Olympic Games at Tokyo, word filtered out of Ethiopia of a warm-up marathon race on May 31 where, once again at 6,000 feet altitude, Bikila had run 2:23:14.8. The Ethiopian Olympic Trials Marathon was held on August 3, again at 6,000 feet altitude, and if the performances were to be believed, the Ethiopians were ready: Bikila ran 2:16:18.8, beating his friend Mamo Wolde by four-tenths of a second. Demissie Wolde (no relation to Mamo) took third in 2:19:30.

Six weeks before the team was to leave for Tokyo, however, Bikila came down with appendicitis, and an appendectomy was performed. Although he would travel to Tokyo with the team, it seemed certain he would not race.

But on October 21, when the Olympic marathoners toed

the line under cloudy skies and with temperatures in the high sixties, Bikila was there—this time wearing shoes.

Ron Clarke, with three Olympic races behind him that week, decided to do the marathon, in hopes of somehow securing a gold medal, something that had eluded him all his life in spite of his holding all distance world records below the marathon. Clarke went out fast, going through 10 kilometers in 30:14. Jim Hogan of Ireland was on his shoulder. Clarke and Hogan went through 15 kilometers in 45:35, with their pursuers a minute back.

Bikila's countrymen were not faring well. Demissie Wolde fell off the pace and Mamo Wolde dropped out. But Bikila, feeling relaxed and strong, caught and passed Clarke and Hogan before the 20-kilometer mark, which he passed in 1:00:58. Hogan was five seconds back and Clarke had faded to forty-one seconds back.

At the turnaround point in Chofu City, Bikila was running smooth as fog over the ground, turning at 1:04:28. At 25 kilometers Hogan was doggedly hanging in fifteen seconds behind Bikila, but Clarke had fallen back and was absorbed by the pursuing pack. Bikila passed 35 kilometers in 1:49:01. Hogan broke and jogged off the course, exhausted. Hogan's departure put Bikila three minutes ahead of his pursuers.

Although his pace slowed in the second half, Bikila remained smooth and steady in his style. As he entered the stadium, the din was terrific. He had become the first marathoner to repeat as Olympic champion, and had done it in convincing style: His 2:12:11.2 was the fastest marathon of all time!

Bikila immediately jogged into the infield, and proceeded to go through a complex series of calisthenics. Many spectators felt Bikila was flaunting the ease with which he had bested the field. In fact, he had learned the hard way that if he did not do a strenuous series of stretches and exercises immediately after a long race, he stiffened terribly within a few hours.

The following year, Bikila and Mamo Wolde returned to

Japan for the May 9 Mainichi Marathon. The temperature was 83 degrees at the start, the way Bikila liked it. Bikila won in 2:22:58.8, three minutes ahead of the second-place finisher.

Bikila's next international race wasn't until July 12, 1966, at Zarauz, Spain, where he won a very tough race in 2:20:28.8, more than five minutes in front of the second-place finisher. On October 30 of that year he went to Seoul and ran a 2:17:04 to again win.

As 1968 approached, with the Olympic Games scheduled at Mexico City, which was both hot and at altitude, speculation abounded that Bikila would again best the best and take home the gold. When Bikila arrived in Mexico, however, he was suffering from a severe leg injury. Nevertheless, when the leaders went through the 5-kilometer point, Bikila was with them. But Bikila's leg could not take the stress and at 17 kilometers he limped off the course, suffering from a stress fracture.

Mamo Wolde won the race in 2:20:26.4; Ethiopia had swept Olympic gold in three consecutive Games.

The following year, Bikila's running career came to an end when he was involved in an automobile accident. His neck was broken and he was paralyzed from the neck down. Frequent visits to hospitals in England failed to rectify the problem, and he was confined to a wheelchair.

Bikila was revered within his country, despite the country's official policy of downplaying heroes and heroics in preference to national pride.

At the 1972 Olympics in Munich, Bikila was a guest of honor. As soon as Frank Shorter was presented with his gold medal for winning the marathon, he went directly to Bikila to shake his hand.

A year later, at the age of forty-one, Bikila, the most graceful marathoner the world had ever seen, the personification of all a marathoner can hope to be, suffered a stroke. He died on October 25, 1973, leaving a wife and four children—and an image of the perfect runner's infinite grace that will never be supplanted.

The Marathoner from Hell: Derek Clayton

Australian marathoner Derek Clayton had much in common with the work ethics of Clarence DeMar and Emil Zatopek when it came to his running: He trained long and he trained hard—to the point of incessantly flirting with injury. But while Clarence DeMar would take time out to help his Boy Scout troop and while Emil Zatopek was filled with high humor and a zest for life, Derek Clayton worked diligently on building the aura of a demonic presence—all the better to psych out his opposition.

During his career, Clayton went out of his way to intimidate other runners. If another runner came up to speak with him or shake his hand, he would apply a steely stare (augmented at one point by a very dark Fu Manchu mustache) and walk off. "I never socialized with a runner I was going to compete against," he said. "Sometimes I never shook hands with them before a race, even if they made the gesture. That's just how it was. I was there to race."

His presence was also heightened by his physical size; while most marathoners averaged five feet, eight inches and 130 pounds, Clayton was a giant: six feet two inches tall, weighing in at 160. He was big, he was strong, he was arrogant. "My attitude," he said in the early 1980s, "was that these other people were coming along to take away what was mine [the win], what I had worked for harder than they had. They were not people I wanted to encourage."

He also revealed in 1970 that he liked to have another runner next to him at 15 miles so that he could begin grinding him into the ground.

"I actually did say that," he admitted, the corners of his mouth going up in a cruel smile.

Clayton's well-orchestrated attitude of contempt for the opposition might very well earn him the distinction of being the most despised major figure in marathoning, the Black Bart, the Dirty Derek, as it were.

But whatever one thinks of his public personality, Clayton

rewrote the record books, and for a dozen years held the title of the world's fastest marathoner—a position that may have been established as much by the Stephen King–style horror story he repeatedly told of what it was like down there in the nether regions under 2:09 as by the accomplishment itself.

The place to start with Derek is at his finest moment: Antwerp, Belgium, May 30, 1969, 7:35 P.M. And this being Derek, the best way to experience his greatest moment is through his own words:

I was feeling absolutely great! I was feeling so good that, in discussions with the promoters, I said, "I'm going to go for a faster time, and I want to make sure the course is exactly the right length." I have always been very fussy about the lengths of courses, as marathon courses can quite often be short—and there is nothing worse than having run a marathon and finding out afterward that it was a half-mile short. It then becomes a nonevent. There is nothing worse for an athlete than a non-event, busting your guts and finding out the course is short—because then it is no marathon at all. It's just a waste of time. . . . I said, "I can't promise you a record, but I can promise you one thing. It's going to be fast. I want this course checked out."

It was a perfect night and the conditions were great. The race was to start at 7 P.M. It's no good trying to run a world record in the marathon in 70, 80, or 90 degrees—no one is going to handle 2:08 in those conditions. You've got to have a good field, because a high-class field pushes you. You've got to have a lot of enthusiasm there—everything has to be right for it.

And I felt this night that everything *was* right for me. I was running well, the people were there, the enthusiasm was fan-tastic, and the weather was absolutely right: cold and windless. I said to Jim Hogan, a well-known Irish runner of that time, driving over in the bus, "Jim, I think I'm going to crack 2:09." He didn't believe me. He said, "What do you think you can run?" I said, "I reckon I could run 2:07 or 2:08." He said, "I wish you luck."

It was one race I really went for. We ran through the first 10,000 meters in 30:06, which is a pretty fast pace. I didn't take out the pace. The guy who led the race was a Kenyan who was confident of doing pretty well. He led, and afterward I said, "Do you know what your best 10,000 meters was?" He said, "Well, that's it." I said, "Why did you want to run that fast?" And he said, "You've got to be in it to win it."

He wasn't in it long, I can tell you. He didn't finish. But I was happy because he got me motoring, and I think once you get moving like that, at that sort of pace, and you still feel good, you just keep going on. I had the proper splits, so I knew I was running fast. I knew I was on the world-record pace for sure. It was just a matter of how much. So when I crossed the line in 2:08:33, it wasn't a surprise; it was the result of a lot of hard work.

But the thing I remember most about the 2:08 was two hours later when the elation had worn off. I was urinating quite large clots of blood, and I was vomiting black mucus and had a lot of black diarrhea. What I don't think too many people can understand is what I went through for the next forty-eight hours. I have discussed this with the medical profession, asking them why this should be, and have never received a satisfactory answer. I only know one thing. After that 2:08, I was virtually finished. If anyone ever flattened themselves to run a race, I did on that particular day. I don't think anyone realized just what it took out of my body. When I look back on the week after that race, I wasn't the same person.

It took me a long, long time to recover—I would say up to six months. It worried me that I was urinating large clots of blood. It's quit normal for an athlete to pass a certain amount of blood in his urine, but that forty-eight hours was unbelievable.

It made me wonder if anyone would get close to this for quite a while. I knew I had a certain amount of natural ability for running marathons because it came pretty easy to me. I've run 2:09, I've run 2:11s, I've run 2:10s, but nothing, nothing has come anywhere close to what I went through to win with 2:08. In retrospect, it is no surprise to me that no one has knocked that time off, because training really hasn't advanced that much.

I think I was one of the ones who paved the way for

running 140, 150, 160 miles a week. I don't think anyone has changed that. The top guys still run around those distances, but they're not running any faster than I ran in training. So really, until a guy comes along who is pretty strong, or in fact much stronger, it won't happen.

Derek Clayton's oft-repeated story of what it took to run a marathon in under two hours and nine minutes—a marathon at a pace faster than five minutes per mile—and the whole persona he created for himself may have contributed more to creating the wall between 2:09 and 2:08 in the marathon than did the physiological limitations of the human body.

Clayton's larger-than-life presence and the rumors of his prodigious training regimen were incredibly intimidating. There were rumors, which he did nothing to dispel, of his having done several weeks of 200-plus miles; he admitted years later that he'd never done them, but that he wasn't going to deny them. He said, "My attitude was that if my competition thought I was doing 200 miles a week, they might think they'd have to do 200 miles a week, and 200 miles a week training will kill you, so they would be playing right into my hands."

When Clayton pushed down under 2:09 he was breaking his own world record—a 2:09:36.4 he'd set at the exclusive Fukuoka Marathon in Japan in December 1967. That performance had broken the previous record of Morio Shigematsu by nearly two and a half minutes, raising the cry of "Short course!" (a cry that also dogged Clayton's 2:08:33.6 at Antwerp). Clayton had insisted that both courses be remeasured; he also pointed out that no one was training with his intensity. (Comparison of the performances of other runners in the two races based upon their previous and subsequent times indicates that the courses were reasonably accurate measurements in what has been, at best, an imperfect sport of feet rather than inches. There is no reason to doubt the accuracy of these two world-best courses.)

Clayton's record fell in October 1981 when Alberto Salazar ran 2:08:13 in the New York City Marathon. Clayton remembered how impressed he was the first time he saw Salazar run. "That Salazar is the kind of runner who's built for the marathon," Clayton had said after watching him set a world's best 5-mile mark (22:04) in Los Altos, California, on January 4, 1981. Clayton credited Salazar's success to his efficient, low-to-the-ground shuffle and his ability to run as fast in the final 10 kilometers as he did in the first 10 kilometers of the marathon.

Clayton was born at Barrow-in-Furness in Britain on November 17, 1942. His family moved to Belfast when he was eight, and they lived there until 1963. In Ireland, Clayton picked up two passions: potatoes and competitive running. "When I trained hard I needed potatoes—I loved to eat potatoes. They're very high in carbohydrates, and I shoveled them in!" His inspiration for running came from watching Gordon Pirie and Herb Elliott on television.

When he and his family moved to Australia, Clayton wanted to be a miler. He worked at it tirelessly, a habit that would be his trademark and his nemesis. One year he ran interval workouts every day, attempting to force his body to develop speed it did not naturally possess. His best quarter mile was 52.8 seconds. It was obvious that no amount of training was going to make him a miler. Always a realist, Clayton moved up to 5,000 meters.

He didn't break three hours in his first marathon, which he claims he did as a lark. His time was 3:00:02.

Nearly three years later, Clayton was training 70 to 80 miles a week, hoping to qualify for the Commonwealth Games in either the mile or the 3-mile. He decided to enter the Victorian Marathon Club Championships, figuring to run it hard to see how far under three hours he could go. The date was October 2, 1965. Clayton not only won the marathon with a 2:22:12, but set an Australian record.

Overnight he gave up his plans to be number one at 5,000 meters. He had found something in which he was already number one.

The intensity of both his ambition and his training took a

profound toll on his body. Patterns in the recoveries from his injuries hinted at training methods he should have been employing in place of his death-march tactics. Both of his world-best marathon marks came in the wake of recovery periods from serious training injuries; had he possessed the insight to interpret the patterns of his success in the wake of forced rest, one wonders at what he could have accomplished. (Unfortunately, elite runners are often their own worst enemies when it comes to training.) His 1967 Fukuoka win came six months after having a ruptured Achilles tendon operated on, and his 1969 Antwerp performance came in the wake of a knee operation that forced him to lay off and get well. His 2:08:33.6 came a mere eleven days after an excellent 2:17:26 tune-up performance in Ankara, Turkey, where the conditions were stacked against him: heat, humidity, and altitude.

Following his 2:08:33.6, instead of returning to Australia to rest, he stayed in Europe to fulfill track commitments. The tour culminated in a marathon duel with British champ Ron Hill, which Clayton lost by two minutes, hauling himself through the final 3 miles on sheer willpower.

He never ran to his potential again.

"If I had it to do over, I would plan more carefully," he said. "I certainly wouldn't do what I did on that [European] tour. That was reckless, to say the least. Toward the end, I retired from racing, not because I was too tired, not because I was too old; I just felt I'd had enough."

While he had the world record in the marathon, what he wanted most of all was an Olympic gold medal. Unfortunately, most Olympic marathons are run in hot weather—conditions under which Clayton, like most large-frame runners, wilted. "I don't think a big person can handle running long distances in hot weather as well as someone more lightly built," he concluded. "I have a lot of energy that I have to expend. I don't run smoothly, and my style is rugged, toughish. Consequently, I generate a lot of body heat. When the sun is out, I generate even more heat. In hot weather, I can never expect to do better than a 2:17."

In the heat, humidity, and altitude of the Mexico Olympics in 1968, he ran 2:27 for seventh place. Munich in 1972 was hot and sticky. He ran 2:19:49 for thirteenth place.

Clayton worked at various jobs in Australia for seventeen years, most of them associated with civil engineering. He also dabbled in real estate, but he did not make a go of it. He and his wife emigrated to the United States in 1979, where Clayton took a job as assistant to the publisher at *Runner's World* magazine. When publisher Bob Anderson sold the magazine to Rodale Press in 1986, Clayton returned to Australia, where he is engaged in several businesses.

With his 2:08:33.6 now a distant memory, broken more than a dozen times since Alberto Salazar burst the psychological dam in 1981, Derek Clayton no longer wastes time justifying Fukuoka in 1967 and Antwerp in 1969 as accurate courses. He held the world's best marathon time on two occasions, covering fourteen consecutive years. What's left to prove?

Lady in Waiting: Grete Waitz

In the 1984 Los Angeles Olympic Games, American runner Joan Benoit won the first women's marathon event.

It is a sport axiom that no one ever remembers who came in second. That axiom couldn't be more wrong when applied to the first women's Olympic marathon.

The second-place finisher was Grete Waitz of Norway, the woman runner who, almost by accident, became the symbol of the push to expand the women's distance-running movement to the hallowed halls of Olympic competition. Grete Waitz became the symbol of that movement because she was at the right place at the right time—and because she was talented, gracious, and stalwart enough to bear up under the weight of the crown with an unpretentious style, an engaging grace, and an intelligence and maturity that might well have been lacking in any other candidate.

The modern history of women attempting to make their mark in the marathon event began at the Boston Marathon (which flatly excluded women) in 1966 and 1967. In 1966, Roberta Gibb hid in the bushes near the start and when the gun went off she jumped out and ran the race in 3:20. The following year Kathrine Switzer applied for a number as "K. V. Switzer," received the number, and dressed in a baggy gray sweatsuit in order to go unnoticed. During the race, it became apparent that there was a woman running with a number (a situation punishable by whatever dire consequences the race officials could conceive), the race policeman, Jock Semple, jumped off the press bus and attempted to physically remove Ms. Switzer from the course. He was butted onto the side of the road by a male friend accompanying Kathrine.

The long-suffering frown on women running in distance events was not Jock Semple's fault—he was merely enforcing the rules. (In later years, once the ban against women marathoners was lifted, Jock and Kathrine Switzer became close friends.) The obstacle to women moving up to longer distances can be traced to the disastrous introduction of women's track and field events into the 1928 Amsterdam Olympic Games. Several competitors in the 800 meters collapsed as a result of going out too fast and were given emergency aid on the track. Fearing the repercussions of a woman runner dying during the Olympic Games and building upon the myth of the "weaker sex," Olympic officials remained adamant against allowing longer events for women. There was even talk of removing the 800 meters from the Games; it was only through a good deal of back-room politics that the 800 was retained and the 1,500 meters eventually installed.

During the 1970s, things began to change. In October 1974, a West German doctor by the name of Ernst Van Aaken, a staunch supporter of women's running, sponsored the first Women's International Marathon Championship in Waldniel. Forty women from seven countries took part. The winning time was a respectable 2:50:31. This came on the heels of Boston accepting women in 1972 and women's national marathon championships in both the United States and West Germany. Two years later, Van Aaken again hosted an international championship in Waldniel. This time forty-five women from nine countries took part. And in 1977, the women's world-best time in the marathon was lowered twice. The record holder was West Germany's Christa Vahlensieck, with a 2:34:47.5.

Meanwhile, American men weren't the only ones embracing the running revolution. They were joined on the roads by literally thousands of women. In order to allow women to compete against each other instead of in the midst of men, several women-only road races were established in America by companies such as Avon and Bonne Bell.

Behind the scenes, a great deal of politicking (much of it done by American men who'd long championed women's rights), went on at the Olympic level toward adding either the 5,000 meters or the 10,000 meters for women to the 1984 Los Angeles Olympic Games. (The host city is allowed to add one event of its choice to the Games.) In order to persuade the often stodgy members of the International Olympic Committee that women should have their own distance events, they would have to be shown that women could safely run longer distances.

The New York City Marathon in October 1978 proved pivotal. The race that had moved out of Central Park and onto the streets of the five boroughs in 1976 was organized by Fred Lebow, a man who has been a staunch supporter of women's running. Among the 1,134 women entered in 1978 was Grete Waitz, a Norwegian schoolteacher who had been an Olympian at 1,500 meters; she had never done a run of more than 18 miles. In 2:32:30, Grete Waitz would do more to move women's running forward than a dozen years of politicking had done.

Grete Waitz's strategy for her first marathon was characteristic of the track runner she was: Go out cautiously, since it was a new event for her, and stick behind the best runner—in this case, world-record holder Christa Vahlensieck—with the hopes of outsprinting her at the end.

The huge crowds were somewhat confusing and Grete soon lost contact with the other women. She found herself out in the lead, running among men. As the miles rolled under her, Grete Waitz became tired and sore as she'd never been before. She worked her way through Central Park, concentrating on staying smooth and in control, pushing away the weariness and the pain. When she crossed the finish line adjacent to Tavern on the Green, her finishing time had destroyed the world record by two minutes and eighteen seconds.

The heroine presented to all the American marathon fans and runners who didn't even recognize her name remained something of an enigma for several years. Shy and soft-spoken, Grete Waitz contended that she was *not* a road runner; she was a track runner. She insisted that she had nothing significant to say about her victory. During the Christmas holidays following her 1978 New York City victory, she was invited to National Running Week in Los Altos, California, sponsored by *Runner's World* magazine. She ran in the New Year's Eve 5-Mile Invitational Race and set a world's best time of 25:28. Again, she insisted that she was not a road racer. She felt that road racing was not really a form of racing. Racing was something done on the track, on that mathematically perfect oval where one tests oneself against the clock, the distance, the other real runners. Grete, competing in a world far removed from road racing, considered her runs at New York and in Los Altos as larks. She not only downplayed them, she had very little to say about them.

All the attention was somewhat disconcerting to Grete, who traditionally goes to bed at 9 P.M. and avoids the bright lights and parties. She was gracious but reserved, wanting to please but wanting to make certain that people knew she was a track racer. Road races did not fall under the International Amateur Athletic Federation's rules, after all, and therefore didn't really count.

That's just the way Grete Waitz had been trained.

One of three children in a family loyal to the Norwegian ideal of sport, she began running at a very early age. Grete's father was a pharmacist and her mother worked in a grocery store. When she was eleven, a neighbor, Terje Pedersen, a former world-record holder in the javelin, lured her onto his track team. Within a year she was Norway's best junior track runner. She began as a sprinter but then moved up to the longer distances in order to take advantage of her tremendous endurance. Grete eventually found herself stalled at 1,500 meters, the longest distance women were allowed to run at the Olympic Games. She knew that she would be a superior 5,000- and 10,000-meter runner, but these events were not contested, and for the track runner, the Olympic gold medal is the ultimate goal.

In 1972, as a nineteen-year-old, Grete (then Grete Andersen) went to the Munich Olympics lightheartedly. Here were the world's most famous athletes, a cosmopolitan city to explore, the camaraderie of the Olympic Village, and all the food you cared to eat. She had trained faithfully and the excitement of the Games inspired her. In her 1,500-meter heat, she ran a 4:16, a personal best for her by a full second. She returned to Oslo 6 pounds heavier but with some happy memories.

In 1975, Grete graduated from college and went off to summer track season. At the Bislett Games in Oslo, she ran the 3,000 meters in 8:46.6, her first world record. A few days later she married Jack Weitz and soon thereafter began her teaching career.

She increased her training to get ready for the 1976 Montreal Olympics. She began doing two workouts a day, training much as her male counterparts did. She usually ran a morning wake-up run of 5 or 6 miles, then did a quality workout in the afternoon. In hopes of improving, however, Grete and Jack began to run the morning wake-up runs at a six-minute pace. Early in 1976, the Norwegian team traveled to Spain to train in an environment free of snow and ice. Grete increased her weekly mileage to 150. Her afternoon workouts were intense. She frequently ran forty repeat 200 meters with a mere ten-second rest between. She began to mentally defeat herself, the pain and discomfort of the intense training exhausting her.

In Montreal, Grete failed tactically. In her 1,500-meter semifinal, she allowed herself to get boxed in, and Jan Merrill of the United States scooted around her to run 4:02.62, an American record. Grete finished in sixth in 4:04.6, and was out of the running for the finals.

Fortunately, the 3,000 meters had been added to international competition for women. The 1976 experience taught Grete that she had the will but not the physical speed needed to compete at 1,500 meters; she moved up to the 3,000. In her first 3,000 at the World Cup Games in Düsseldorf in September of 1977, Grete dominated the event and won handily in 8:43.5. She began 1978 by winning the World Cross-Country Championships in Glasgow, Scotland, thirty seconds in front of Romania's Natalia Maracescu.

Grete looked forward to the European Championships in Prague, where she would run the 3,000. But she was outsprinted there by the Russian Svyetlana Ulmasova and by Maracescu. Knut Kvalheim, Norwegian record holder in the mile, had placed ninth in the 10,000 meters that same day after coming into the race having run the eighth-fastest time in history the day before (27:41.3). Knut and Jack and Grete walked through Prague that evening, consoling one another on their losses. Knut told the Waitzes about his experiences at the 1976 New York City Marathon, where he had dropped out at 10 miles after going out too fast. He said that if Grete were interested in running the race, he could probably get her an invitation from race director Fred Lebow. Grete showed more curiosity than outright interest.

Back home in Norway, while she concentrated on her track racing, Jack began to devour everything he could about marathoning, especially in American running magazines. "I told her that her training was as good or better than the other girls'," Jack remembered. "I was pretty sure she could beat them."

Grete began to look at the New York City Marathon as probably the only chance she and Jack would ever have to see the city of New York. She began to talk to friends at Finnair about the possibilities of her and Jack going. "I would not go alone, a single girl, to New York," she recalled.

Fred Lebow remembers a late night in 1978 at the New York City Road Runners Club, preparing for the marathon. An aide rattled off the day's rejections and acceptances. "I rejected the girl who wants expenses for her husband."

When Fred asked who that was, the aide searched her records. The applicant was a cross-country runner from Norway who had never even run a marathon by the name of Grete Waitz.

Fred Lebow's mind went into overdrive. He knew Grete's name and her performances for the year. The thing that impressed him was her cross-country win. After all, Bill Rodgers's American marathon record in 1975 had come on the heels of his third-place finish in the World Cross-Country Championships. Although track runners tended to blow a marathon by going out too fast, Lebow felt having Grete Waitz would be terrific, because it might push world-record holder Vahlensieck to a new record, which always looked good in a marathon's record books.

Lebow authorized the expenses for Grete and Jack, and the rest is history.

It is not difficult to appreciate Grete Waitz's astonishment at what happened to her life once she won the New York City Marathon. If it was frustrating for Grete to get across the message that she was not a road racer, it was more frustrating for the leaders of the women's running movement, who swarmed over her every time she returned to the United States. They hoped to find in her the symbol, the spokeswoman they needed to take a giant step toward their goal of getting the women's distance events into the Olympic Games. Grete Waitz did not see herself as a savior come to raise the women's running movement to its goal by virtue of her miraculous running ability. She was polite but adamant about her position.

Over the next two years Grete became a legend. She returned to the United States to race in Central Park in the L'eggs Mini-Marathon, defended her titles at the New York City Marathon and the *Runner's World* 5-Mile Invitational, and entered her first Falmouth Road Race in Massachusetts. The closest she came to defeat (or actually, the closest anyone came to staying with her) was at the 1980 Falmouth Road Race, a 7.1-mile course on Cape Cod. America's Jan Merrill came within forty-five seconds of Grete while Grete was breaking the course record by sixty-three seconds—it was during a week when she was suffering a very sore Achilles tendon. She also managed to win the World Cross-Country Championships three years in a row, 1978–80, always by thirty seconds or more.

Her 1979 New York City Marathon race (her forty-first race in nine months) was typically meticulous. She ran 2:27:33 to break her own world record by four minutes and fifty-seven seconds.

Meanwhile, the politicking at the Olympic level took some interesting turns. Instead of pushing for a women's 5,000-meter or 10,000-meter race at Los Angeles in 1984, the strategy changed to going for the marathon. The thinking was twofold: If the supporters of women's running could get the marathon on the schedule, there would be no argument against the shorter distance events; *and* the women's marathon would be easier to fit into the overall Olympic Games schedule than would be the heats, semifinals, and the final of a long track event.

As Grete Waitz's career moved from her new association with road racing in 1978 to the Olympic Games in L.A. in 1984, her discomfort with the media began to evaporate and she gradually began to accept that, indeed, she *was* a road racer—and the world's best, at that.

Her dedication to her training, her soft-spoken and low-key approach to life, and her acceptance of her growing role in women's running came together to make her the ideal standard-bearer. Her very presence as a symbol of what women could accomplish while remaining feminine and gracious earned wide support. Her second-place finish at Los Angeles was a disappointment to some of her supporters who felt she deserved to win the gold medal, but in typical fashion, she was the first to congratulate Joan Benoit for her courageous run for the glory on the heels of major leg surgery.

During recent years, Grete Waitz has continued to compete at a high level in spite of persistent injuries that have limited her racing. No other marathoner in the world has dominated a specific marathon the way she has New York: between 1978 and 1990, Grete Waitz won the race nine times.

18

Beyond 26.2 Miles

> For you, as for me, a mere 26.2-mile marathon may offer
> all the challenge and agony we need for the time being. But
> isn't it cheering to know there's more awaiting us if we
> should ever decide to find out what we're really made of?
>
> —JIM FIXX, *Jim Fixx's Second Book of Running*

Strictly speaking, the ultramarathon is any race beyond the
standard 26.2-mile marathon distance. To purists, however,
the ultramarathon distance begins at 50K, or 31 miles. (Where
that leaves distances between 26.2 and 31 miles, I'm not exactly certain. Based upon its degree of difficulty and the fact
that it is measured at 26.3 miles, I'd be inclined to place the
Pike's Peak Marathon into the ultramarathon category.)

The tradition of ultramarathoning, although practiced fit-
fully and not in very great numbers until recent years, enjoys
a longer history than marathoning. The Greek *hemerodromoi*
(or "all-day runners") were used as messengers long before
Pheidippides supposedly ran from the Plains of Marathon to
the city of Athens in 490 B.C. In fact, there is evidence that
Pheidippides can more legitimately be claimed by the ultramarathoners. The *hemerodromoi* who actually made that
relatively short historic jaunt was never named in contemporary accounts. It was historians writing more than five centu-
ries later and nineteenth-century poets who attributed the run
to Pheidippides. It *is* plain from the extant accounts of the
battle by the Greek historian Herodotus that Pheidippides is

the *hemerodromoi* who ran to Sparta and back (a distance of roughly 260 miles) in hopes of enlisting Spartan aid to go up against the Persians.

In other cultures, messengers have run extremely long distances under sometimes extreme conditions. In Africa, messengers ran enormous distances carrying messages in the split of sticks they held aloft; in Tibet, messages between remote monasteries were delivered by runners; and in northern Mexico, the Tarahumara Indians would think nothing of running 50 miles to visit a relative in a remote village, and then turn around to run 50 miles home. In its ability to travel great distances on foot, the human animal is not unrelated to the Monarch butterfly, which migrates thousands of miles in a year.

Because of the almost mind-boggling distances covered by ultramarathoners, the sport has until recently been considered more of a fad. And as such, it has gone through various incarnations and reincarnations, each time emerging, like a butterfly at the far end of metamorphosis, in a radically different form.

Modern ultramarathoning can be traced back to eighteenth-century England, when it was referred to as "pedestrianism," since, at the distances these athletes were going, walking became an integral part of their strategy. In 1788, Foster Powell covered 100 miles in twenty-two hours. In 1806, Captain Barclay lowered the 100-mile time to nineteen hours; still later, on a bet, Barclay covered 1,000 miles in a thousand hours!

By the turn of the twentieth century, a fanatical following accompanied pedestrian races in both England and America. The six-day race, the event of choice, drew thousands of spectators; tens of thousands of dollars changed hands in betting on the outcome, and the winning pedestrians earned what were at that time fabulous prizes.

For a time, six-day races were dominated by two Americans. Daniel O'Leary, who had emigrated from Ireland to the United States when he was twenty, made a name for himself by challenging America's pedestrian champion, Edward Weston. O'Leary beat Weston in a showdown in 1875, 503 to 451 miles.

O'Leary traveled to England in March 1878 and easily won the first Astley Belt Race. This race, held at the Agricultural Hall in Islington, London, became the Boston Marathon of the six-day craze. At that initial Astley, O'Leary turned in a 520-mile performance, while Weston came up with a flimsy medical excuse for not starting. During the race, it is estimated that Britons bet some $500,000 on the outcome.

A series of six-day races named in honor of O'Leary were begun at New York's Madison Square Garden in 1879. World records were frequently set there, culminating in the astonishing 623.75 miles G. Littlewood totaled up late in 1888.

The six-day races reached a peak in the 1880s but afterward they began to degenerate with overpromotion and inferior facilities.

Some feeble attempts to revive the six-day races in the 1920s failed to generate enthusiasm. Nevertheless, an American organizer put together an even more ambitious event in 1928.

At 3:30 P.M. on March 4, 1928, at Ascot Speedway in Los Angeles: a 3,400-mile stage race got under way. The event, which would cross the entire United States, drew 199 competitors and offered $25,000 to the winner. It was organized by C. C. "Cash and Carry" Pyle, a sports promoter who had moved football and tennis into the professional side of the sports pages and who had made Red Grange a household name. In fact, Grange himself set off the bomb that signaled the start of what came to be known as the Bunion Derby.

Pyle promoted and financed the race as he went, using every trick he could muster, from selling Maxwell House Coffee the right to caffeinate the runners from a mobile coffeepot said to be the world's largest to cajoling towns and cities to sponsor the race to come through their town, even if it meant detouring the runners from the original course. Although it sported an international field, the race was won by Andrew Hartley Payne, an Oklahoma Cherokee Indian. Because of Pyle's money problems, Payne did not receive his prize money until ninety days after the race was over, in front of perhaps the smallest crowd ever assembled at Madison Square Garden—some three hundred faithful.

Pyle would attempt to field another Bunion Derby the following year, but he was never again to match his transcontinental race of 1928.

By the 1970s, ultramarathoning was marginally alive in America, England, and South Africa. All three countries hosted several twenty-four-hour runs on tracks and a number of road races of 50K and above. Except for South Africa's 52-mile Comrades' Marathon and England's London-to-Brighton ultra, the fields rarely topped a dozen. Ultramarathoning was pretty much all one big family, as competitors traveled huge distances to race *with* more than *against* each other, and there was a steady stream of correspondence and training advice crossing the country between ultra practitioners.

The foremost proponents of the sport in America were Ted Corbitt, a physical therapist in New York City who is considered the godfather of modern ultrarunning; Tom Osler, a math professor at Glassboro State College in New Jersey who did pioneer work on what food fuels keep ultrarunners on the go best; Nick Marshall of Harrisburg, Pennsylvania, who won ultraevents, but even more important was obsessive about keeping and publishing statistics for the sport; and another Pennsylvanian, Park Barner, a tall, quiet, intensely competitive runner whose image of drab running clothes, anonymous black running shoes, eyes staring straight ahead, and frequently bloody nipples seeping scarlet through his T-shirt probably did much to frighten the tentative away from the sport and to draw the fanatical marathoner looking for the next challenge.

During the same period, an adventure-running movement on the West Coast was fermenting; it would ultimately blend with the East Coast track and road running ultras to further expand and add texture to the incredible variety offered by ultrarunning. Kenneth Crutchlow, a British expatriate, created athletic adventures that escalated in their brazenness and peculiarity. He challenged a steamship to a race from San Francisco to Alaska while he rode a bicycle (he beat the steamship). He also established a midsummer running course in Death Valley that ran from Shoshone in the South to Scotty's Castle in the North. Growing tired of that, Crutchlow ran an insane 150-mile course relay-style with Paxton Beale of San Francisco in the summer of 1973. They ran from Badwater in Death Valley (the lowest point in the Western Hemisphere and the hottest and driest place on earth) to the peak of Mount Whitney (at 14,494 feet, the highest point in the contiguous United States). Inspired by this deed, a health club manager from Walnut Creek, California, named Al Arnold began attempts to run it solo in 1974; he succeeded in 1977.

Farther north in the Sierra Nevada range, a 100-mile endurance horse race from Squaw Valley to Auburn, known as the Tevis Cup, had been held for years. In 1974, when his horse came up lame a few weeks before the race, Gordon Ainsleigh, who also dabbled in ultrarunning, decided to cover the trails and fire roads on foot, hoping to break twenty-four hours. He succeeded, and the Western States 100 was born. This race quickly caught the imagination of distance runners across the country, becoming America's premiere ultraevent.

As the running revolution took off, ultramarathon fields began to grow steadily if not spectacularly, as did the sport's variety of potential challenges. (This was the same era that spawned the Ironman Triathlon, the precursor of all triathlons.)

Ultramarathoning offered an alternative to mass marathons. The fields were small, the challenge was great, the variety was limited only by the imagination. In response to the tremendous growth in road racing in this country, many of the ultras moved in the opposite direction: to the tracks and more often to the trails.

The urge to escape to challenges beyond the standard

marathon has, relativly speaking, swelled the ranks of ul-tramarathoning. *UltraRunning* magazine, the sport's prime source of information, grew from 4,200 subscribers in January 1990 to 5,000 in 1991. Nearly 1,500 runners apply each year to enter the Western States 100; a lottery brings the starting field down to a more manageable 350.

The Challenges of Ultramarathoning

A careful examination of the starting field of an ultramara-thon elicits a universal observation: There's a lot of gray hair here.

Runners who participate in the ultraevents are typically older than those who participate in marathons (and mara-thoners are typically older than those who participate in 5K and 10K races). The longer the distance, the greater the need for pacing, and judicious pacing is not usually a characteristic of the younger runner.

Ultrarunning poses unique challenges to the marathoner beyond pacing. The ultrarunner must develop a tremendous capacity for endurance and an appreciation for the care and feeding of the body over tremendous distances; he or she must be able to push back or absorb discomforts experienced by few other athletes. The ultrarunner must also learn to become more self-sufficient. Whereas the marathoner enjoys aid every three miles or so and has a clear course to follow, the ultrarun-ner must learn to carry whatever he or she needs and to study maps and read trails. There may be 10 or 15 miles between aid stations and many races run through minimally marked forest or wooded areas.

The skills needed to complete an ultramarathon come with experience and with a resourcefulness that comes with age.

Certainly the greatest challenge that faces any ultrarunner is to face the course and to complete it. More than in the marathon, just finishing (and sometimes merely surviving) an ultrarun is considered a victory. This is especially true when you consider the fact that an ultra often runs up and down the sides of mountains. The challenge is complicated by the extreme length of time an ultra consumes; the longer the runner is out there, the greater the chance that, even if the race began under favorable conditions, the weather will take a turn for the worse—often just at the time the athlete is coming down to his or her last ounces of reserve energy.

The Western States 100, for example, begins at Squaw Valley, where the first 5 miles are uphill to Emigrant Pass (8,750 feet) and where runners occasionally find themselves chugging through snowfields. Later that day, as the course drops through the canyons of the California Street loop between 60 and 80 miles, runners contend with temperatures of more than 100 degrees. Even when the event is held on a track, similar problems can be encountered: a twenty-four-hour track run can experience pleasant 72-degree temperatures and warm skies at noon and quickly sink to chilly downpours barely above freezing during the middle of the night.

When the ultra moves into the realm of adventure runs, the challenges multiply even further, because the runner is forced to plan the run as though it's a well-orchestrated military operation, arranging for aid drops and support crews, anticipating clothing needs for different conditions, securing necessary permits for wilderness areas, and covering his or her own ass for the unexpected. Adventure runs include the 212-mile John Muir Trail along the ridge line of the Sierra Nevada (which seldom drops below 10,000 feet); running the length of the Appalachian Trail; running from the lowest to the highest points in the lower forty-eight states; and running across Canada. The challenges the runner will face must all be anticipated and prepared for—and then suffered stoically. Ultramarathoning is the epitome of a sport requiring persistence, good planning, and patience.

The Variety of Ultramarathoning

Ultramarathoning appeals to the runner who does not want to get caught in a rut. The variety the sport offers is immense;

for instance, the June 1991 issue of *UltraRunning* included reports on these races:

- Sri Chinmoy 100-Mile, Queens, New York; 1-mile loop, flat, paved, certified, with 50-mile and 100K splits.
- Strolling Jim 40, Wartrace, Tennessee, 41.2 miles; 75 percent paved, 25 percent gravel, hilly.
- American River 50, Sacramento, California; 50 miles; bike and horse trails.
- Cuyamaca 50K, Descanto, California; trails and dirt roads at an altitude of 3,400 to 6,400 feet.
- Old Pueblo 50 Mile, Tucson, Arizona; jeep roads, trails, and sand.
- Collegiate Peaks Runs, Buena Vista, Colorado; 25-mile loop; trails, jeep roads, cross-country.
- Zane Grey Highline Trail 50, Pine, Arizona; 29 miles on trails, 21 on roads.
- Massanutten Mountain Massacre IV, Fort Valley, Virginia; 50 miles; rocky, hilly trails.
- The Reservoir 50, Baltimore; rocky and hilly trails.
- Ruth Anderson 100K, San Francisco; 4.48-mile loop (with 50-mile splits).

The variety available in ultramarathoning is limited only by one's imagination: 50 kilometers on the roads, on a track, on trails; 50 miles on roads, track, trails, or a combination; 100-mile trail runs; 6-, 8-, 12-, 24-, 48-, 72-hour or six-day races on a track (sand, dirt, clay, all-weather tartan) or loop course of some type; or any middle distance that happens to strike your fancy or that characterizes the available course: a special birthday ultra of 57 miles or a 37-mile ultra because that just happens to be how long a trail or road is between two points.

Ultrarunning has something for everyone who wants to push beyond the marathon and who wants to occasionally—or permanently—get away from the maddening crowds.

The Future of Ultrarunning

The marathoner who wants to sample the varied world of ultrarunning needs only a subscription to *UltraRunning* magazine and the dedication to regularly set aside an entire day to training. Where marathon training monopolizes three hours on a Saturday afternoon, training for the ultradistances can take from dawn to dusk, although the novice does not necessarily need to become so obsessive in order to sample the ultradistances.

If you are trained to run a marathon, by combining slow running with occasional walking, you can comfortably step up to a 50-miler. The ultranovice would do best to begin with a relatively flat road or trail 50-miler that has a reputation for good aid services along the way. It also helps if the race has a relatively large starting field, so that you will be in the company of other runners during most of the race. Even more than in marathoning, it is important to make inquiries before entering to be certain an ultra is well organized. Some ultraraces are not well organized, and it doesn't seem to bother many of the entrants (who are often more interested in a beautiful and inspiring course than in the basic amenities, but who are experienced and self-sufficient enough that they can take care of themselves), although it's not something an ultranovice should want.

The ultramarathoning world is still relatively small and intimate, but its obvious get-away-from-it-all aspect in today's increasingly complex world will continue to draw many marathoners into its embrace. Fortunately, enough ultramarathons exist in enough out-of-the-way places that any interested runner is still able to find one that features small fields, intimate awards ceremonies, and a camaraderie that is eroding in the larger world of marathons.

If there is no ultra available at the time of year and at the distance you want, it is extremely easy to put one together and invite a few friends. Just send out announcements of the race, draw the course on a map, send out copies of the map, draw a chalk line on the ground, and at the appointed hour, count down to the start. That's essentially how simple road racing was in the 1960s, and it's not too far afield from how most ultramarathons are in the 1990s. If the dancer cannot be separated from the dance, or the runner from the run, the ultramarathoner cannot be separated from the landscape.

An Ultramarathoner's Creed

Tom Osler, one of the pioneers of American ultrarunning, developed the following philosophy back in the 1970s "based upon the faith that if I take good care of my body, it will reward me with robust health and respectable athletic performances."

1. My body is the source of my running joy. I will respect its needs and not subject it to foolish abuse.

2. Pain, discomfort, and fatigue are my body's signals that it is being overtaxed. When these arise, I will take appropriate action by slowing down, resting, or quitting as the degree of the symptoms indicates.

3. Running is to be enjoyed. I will endeavor to maintain a playful attitude toward competitive races, and not take victory or defeat seriously.

4. I am a trained athlete. I realize that my appearance in competition provides an example to others of what the healthy body can achieve. For the good of the sport as well as my own health, I will at all times endeavor to walk and run in good form. I will quit rather than give the public a degrading display of overfatigue.

5. Running myself to the point where I stagger or am totally drained is not heroic but a poor show of misused energy. I will retire from the race long before I reach such a state.

When faced with the prospect of annihilation during a race, retreat with valor and return another day. Running, especially running long, should ultimately be a reviving and enjoyable adjunct to our lives, not a substitution for a full life. Train with determination and a sense of joy! Smile tolerantly at unsuccessful quests and humbly accept the occasional success as a boon and a bonus—and not as an end in itself.

Run often, run long, but never outrun your joy of movement.

Appendixes

I: North American Marathons

There are well over two hundred marathons in North America each year. The following are arranged alphabetically by state; Canadian marathons are at the end of the state listings. There are only two states that do not currently offer at least one marathon: Delaware and Wyoming.

All known North American marathons were surveyed for this directory. Most responded. Information for each marathon is listed as follows:

Name of marathon
Mailing address
Phone number
Month in which marathon is typically held
Race director
Year marathon was begun
Certification
Type of course
Description of course
Sanctioned by
Number of entries in 1991
Number of volunteers at 1991

In instances where marathon directors did not respond with additional information, basic information, gathered from other sources, is given.

If you are interested in a specific marathon, send a legal-sized stamped, self-addressed envelope to the address listed in order to receive an entry form and other available information for the next edition of the race.

Alabama

Rocket City Marathon
Huntsville Track Club
8811 Edgehill Drive
Huntsville, AL 35802
205/881-9077
December
Harold and Louise Tinsley
1977
Certified
Out and back and loop: First
7 miles lead to 14-mile loop
before returning on original
miles to finish; relatively
flat, with a mere 21-foot
elevation change per mile;
course runs mostly on city
streets and tours the city of
Huntsville.
TAC, RRCA, and USRA
Masters Circuit sanctions
1,279 entries in '91
1,000 volunteers

Vulcan Marathon
Birmingham Track Club
P.O. Box 360044
Birmingham, AL 35236
205/995-5344
November

Alaska

Equinox Marathon
105 Patty Center
University of Alaska
Fairbanks, AK 99775
907/474-7205
September

*Mayor's Midnight Sun
Marathon*
Parks and Recreation
Department
Municipality of Anchorage
Box 196650
Anchorage, AK 99519
907/343-4474
June
John McCleary
1974
Certified
Point to point: Course is run
on a variety of trails and
surfaces through scenic
woodlands with mountain
vistas; runners have in the
past experienced a variety of
wildlife along the course:
moose, black bears,
porcupine, eagles; total
uphills is 500 feet, downhills
600 feet.
TAC sanction
193 entries in '91

Snowgoose Marathon
Anchorage Running Club
P.O. Box 211923
Anchorage, AK 99521
907/561-7652
August
Betty Bailey

Arkansas

Arkansas Marathon
Chamber of Commerce
2nd and Bennett
Booneville, AR 72927

501/675-2666
March

Hogeye Marathon
2139 Ora Drive
Fayetteville, AR 72701
501/442-4612
April
Andy Lucas
1976
Certified
Out and back: Begins in
    downtown and runs
    through University of
    Arkansas campus, out
    through the country, and
    back to downtown.
600 entries in '91
25 volunteers

Arizona

Arizona Marathon
2801 West Medlock Drive
Phoenix, AZ 85017
602/246-7697
January
Bob Porter

Lake Powell Marathon
P.O. Box 3148
Page, AZ 86040
602/645-5770
April
Dave Ruiz
1989
Certified
Point to point: Primarily flat,
    with some varied hills, 300
    feet elevation gain overall;

scenic: mountains, desert,
    sandstone cliffs.
TAC sanction
200 entries in '91
250 volunteers

Mule Mountain Marathon
P.O. Box 100
Fort Huachuca, AZ 85613
602/533-2541
April

Tucson Marathon
Southern Arizona Road
    Runners Club
4625 East Broadway, Suite 112
Tucson, AZ 85711
602/299-6731
January
Barbara Liquori

Whiskey Row Marathon
P.O. Box 3732
Prescott, AZ 86302
602/445-7221
May
Committee directs race
1979
Not certified
Out and back
RRCA sanction
111 entries in '91
120 volunteers

California

Aptos Marathon
Team Challenge
P.O. Box 20963
El Sobrante, CA 94803
510/841-1190

May
1991
Not certified
Course includes 1.2 miles on asphalt roads, 7 miles of very difficult but exciting trails, and 18 miles of tree-covered winding fire trails.
TAC sanction

Avenue of the Giants Marathon
Six Rivers Running Club
P.O. Box 214
Arcata, CA 95521
707/443-1226
May
Gaye Gilchrist
Certified
Two out and backs: Some gentle hills, runs on narrow paved roads through redwood groves and along Eel River.
TAC sanction
380 finishers in '91

Big Sur Marathon
Box 222620
Carmel, CA 93922
408/625-6226
April
William Burleigh
1986
Certified
Point to point: Spectacular, hilly, challenging, rural ocean views.
TAC sanction
2,445 entries in '91
1,200 volunteers

Burney Classic Marathon
P.O. Box 217, Department M
Burney, CA 96013
916/335-2825
September
Don Jacobs
1990
Certified
Point to point
TAC sanction
15 entries in '91
80 volunteers

California International Marathon
P.O. Box 161149
Sacramento, CA 95816
916/447-2786
December
Norman and Helen Klein

Catalina Marathon
California Athletic Productions
21 39th Place
Long Beach, CA 90803
213/433-4557
March
Not certified
Point to point: 95 percent paved, very hilly; mountains with seascape views.
450 entries in '91

Forest of Nisene Marks Marathon
Box 477
Santa Cruz, CA 95061
408/458-9984
June
Valerie Johnson
1991
Not certified

Loop with out and back:
Scenic, forest trails, hilly,
difficult.
No sanction
400 entries in '91

Humboldt Redwoods Marathon
351 Roundhouse Creek Road
Trinidad, CA 95570
707/442-6463
October
Karen Angel
Certified
Two out and backs: Paved,
shaded on Avenue of the
Giants; miles 1–13 flat and
fast; miles 13–20 gentle
uphill with 185-foot
elevation gain; miles 20–26
gentle downhill with
185-foot elevation loss.
TAC sanction
250 entries in '91
200 volunteers

*Jimmy Stewart Relay
Marathon*
St. John's Hospital and Health
Center
1328 22nd Street
Santa Monica, CA 90404
213/829-8968
March
Susan Wilson
1982
Certified
Loop: Flat, fast, around scenic
Griffith Park. This race is
run as a relay event with
five members to a team.
TAC sanction

780 teams in '91
400 volunteers

Long Beach Marathon
1825 Redondo Avenue
Long Beach, CA 90804
213/494-2664
February
Joe Carlson
1982
Certified
Combination of loops and out
and backs: Relatively flat;
very scenic: along Pacific
Ocean and adjacent
waterways.
TAC, AIMS, and ARRA
sanctions
3,421 entries in '91
2,400 volunteers

City of Los Angeles Marathon
11110 West Ohio Avenue,
Suite 100
Los Angeles, CA 90025
213/444-5544
March
Joe Blackstone
1986
Certified
Loop: Course begins in
Coliseum/Sports Arena area,
winds through a diverse
collection of areas, including
downtown L.A.,
Chinatown, and Hancock
Park; concludes in front of
Coliseum.
TAC sanction
18,380 entries in '91
17,149 volunteers

*Mammoth Mountain Trail
    Marathon*
Team Challenge
P.O. Box 20963
El Sobrante, CA 94803
510/841-1190
August
1991
Not certified
Out and back: Begins at
    Mammoth Mountain Inn
    (9,000 feet) and follows
    scenic fire roads through
    Inyo Craters and Lower
    Dead Man Pass to
    Crestview (7,500 feet), then
    returns.
No sanction

Modesto Marathon
Shadowchase Running Club
P.O. Box 3605
Modesto, CA 95352
209/578-4575
April
Joann Hull
1983
Certified
Multiple loop: Flat and fast
    along rural roads among
    orchards and farmland.
TAC sanction
200 entries in '91
100 volunteers

Napa Valley Marathon
1325 Imola Avenue
Napa, CA 94559
707/255-2609
March
Norman and Helen Klein

1978
Certified
Point to point: From Calistoga
    to Napa along the historic
    and scenic Silverado Trail
    (asphalt road), covers the
    length of Napa Valley,
    north to south; 348-foot
    elevation loss.
TAC sanction
1,761 entries in '91
700 volunteers

Orange County Marathon
567 San Nicholas, Suite 101
Newport Beach, CA 92660
714/640-2593
November
Michael Marckx
1991
Certified
Point to point: Flat, through
    six cities in Orange County,
    92-foot drop in elevation
    through suburban landscape,
    ending across from
    University of California
    Irvine campus; begins
    outside Anaheim Stadium.
TAC sanction

Palos Verdes Marathon
P.O. Box 153
Palos Verdes, CA 90274
213/377-3419
June
George Owens
1966
Certified
Point to point: Hilly.
TAC sanction

800 entries in '91
400 volunteers

Russian River Marathon
P.O. Box 204
Ukiah, CA 95482
707/462-1954
June
Dennis Huey
1978
Certified
Out and back: Paved road
through scenic wine country
terrain and country back
roads; flat to gently rolling;
less than 200-foot elevation
change.
TAC sanction
75 entries in '91
200 volunteers

Sacramento Marathon
P.O. Box 995
Dixon, CA 95620
916/678-5005
October
Ron Sturgeon

San Diego Marathon
In Motion
7847 Convoy Court, Suite 105
San Diego, CA 92111
619/268-5882
January
Lynn Flanagan

*City of San Francisco
   Marathon*
650 5th Street, Suite 514
San Francisco, CA 94107
415/896-0587
August

John Mansoot
1989
Certified
Point to point: 100 percent
paved, primarily flat but
some rolling with
outrageous views of the city.
TAC sanction
3,500 entries in '91

*Santa Monica Sports/Art
   Festival Marathon*
Recreation Division
Cultural and Recreation
Services
2600 Ocean Park Boulevard
Santa Monica, CA 90405
213/458-8315
August
Clayton Iske
1972
Certified
Multiple loop: Flat, runs past
ocean.
TAC sanction
2,290 entries in '91
200 volunteers

Sri Chinmoy Marathon
1995 20th Avenue
San Francisco, CA 94116
415/753-5998
September
Amaless Krien
1984
Not certified
Loop: Absolutely flat 1-mile
loop on asphalt.
TAC sanction
32 entries in '91
12 volunteers

Summit Marathon
California Runners Factory
51 University Avenue
Los Gatos, CA 95030
408/395-4311
November

Valley of the Flowers Marathon
P.O. Box 964
Lompoc, CA 93436
805/736-4567
June
Jim Small
1979
Certified
Loop: 99 percent paved,
   mostly flat, runs through
   farmlands.
TAC sanction
950 finishers in '91

Western Hemisphere Marathon
4117 Overland Avenue
Culver City, CA 90230
213/202-5689
December
Jack Nakanishi
1948
Not certified
Out and back: Flat.
TAC sanction
501 entries in '91
300 volunteers

Wild Wild West Marathon
Chamber of Commerce
P.O. Box 749
Lone Pine, CA 93545
619/876-4444
May
Mary Sinclair

1978
Not certified
Loop: Through the desert and
   the Alabama Hills
   (backdrop for numerous
   films and television shows)
   at the base of Mount
   Whitney; course runs from
   high desert (4,000 feet) to
   6,200 feet.
No sanction
95 entries in '91
35 volunteers

Note: David Horning of
   Enviro-Sports (P.O. Box
   1040, Stinson Beach, CA
   94970; 415/868-1829) puts on
   a series of more than a
   dozen "marathons" each
   year. Although held in
   extremely scenic areas, the
   courses are not certified, aid
   is limited, and runners who
   enter these races should be
   self-sufficient. A postcard
   sent to Dave will get you
   on his mailing list.

Colorado

Arbor Day Aurora Marathon
City of Aurora Forestry
   Division
1470 South Havana Street,
   Suite 520
Aurora, CO 80012
303/695-7143
April
1986

Certified
Out and back: 100 percent
    paved, rolling, suburban.
210 entries in '91

Collegiate Peaks Marathon
Box 3134
Buena Vista, CO 81211
719/395-2656
April
1991
Not certified at this time
Loop: Runs from the
    Community Center to
    Davis Face (8,000 feet to
    9,400 feet), then down to
    Lenharty (8,500 feet), then
    up Lenharty Cutoff (9,400
    feet) and back to town;
    tough but beautiful course.
    A 50-miler is also offered.
108 entries in '91
20 volunteers

Denver Marathon
BKB Limited
8400 East Prentice Avenue,
    Suite 202
Englewood, CO 80111
303/741-3587
September

Pueblo River Trail Marathon
YMCA
700 North Albany Street
Pueblo, CO 81003
719/543-5151
October
Ben Valdez
1984
Certified

Point to point: First 12 miles
    are on paved roads, slightly
    rolling but basically
    downhill; runners then join
    trail along Lake Pueblo and
    the Arkansas River; path
    takes runners through
    rolling hills and a beautiful
    wildlife area along river to
    downtown Pueblo.
TAC sanction
560 entries in '91
125 volunteers

Pikes Peak Marathon
P.O. Box 38235
Colorado Springs, CO 80937
719/473-2625
August
Carl McDaniel and Nancy
    Hobbs
1956
Not certified
Out and back: Starts at 6,200
    feet and ascends on narrow
    rocky footpath to summit
    of Pikes Peak (14,110 feet)
    and returns along same trail;
    first 1.6 miles and last mile
    on paved road.
No sanction
708 entries in '91
500 volunteers

Steamboat Marathon
Steamboat Springs Chamber
    Resort
P.O. Box 774408
Steamboat Springs, CO 80477
303/879-0882
June

Lane Schrock
1982
Certified
Point to point: Course begins at Hans Peak (8,100 feet) and ends at 6,700 feet; includes winding hills and valleys and is a scenic course along lakes, mountains, rivers, and ranches.
TAC sanction
315 entries in '91
200 volunteers

Connecticut

East Lyme Marathon
Box 186
East Lyme, CT 06333
203/739-2864
September
Way Hedding

Nipmuck Trail Marathon
234 Singleton Road
Chaplin, CT 06235
203/455-1096
June
David Raczkowski
1983
Not certified
Multiple loop: Trails, a mile of roads, no extreme hills.
TAC sanction
110 entries in '91
14 volunteers

District of Columbia

Marine Corps Marathon
P.O. Box 188

Quantico, VA 22134
703/640-2225
November
Captain Salgado
1976
Certified
Loop: Relatively flat, winds through Arlington, Georgetown, and District of Columbia, passing such attractions as the Capitol, White House, Jefferson and Lincoln memorials; course nickname is the Marathon of the Monuments.
TAC sanction
13,000 entries in '91
35,000 volunteers

Florida

Blue Angel Marathon
Naval Air Station
MWR, Building 632, Radford Boulevard
Pensacola, FL 32508
904/452-3922
February
Judith Bagshaw

Brandon Marathon
Brandon Running Association
P.O. Box 1564
Brandon, FL 33509
813/681-4279
December
Bill McKnight
1980
Certified
Out and back: Runs on the toll road that joins the city

of Tampa and Brandon
suburb; marathon relay race
follows the same course.
262 entries in '91
120 volunteers

Jacksonville Marathon
3853 Baymeadows Road
Jacksonville, FL 32217
904/739-1917
January
Doug Alred
1983
Certified
Out and back with loop: 100
    percent paved, flat,
    suburban and semirural.
518 entries in '91

Miami Marathon
Miami Runners Club
7920 Southwest 40th Street
Miami, FL 33155
800/940-4RUN or 305/227-1500
January
Michael Peyton
1989
Certified
Out and back: Flat and fast.
TAC sanction
2,000 entries in '91
200 volunteers

Pinellas Trail Marathon
Sunshine Running Team
P.O. Box 7104
Clearwater, FL 34618
813/536-8585
February

Space Coast Marathon
Space Coast Runners
P.O. Box 2407

Melbourne, FL 32902
407/724-2923
February
Harold Tucker

Tallahassee Marathon
324 Lipona Road, #6
Tallahassee, FL 32304
904/574-1458
February
Michael Fox

Georgia

Atlanta Marathon
Atlanta Track Club
3097 East Shadowlawn
    Avenue, Northeast
Atlanta, GA 30305
404/231-9064
November

Hawaii

Honolulu Marathon
Honolulu Marathon Assn.
3435 Waialae Avenue, #208
Honolulu, HI 96816
808/734-7200 Fax: 808/732-7057
December
1973
Certified
Out and back: Scenic course
    that includes spectacular
    ocean views alongside
    world-famous Waikiki Beach
    and Diamond Head and
    Koko Head craters; level
    terrain except short uphill
    grades along Diamond

Head; 17 aid stations
offering water, cold sponges.
TAC sanction
14,605 entries in '91
2,000 volunteers

Kilauea Volcano Marathon
P.O. Box 106
Hawaii National Park, HI
  96718
808/967-8222
July
Susan McGovern
1983
Certified
Loop: Known as the "world's
  toughest measured
  marathon," this race is held
  over extremely rough and
  uneven terrain, major lava
  fields in the Ka'u Desert,
  and is a challenge to the
  most advanced and hardy
  runners.
TAC sanction
104 entries in '91
200 volunteers

Maui Marathon
Valley Isle Road Runners
P.O. Box 330099
Kahului, HI 96732
808/871-6441
March
1970
Not certified
Point to point: First 15 miles
  are beautifully scenic with
  slight hills; the remainder of
  the race can get hot and
  there is a 1,000-foot hill at

mile 24; the finish is in a
beautiful resort area.
120 finishers in '91
200 volunteers

Idaho

Coeur D'Alene Marathon
P.O. Box 2393
Coeur d'Alene, ID 83814
208/765-6019
May
Mark Cataldo
1978
Certified
Loop: Runs through city and
  rural subdivisions; very
  scenic; 99 percent paved; flat
  with one hill at 9 miles.
TAC and RRCA sanctions
523 entries in '91
215 volunteers

Great Potato Marathon
YMCA
1050 West State Street
Boise, ID 83702
208/344-5501
May
Tim Sevena
1978
Certified
Point to point: Very fast with
  two small uphills; starts
  outside of town and finishes
  at the BSU Stadium in
  Boise.
TAC sanction
100 entries in '91
150 volunteers

*Salmon River Summer
Marathon*
Chamber of Commerce
200 Main Street
Salmon, ID 83467
208/756-2100
July
Dick and Pat Hauff
1980
Certified
Point to point: Course follows
the Salmon River
downstream through
breathtaking mountains and
valley scenery, ends at the
junior high school track.
TAC sanction
81 entries in '91
46 volunteers

Illinois

Chicago Marathon
214 West Erie
Chicago, IL 60610
312/951-0660
October
Carey Pinkowski
1977
Certified
Loop: Flat, fast course winds
through the city of Chicago,
beginning at the Daley
Plaza and finishing at Grant
Park.
TAC sanction
8,007 entries in '91
2,445 volunteers

Lake County Moore Marathon
P.O. Box 349
Deerfield, IL 60015
708/317-1060
April
Gretchen Bercaw
1980
Certified
Point to point: Begins in town
of Zion (30 miles north of
Chicago) and follows Lake
Michigan south through
two military facilities and
the north suburbs of
Chicago.
650 entries in '91
1,200 volunteers

Indiana

Anderson-Muncie Marathon
Anderson Roadrunners
P.O. Box 282
Anderson, IN 46015
317/644-7796
October

Sunburst Marathon
225 West Colfax Avenue
South Bend, IN 46601
219/233-6161
June
Joyce Fox

Iowa

Drake Relays Marathon
1631 38th Street
Des Moines, IA 50310
515/274-5379

April
Cal Murdock
1969
Certified
Multiple loop: Starts at
    stadium, runs two-plus
    loops, then heads to
    downtown finish.
TAC and RRCA sanctions
356 finishers in '91
300 volunteers

*University of Okoboji
    Marathon*
Box 3077
Spencer, IA 51301
712/338-2424
July
Herman Richter
1978
Not certified
Loop: Circles Lake West
    Okoboji; gentle terrain.
60 entries in '91
33 volunteers

Kansas

Wichita Marathon
121 North River Boulevard
Wichita, KS 67203
316/267-6812
October
Clark Ensz
1980
Certified
Out and back: Very flat, all on
    paved path along river.
RRCA sanction
148 entries in '91
45 volunteers

Kentucky

Louisville Marathon
Box 36452
Louisville, KY 40233
502/456-8160
October
Gil Clark

Louisiana

Louisiana Marathon
550 McCormick Street
Shreveport, LA 71104
318/868-2449
February
Lamar Fleming

*Marathon Festival of Louisiana
    Marathon*
P.O. Box 16955
Baton Rouge, LA 70893
504/344-7223
February
Len Bahr

Mardi Gras Marathon
NOTC
P.O. Box 52003
New Orleans, LA 70152
504/482-6682
January
Chuck George

Maine

*Bud Light Marathon at
    Sugarloaf*
Sugarloaf USA
Minister Hill
Kingfield, ME 04947

207/237-2000
May
Chip Carey
1984
Certified
Point to point: Paved, very
rural, mountain peaks, loses
610 feet of altitude overall.
TAC sanction
253 entries in '91
75 volunteers

Maryland

Last Train to Boston Marathon
8 Class Court
Baltimore, MD 21234
410/661-6099
March
Brad Roberts
1977 (no race held in 1985)
Certified
Multiple loop: 4-loop course,
relatively flat; held on the
roads of the Edgewood,
Aberdeen Proving Grounds,
an army base.
TAC and RRCA sanctions
185 entries in '91
21 volunteers

*Washington's Birthday
Marathon*
4204 Breezewood Lane
Annandale, VA 22003
703/256-2327
February
Bill Brogan
1960
Certified

Out and back and multiple
loop: Gently rolling, quiet
countryside, mostly on
grounds of the U.S.
Department of Agriculture,
Beltsville, Md., facility; 100
percent paved roads.
TAC & RRCA sanctions
181 entries in '91
45 volunteers

Massachusetts

Boston Marathon
Boston Athletic Association
P.O. Box 1992
Hopkinton, MA 01748
508/435-6905
April
Guy Morse
1897
Certified
Point to point: The
granddaddy of them all
begins at the green in
Hopkinton and makes its
way over varied terrain to
downtown Boston; first 5
miles downhill, famous
series of hills at 18 miles
topped by Heartbreak Hill,
then downhill to finish;
loses 480 feet overall.
Entrant must qualify based
on age and sex.
TAC sanction
8,686 entries in '91

Cape Cod Marathon
P.O. Box 699

West Falmouth, MA 02574
508/548-0348
October
Courtney Bird

Hyannis Marathon
P.O. Box 1678
Hyannis, MA 02601
508/778-6965
March
Jack Glennon
1984
Certified
Multiple loop: Seaside terrain, mainly flat, with rolling terrain between 10 and 11.5 miles, and 23 and 24.5.
TAC sanction
623 entries in '91
220 volunteers

Lifetime Marathon
250 Dracut Street
Dracut, MA 01826
508/957-3178
October
John Meehan

Race of Champions Marathon
Greater Springfield Harriers
206 West Weymouth Street
Springfield, MA 01108
413/736-9905
May

Michigan

Bayshore Marathon
1019 Pine Street
Traverse City, MI 49684
616/941-5743
May

Deb Seyler
1982
Certified
Out and back: Paved, flat, along the bay.
700 entries in '91

Detroit Free Press/Mazda International Marathon
321 West Lafayette
Detroit, MI 48236
313/222-6676
October
Barbara Bennage
1978
Certified
Point to point: Begins in Windsor, Ontario, Canada, and runs through the Detroit-Windsor Tunnel, finishing in Detroit; the tunnel constitutes the only underwater mile in road racing.
TAC sanction
2,500 entries in '91
2,000 volunteers

Michigan Trail Marathon
43259 Crescent Boulevard
Novi, MI 48375
313/347-4949
April
Jeff Gaft
Not certified
Multiple loops: Two loops, 100 percent paved, very hilly.
400 entries in '91

Northern Shufflers Marathon
234 Rossway Road
Pleasant Valley, MI 12569

914/635-2936
September
Bill Szed

Scotty Hanton Marathon
P.O. Box 611628
Port Huron, MI 48061
313/985-9623
September
Toni Tricomo

Minnesota

Beargrease Snowshoe Marathon
4713 Mungershaw Road
Saginaw, MN 55779
218/729-5247
January
Barb Van Skike

Grandma's Marathon
P.O. Box 16234
Duluth, MN 55816-0234
218/727-0947
June
Scott Keenan
1977
Certified
Point to point: Run on scenic
   Old Highway 61 along
   shores of Lake Superior,
   beginning just outside Two
   Harbors, Minn., and
   finishing in Duluth's Canal
   Park.
TAC sanction
5,300 entries in '91
3,300 volunteers

Twin Cities Marathon
708 North First Street, Suite
   238

Minneapolis, MN 55401
612/673-0778
October
Patricia Goodwin
1982
Certified
Point to point: Begins at
   Hubert H. Humphrey
   Metrodome in downtown,
   follows lakes and parkways
   to Mississippi River, finishes
   at state capitol near
   downtown St. Paul.
TAC sanction
6,500 entries in '91
3,000 volunteers

Walker North Country
   Marathon
Leech Lake Area Chamber of
   Commerce
P.O. Box 1089
Walker, MN 56484
800/833-1118
September

Mississippi

Mississippi Marathon
Mississippi Track Club
P.O. Box 866
Clinton, MS 39056
601/856-9884
December
Bob Coleman
1975
Certified
Out and back: Runs along
   Natchez Trace and back.
TAC and RRCA sanctions
107 entries in '91
41 volunteers

*Mississippi Beach Rotary
   Marathon*
P.O. Box 3504
Gulfport, MS 39505
601/832-6071
November
Lindo Sullivan
1990
Certified
Point to point.
TAC and RRCA sanctions
798 entries in '91

Tupelo Marathon
1007 Chester Avenue
Tupelo, MS 38801
601/842-2039
September
Johnny Dye

Missouri

Heart of America Marathon
Columbia Track Club
2980 Maple Bluff Drive
Columbia, MO 65203
314/445-2684
September
Joe Duncan
1960
Certified
Loop: Extremely hilly, on
   asphalt roads except for 4
   miles on gravel (miles 8–12).
70 entries in '91
30 volunteers

Kansas City Marathon
Humana-Prime Health
5001 State Line
Kansas City, MO 64112
816/531-2387

October
Betsy Titterington
1984
Certified
Out and back and loop
   combination.
TAC and RRCA sanctions
470 entries in '91
600 volunteers

Olympiad Memorial Marathon
Marathon Sports
13453 Chesterfield Plaza
Chesterfield, MO 63017
314/434-9577
February
Jerry Kokesh
1973
Certified
Keyhole: Rolling in the first 7
   miles, four major hills from
   mile 8 to mile 13, downhill
   or flat to 17 miles, rolling
   to 20, with the last 10K
   primarily flat to downhill.
   Part of course is the same
   as the 1904 Olympic
   Marathon course.
TAC and RRCA sanctions
180 entries in '91
125 volunteers

St. Louis Marathon
St. Louis Track Club
2385 Hampton Avenue, Suite
   101
St. Louis, MO 63139
314/781-3726
November
Tom Eckelman
1973
Certified

Out and back: Rolling to flat
on downtown city streets;
hills going west to Forest
Park and returning
downtown.
TAC and RRCA sanctions
1,172 entries in '91
800 volunteers

Montana

Ghost Town Marathon
Governor's Cup Festival
P.O. Box 451
Helena, MT 59624
406/444-8983
June
Hal Rawson
1973
Certified
Point to point: Starts in the
mountains at Ghost Town,
runs through rural hills
toward the city of Helena,
finishing downtown.
TAC sanction
150 entries in '91
350 volunteers

Mountain Goat Marathon
165 Mountain Goat Road
Hamilton, MT 59840
406/363-1262
July
Mario Locatelli

Nebraska

Lincoln Marathon
5309 South 62nd Street
Lincoln, NE 68516

402/423-4519
May
Nancy Sutton

Omaha Marathon
5822 Ohio Street
Omaha, NE 68104
402/553-8349
November
Gary Meyer

Nevada

Las Vegas Marathon
P.O. Box 81262
Las Vegas, NV 89180
702/876-3870
February
Al Boka
1967
Certified
Point to point: Desert,
blacktop, 900-foot elevation
loss.
TAC and AIMS sanctions
2,305 entries in '91
250 volunteers

Silver State Marathon
P.O. Box 21171
Reno, NV 89515
702/825-3006
August
Bob MacMahan

New Hampshire

Clarence DeMar Marathon
188 Pearl Street
Keene, NH 03431
603/357-1215

September
Richard Lecuyer

New Jersey

Atlantic City Marathon
Boardwalk Runners
P.O. Box 2181
Ventnor, NJ 08406
609/822-6911
November
Barbara Altman

New Mexico

Alamogordo Marathon
503 Sunshine
Alamogordo, NM 88310
505/434-5605
December
Clint Burleson and Carol Ann
  Marvsiak
1991
Certified
Point to point: First 9 miles in
  the exotic and bizarre sand
  dunes of White Sands
  National Monument; course
  then follows highway along
  base of Sacramento
  Mountains, and from there
  to the city of Alamogordo,
  past the zoo, finishing in
  the park; flat, fast.
TAC sanction
385 entries in '91
200 volunteers

Duke City Marathon
P.O. Box 14903
Albuquerque, NM 87191

505/888-2448
September

Shiprock Marathon
3005 Northridge Drive,
  Suite K
Farmington, NM 87401
505/326-2273
May
Mark Irwin and Keith
  Peterson
1982
Certified
Point to point: Course features
  rolling hills, begins at
  approximately 6,000 feet and
  has elevation drop of 1,000
  feet, with the last six miles
  downhill; course is scenic,
  run on the Navajo
  Reservation in the high
  plateau country of
  northwest New Mexico.
103 entries in '91
38 volunteers

Turtle Marathon
3100 Main Street
Roswell, NM 88201
505/622-8973
September
Doris Callaway
1988
Not certified
Out and back: Rolling hills,
  3,600-foot elevation change,
  open spaces, clean air, 60–70
  degrees. "We list results in
  reverse turtle order."
No sanction

26 entries in '91
5 volunteers

New York

Buffalo Marathon
1776 Statler Towers
Buffalo, NY 14202
716/882-3365
May
Tom Palmer

Dutchess County Classic Marathon
234 Rossway Road
Pleasant Valley, NY 12569
914/635-2936
September
Charles Sprauer
1979
Certified
Loop: Two circuits of loop; mostly flat, hills are rolling.
TAC sanction
117 entries in '91
125 volunteers

Finger Lakes Marathon
301 The Clinton House
Ithaca, NY 14850
607/272-3442
October
Henry Theisen
1969
Certified
Point to point
TAC and RRCA sanction
43 entries in '91
25 volunteers

Hilton Marathon
74 Dunsmere Drive
Rochester, NY 14615
716/865-8723
October
Walt Check
1990 (for previous eighteen years held in Rochester)
Certified
Multiple loop: Essentially flat with a few mild hills.
TAC sanction
205 entries in '91
175 volunteers

Hudson Mohawk Marathon
547 Watervliet-Shaker Road
Latham, NY 12110-4620
518/783-1729
February
Carl Poole
1974
Certified
Multiple loop: Mostly flat; start and finish near Phys Ed building of State University of New York, Albany; four 6.3-mile loops.
TAC sanction
82 entries in '91
19 volunteers

Long Island Marathon
Sports Unit
Eisenhower Park
East Meadow, NY 11554
516/542-4439
May
Parri Kemler

*Mohawk-Hudson River
    Marathon*
63 Meadowbrook Road
Watervliet, NY 12189
518/235-8864
October
Ed Mulheren
1983
Point to point: 16 miles of
    asphalt bike paths along
    Mohawk and Hudson rivers,
    10 miles of city streets;
    overall elevation loss of 370
    feet; one moderate hill at
    12.5.
TAC and RRCA sanctions
374 entries in '91
200 volunteers

Monster Marathon
1189 Dryden Road
Ithaca, NY 14850
607/272-8957
Joe Dabes
1990
Not certified
Out and back: Double out and
    back; toughest trail
    marathon in the East, with
    5,560 feet of climb; the race
    also features an age/sex
    handicapped start (per
    National Masters' News
    age-graded table). Not for
    the faint of heart.
RRCA sanction
70 entries in '91
10 volunteers

New York City Marathon
New York Road Runners
    Club

9 East 89th Street
New York, NY 10128
212/860-4455
November
Fred Lebow
1970
Certified
Point to point: Starts at
    Verrazano-Narrows Bridge
    on Staten Island, then runs
    through Brooklyn, Queens,
    Manhattan, the Bronx, and
    finishes back in Manhattan
    in Central Park; largest hill
    is center of Verrazano
    Bridge. The world's largest
    marathon.
TAC sanction
26,900 entries in '91
9,000 volunteers

Super Bowl Marathon
48 Halgren Crescent
Haverstraw, NY 10927
914/429-1579
January
Brian Adler
1987
Certified
Out and back: Totally flat; 1
    mile out and 1 mile back,
    repeated 13 times plus
    additional 385 yards at end.
TAC and RRCA sanctions
180 entries in '91
50 volunteers

Taylor Wineglass Marathon
P.O. Box 98
Corning, NY 14830
607/936-9971

October
Allen Togut

*Under the Lights for Charity
  Marathon*
615 Pinegrove Avenue
Irondequoit, NY 14617
716/342-1533
May
Don McNelly
Race is part of a 24-hour
  event.

Virgil Trail Monster
3 Eagles Head Road
Ithaca, NY 14850
315/443-3444
September
Dan Mittler

Yonkers Marathon
Yonkers Parks and Recreation
  Department
285 Nepperham Avenue
Yonkers, NY 10701
914/964-3501
April
1935 (Can actually trace its
  origin back to Thanksgiving
  Day 1907 but the marathon
  died after the 1914 running,
  to be revived in 1935.
  Incredibly, in 1909 the
  marathon race was so
  popular that Yonkers was
  forced to stage two
  marathons.)
Certified
Loop: Most of the course is
  run on Saw Mill River
  Road (Route 9A) and
  Broadway (Route 9); the last

5 miles are tough (i.e.,
  uphill).
TAC sanction

North Carolina

Charlotte Observer Marathon
Observer Promotion
P.O. Box 32188
Charlotte, NC 28232
704/358-5425
January
Don King
1977
Certified
Loop: Tough, with generous
  hills; long, gradual uphill
  between 24.5 and 25.5.
  "Personal records are rare."
TAC sanction
1,163 entries in '91
900 volunteers

Fireworks Marathon
Recreation Department
Box 67, 1 North Lake Drive
Lake Junaluska, NC 28754
704/452-2881
July
Rev. Millsaps Dye
1991
Not certified
Multiple loop: 11 loops on
  2.388-mile course plus
  portion to fill out 26.2 mile;
  drinking fountains and
  facilities every loop; loops
  around small, beautiful lake;
  one small hill, otherwise
  flat; minimum traffic.
USMMA sanction

40 entries in '91
25 volunteers

*Grandfather Mountain
Marathon*
Route 2, Box 590
Boone, NC 28607
704/264-7528
July
Al Fereshetian
1967
Not certified
Point to point: Very hilly, very
    scenic; starts at 3,333 feet
    and finishes at 4,279 feet;
    race finish is at Scottish
    Highland Games, with
    crowd of 20,000.
No sanction
300 entries in '91
60 volunteers

Greensboro Marathon
Greensboro Running Club
P.O. Box 178
Greensboro, NC 27402
919/282-2074
November
John Dyson

North Dakota

Bismark Marathon
YMCA
P.O. Box 549
Bismarck, ND 58502
701/255-1525
September
Bill Bauman
1981
Certified

Out and back: Flat and
    fast—and scenic, run on the
    Missouri River bottoms.
TAC sanction
150 entries in '91
30 volunteers

Ohio

Athens Marathon
P.O. Box 2282
Athens, OH 45701
614/593-6120
April
Mark Graham

Blue Ash Marathon
10119 Crosier Lane
Cincinnati, OH 45242
513/793-0508
April
Greg McCormick

Cincinnati Holiday Marathon
7581 Glenhurst Drive
Dayton, OH 45414
513/898-7015
November
Denny Fryman

Cleveland Marathon
1925 Enterprise Parkway
Twinsburg, OH 44087
216/425-9811
May
Chris Tatreau

Columbus Marathon
P.O. Box 26806
Columbus, OH 43226
614/433-0395
October

Doug Thurston
1980
Certified
Loop: Mostly flat, scenic
  through Ohio State
  University, Victorian
  Village, German Village, and
  communities of Upper
  Arlington and Bexley.
TAC sanction
5,572 entries in '91
2,800 volunteers

Englewood Reserve Marathon
7581 Glenhurst Drive
Dayton, OH 45414
513/898-7015
January
Denny Fryman

Fall Fantasy Marathon
7581 Glenhurst Drive
Dayton, OH 45414
513/898-7015
September
Denny Fryman

Glass City Marathon
Toledo Roadrunners
P.O. Box 5656
Toledo, OH 43613
419/691-6064
April
Pam Graver
1990 (previously run from 1971
  to 1983)
Certified
Loop: Flat, fast; begins and
  ends in downtown, runs
  along Maumee River.
TAC sanction

518 entries in '91
600 volunteers

Leprechaun Marathon
7581 Glenhurst Drive
Dayton, OH 45414
513/898-7015
November
Denny Fryman

Mid-Winter Marathon
7581 Glenhurst Drive
Dayton, OH 45414
513/898-7015
February
Denny Fryman

Ohio/Michigan Run Marathon
Cystic Fibrosis Foundation of
  NW Ohio
1 Stranahan Square, Suite 518
Toledo, OH 43604
419/241-4342
July
Tom Falvey
1988
Certified
Loop
TAC sanction
36 entries in '91
20 volunteers

Ohio River Marathon
1042 Pripz Avenue
Dayton, OH 45410
513/253-2180
February
Clint Jett
1967
Certified
Out and back: Continuous
  hills combined with nasty

and cold February weather makes this an experience to remember.
TAC sanction
65 entries in '91
50 volunteers

Park of Roses Marathon
7581 Glenhurst Drive
Dayton, OH 45414
513/898-7015
June
Denny Fryman

Spring Fling Marathon
7581 Glenhurst Drive
Dayton, OH 45414
513/898-7015
May
Denny Fryman

Summer Spree Marathon
7581 Glenhurst Drive
Dayton, OH 45414
513/898-7015
August
Denny Fryman

Union Terminal Marathon
7581 Glenhurst Drive
Dayton, OH 45414
513/898-7015
August
Denny Fryman

Vandalia Holiday Marathon
7581 Glenhurst Drive
Dayton, OH 45414
513/898-7015
December
Denny Fryman

Vandalia Winter Marathon
7581 Glenhurst Drive
Dayton, OH 45414
513/898-7015
January
Denny Fryman

Winter Fun Marathon
7581 Glenhurst Drive
Dayton, OH 45414
513/898-7015
February
Denny Fryman

Oklahoma

Andy Payne Marathon
United National Indian Tribal
    Youth
P.O. Box 25042
Oklahoma City, OK 73125
405/424-3010
May

Bulldog Marathon
2610 Northwest Expressway,
    #B
Oklahoma City, OK 73112
405/946-5623
December
Dan Metcalf
1985
Certified
Point to point: Begins at the
    base of the Quartz
    Mountains and runs south.
TAC sanction
3 entries in '91
5 volunteers

Jim Thorpe Marathon
P.O. Box 24045
Oklahoma City, OK 73124
405/232-3060
November
W. L. Draper
1990
Certified
Out and back.
TAC sanction
200 entries in '91
400 volunteers

Tulsa Marathon
5123 South Detroit Avenue
Tulsa, OK 74105
918/742-4127
November
John Castillo

Oregon

Crater Lake Rim Marathon
5830 Mack Avenue
Klamath Falls, OR 97603
503/884-6939
August

Harvest Festival Marathon
P.O. Box 523
Talent, OR 97540
503/535-4854
September
Jerome Ellison

Lost Soles Marathon
P.O. Box 523
Talent, OR 97540
503/535-4854
February
Jerome Ellison

Portland Marathon
P.O. Box 4040
Beaverton, OR 97201
503/226-1111
September
Les Smith
1972
Certified
Loop with 2 out and backs
TAC and RRCA sanctions
5,226 entries in '91
3,500 volunteers

Trail's End Marathon
Oregon Road Runners Club
P.O. Box 549
Beaverton, OR 97075
503/531-0133
February
Gordon Lovie
1970
Certified
Figure-8s: Fairly flat, with
   views of the ocean, and one
   short hill at 18 miles.
RRCA sanction
306 finishers in '91

Pennsylvania

Eriesistible Marathon
319 West 10th Street
Erie, PA 16502
814/454-5868
September
Ken Chestek

God's Country Marathon
Potter County Recreation
   Department
P.O. Box 245

Coudersport, PA 16915
814/435-2290
June
Jeff and Carol Carts

Great Valley Marathon
5645 Stamy Hill Road
Waynesboro, PA 17268
717/263-5631
January
Mike Witter
1989
Certified
Out and back: Gently rolling
   with hills coming between
   3.0 and 4.2 miles.
TAC sanction
150 entries in '91
30 volunteers

Harrisburg Marathon
5906 Fox Street
Harrisburg, PA 17112
717/652-7002
November
Robert Mahady

Johnstown Marathon
YMCA
100 Haynes Street
Johnstown, PA 15901
814/535-8381
October
Norm Snyder
1975
Certified
Point to point: Covers both
   urban and rural areas; fairly
   level, with "terrific"
   downhill between miles 5
   and 6.

TAC sanction
164 entries in '91
200 volunteers

City of Pittsburgh Marathon
429 4th Avenue, Suite 1001
Pittsburgh, PA 15219
412/765-3773
May
Leonard Duncan
1985
Certified
Point to point: Course is fast
   and challenging with first 5
   miles gradual downhill;
   levels off and then climbs at
   mile 11, then again levels,
   until descent begins at mile
   22 to finish.
TAC sanction
3,315 entries in '91
1,500 volunteers

Rhode Island

Rhode Island Marathon
80 Lincoln Street
North Kingstown, RI 02852
401/885-1382 FAX
   401/885-5506
November
Meridith Nelson
1976 (formerly Ocean State
   Marathon)
Certified
Point to point
TAC sanction
1,055 entries in '91
150 volunteers

South Carolina

Carolina Marathon
P.O. Box 5290
Columbia, SC 29250
803/777-2456
February
Russ Pate
1977
Certified
Out to a loop, then back:
   Rolling terrain, residential
   neighborhoods, all macadam
   surface.
TAC sanction
225 entries in '91
150 volunteers

Kiawah Island Marathon
P.O. Box 12001
Charleston, SC 29412
803/768-3400
December

Upstate Marathon
P.O. Box 8516
Spartanburg, SC 29305
803/244-8994
December
Darrell Jennewine

South Dakota

Black Hills Marathon
P.O. Box 9243
Rapid City, SD 57709
605/348-7866
September
Dennis Lunsford

Longest Day Marathon
1345 First Street

Brookings, SD 57006
605/692-2334
April
Charles S. Roberts, Jr.
1969
Certified
Multiple loop: Two loops on
   pavement with 2 miles of
   gravel; elevation gain and
   loss of 75 feet each loop.
TAC sanction
75 entries in '91
70 volunteers

Tennessee

Andrew Jackson Marathon
Jackson Roadrunners
P.O. Box 3832
Jackson, TN 38303
901/668-1708
November
Bob Saffel

*Chickamauga Battlefield
   Marathon*
The Front Runner
3903 Hixson Pike, Suite C
Chattanooga, TN 37415
615/875-3642
November

Memphis Marathon
First Tennessee Bank
P.O. Box 84, Suite 1001
Memphis, TN 38101
800/489-4040 ext. 4726
December
Terry Lee and Ernie Lee, Jr.
1988
Certified

Loop: Mostly flat with a few gentle rolling hills but nothing major; winds through residential areas, a park, and along major city streets.
RRCA sanction
508 entries in '91
800 volunteers

Music City Marathon
205 Woodland Court
Hermitage, TN 37076
615/889-1306
March
Thomas de Paulis
1987
Certified
Out and back: Start and finish at Edwin Warner Park; runs through scenic country setting; moderate hills.
TAC sanction
650 entries in '91
60 volunteers

Smoky Mountain Marathon
4132 Forest Glen Drive
Knoxville, TN 37919
615/524-5040
February
Chuck Pate
Certified

Texas

Austin Marathon
Run Tex
908-B West 12th Street
Austin, TX 78703
512/472-3272

March
Paul Carrozza

Cowtown Marathon
P.O. Box 567
Fort Worth, TX 76101
817/735-2033
February
Jim Gilliland
1979
Certified
Loop: Scenic loop beginning and ending in historic stockyards of Fort Worth; course is hilly and challenging as it winds through downtown, including the cultural district, the zoo, and Sundance Square.
TAC sanction
800 entries in '91
1,000 volunteers

Dallas White Rock Marathon
3607 Oak Lawn
Dallas, TX 75219
214/526-5318
December

Great Southwest Marathon
YMCA
Box 3137
Abilene, TX 79604
915/677-8144
March
Mike Osborn
1977
Certified
Loop: Flat, circular course around the city of Abilene.

TAC sanction
180 entries in '91
50 volunteers

Houston-Tenneco Marathon
P.O. Box 2511
Houston, TX 77252-2511
713/757-2700
January
David Hannah
1972
Certified
Loop: Fast, flat, single-loop beginning and ending in downtown.
TAC, RRCA, and ARRA sanctions
5,075 entries in '91
3,000 volunteers

San Antonio Marathon
121 Joliet
San Antonio, TX 78209
512/821-6046
November
John Purnell
1988
Certified
Out and back
TAC sanction
1,200 entries in '91
600 volunteers

Woodlands Marathon
South Montgomery County YMCA
6145 Shadowbend Place
The Woodlands, TX 77381
713/367-9622
January
Dan Green

1979
Certified
Loop: Flat and fast on concrete streets and asphalt shoulders through tree-lined streets of The Woodlands, 35 miles north of Houston.
TAC sanction
329 entries in '91
300 volunteers

Utah

Deseret News Marathon
P.O. Box 1257
Salt Lake City, UT 84110
801/237-2135
July
1970
Certified
Point to point: Begins at Washington Park (5,650 feet), climbs to 6,227 feet (at 11-mile mark), then drops over the remainder of the course to 4,200 feet.
TAC sanction
403 entries in '91
250 volunteers

St. George Marathon
St. George Leisure Services Dept.
86 South Main Street
St. George, UT 84770
801/634-5850
October
Kent E. Perkins
1977
Certified

Point to point: Race begins at 5,000 feet near majestic Pine Valley Mountain; downhill course, winding through Snow Canyon State Park; finish line elevation is 2,600 feet.
TAC sanction
2,461 entries in '91
1,000 volunteers

Vermont

Green Mountain Marathon
Box 209
Huntington, VT 05462
802/434-3228
October
Howie Atherton
1986
Certified
Out and back: Gently rolling back roads along Lake Champlain; race is actually on an island in the lake; 60 percent gravel, 40 percent paved; low-key race through fall foliage.
TAC sanction
100 entries in '91
50 volunteers

Vermont City Marathon
Bank of Vermont
P.O. Box 152
Burlington, VT 05402
802/638-1815
May
1989

Certified
Out and back and loop: Start and finish at Battery Park; runs on city streets, roads, and bike path; 85 to 90 percent flat, gentle hills, downhill at mile 2 and uphill at mile 21.
TAC sanction
733 entries in '91
550 volunteers

Virginia

Richmond Marathon
P.O. Box C-32333
Richmond, VA 23293
804/649-6325
October
DeWayne Davis
1978
Certified
Loop: Rolling, scenic, along river and monuments; plenty of spectators to cheer runners on.
TAC sanction
3,000 entries in '91 (combined marathon, half marathon, and 5-miler)
1,100 volunteers

Shamrock Sportsfest Marathon
2308 Maple Street
Virginia Beach, VA 23451
804/481-5090
March
Jerry Bocrie
1972
Certified

Out and back: Flat and fast, runs through oceanfront resort and homes, and finishes inside 70,000-square-foot Pavilion Convention Center.
TAC and RRCA sanctions
1,400 entries in '91
1,000 volunteers

Washington

Capital City Marathon
P.O. Box 1681
Olympia, WA 98507
206/786-1786
May
Russ Chadwick

Skagit Flats Marathon
1048 Gardner Road
Burlington, WA 98233
206/757-8052
September
Jim Taylor
1978
Certified
Loop: A small country marathon starting in a rural town, traverses a completely flat course along country roads and along farmlands; highest point is a freeway overpass; ends at high school football stadium.
TAC sanction
52 entries in '91
40 volunteers

Seattle Marathon
P.O. Box 31849
Seattle, WA 98103
206/547-0885
November

Tri-Cities Marathon
1205 Ryan Avenue
Pasco, WA 99301
509/545-5693
October
Kathleen Leonard

West Virginia

Almost Heaven Marathon
19 Riverside Drive
South Charleston, WV 25303
304/744-6502
December
Pat Board

Ridge Runner Marathon
North Bend State Park
Cairo, WV 26337
304/643-2931
June
Jane D. Ostyre
Not certified at this time
Loop

Wisconsin

American Odyssey Marathon
3842 Crestwood Drive
Wausau, WI 54401
715/675-6977
September
Roger Ross
1978
Not certified
Point to point: Rolling hills, some of them impressive;

race begins in Marathon, Wis., and ends in Athens, Wis., something no marathon outside of Greece can claim.
No sanction
100 entries in '91
30 volunteers

Dairyland Marathon & Volksmarsch
Medford Chamber of Commerce
P.O. Box 172
Medford, WI 54451
715/748-3496
April
Ann K. Dillon
1991
Not certified
Point to point: Run on beautiful pine-tree-lined trail and old railroad bed.
No sanction
100 entries in '91
25 volunteers

Fox Cities Marathon
316 North Appleton Street
Appleton, WI 54911
414/739-6222
October
Gloria West
1991
Certified
Point to point: Begins in Neerah, runs through seven cities and crosses rural settings with rolling hills before ending in Appleton.
TAC sanction

1,700 entries in '91
1,000 volunteers

Lakefront Marathon
Running on Prospect
2111 North Prospect Avenue
Milwaukee, WI 53202
414/272-7867
October
Armen Hadjinian
1980
Certified
Point to point: Relatively flat.
TAC and RRCA sanctions
900 entries in '91
300 volunteers

Lake Geneva Marathon
P.O. Box 1134
Lake Geneva, WI 53147
414/248-4323
May
Barbara and Frank Dobbs
1986
Certified
Loop: Hilly and beautiful, circles one of the deepest—and cleanest—lakes in Wisconsin.
TAC sanction
1,000 entries in '91
200 volunteers

Paavo Nurmi Marathon
Chamber of Commerce
110-A 2nd Avenue South, Highway 51
Hurley, WI 54534
715/561-4334
August

Kay Decker
1968
Certified
Point to point: Moderate to
hilly; runs from Upson,
Wis., and finishes in Hurley,
Wis.
TAC sanction
375 entries in '91
375 volunteers

Canada

Calgary Stampede Marathon
Box 296, Station M
Calgary, Alberta
Canada T2P 2H9
403/270-8828
July
Ian Hamilton
1964
Certified
Out and back: Flat, fast; paved
city streets in scenic Bow
River valley; only elevations
changes are highway over-
and underpasses.
Athletics Alberta sanction
600 entries in '91
1,000 volunteers

Fort McMurray Oilsands
Marathon
P.O. Box 5792
Fort McMurray, Alberta
Canada T9H 4V9
403/791-6414
September
Fred Payne
1990

Certified
Out and back: Relatively flat;
starts at MacDonald Island,
passes through downtown
Fort McMurray before
heading north on Highway
63 to the turnaround, then
returns to MacDonald
through a shorter
downtown section.
Athletics Alberta and
Canadian Track & Field
Association sanctions
55 entries in '91
113 volunteers

Johnny Miles Marathon
P.O. Box 7
New Glasgow, Nova Scotia
Canada B2H 5E1
902/752-8209
May
George Manos
1975
Certified
Multiple loop
Canadian Track & Field
Association sanction
80 entries in '91
275 volunteers

Lakeland Runaway Marathon
Recreation Department
Lakeland College
Vermilion, Alberta
Canada T0B 4M0
403/853-8471

Manitoba Marathon
200 Main Street
Winnipeg, Manitoba

Canada R3C 4M2
204/985-4183
June

National Capital Marathon
P.O. Box 426, Station A
Ottawa, Ontario
Canada K1N 8VS
613/234-2221
May
Chantal Bourbonnaire
1973
Certified
Out and back
Athletics Canada sanction
2,000 entries in '91
800 volunteers

*New Brunswick Heart
    Marathon*
340 MacDonald Avenue
Oromocto, New Brunswick
Canada E2V 2J3
506/422-3086(W) or
    506/357-6566(H)
May
Terry Goodlad
1979
Certified
Loop followed by an out and
    back: Primarily flat, two
    hills on the out and back
    portion of the course. Very
    scenic.
Athletics Canada sanction
390 entries in '91
70 volunteers

Nova Scotia Marathon
P.O. Box 100
Barrington, Nova Scotia

Canada B0W 1E0
902/637-3254
July
Raymond Green
1970
Certified
Figure-8: Mostly flat with
    rolling hills passing through
    small fishing villages; passes
    along coast for most of the
    distance, with offshore
    breezes; two steep hills of
    500 feet in the later part of
    the course.
N.S.T.F. and R.N.S. sanctions
54 entries in '91
40 volunteers

*Prince Edward Island
    Marathon*
YMCA
252 Prince Street
Charlottetown, Prince Edward
    Island
Canada C1A 4S1
902/566-3966
September
Fred Hughes

Royal Victoria Marathon
182-911 Yates Street
Victoria, British Columbia
Canada V8V 4X3
604/382-8181
October
Rob Reid
1980
Certified
Double loop: Initial loop of
    roughly 10K followed by a
    much larger loop that

contains some out-and-back portions; starts and finishes beside Victoria's Inner Harbour, includes historic Old Town, Beacon Hill Park, the Songhees Community of the Inner Harbour, two small bridge crossings, the waterfront, downtown, the Victoria Golf Club Links, and passes through residential communities before finishing in front of provincial legislative buildings.
868 finishers in '91
73 volunteers

Saskatchewan Canada Goose Marathon
128 Ottawa Avenue South
Saskatoon, Saskatchewan
Canada S7M 3L5
306/382-2962
September
Ray Risling
1979
Certified
Double out and back
Athletics Canada sanction
62 finishers in '91
40 volunteers

Toronto Marathon
Ontario Track & Field Association
1220 Sheppard Avenue East
Willowdale, Ontario
Canada M2K 2X1
416/495-4311
October
John Craig
1978
Certified
Loop: Flat and fast; bow-tie-shaped loop with uphill at 15K and 32K; final 10K is flat or gentle downhill; finishes in sports stadium.
Athletics Canada sanction
2,084 entries in '91
1,100 volunteers

Twin Cities Marathon
9 Fair Haven Place
St. John's, Newfoundland
Canada A1E 4R9
709/368-9234
September
Gary Sabin

Vancouver International Marathon
099-555 West 12th Avenue
Vancouver, British Columbia
Canada V6H 1E1
604/872-2928 Fax: 604/731-8517
1972
Certified
Loop: Begins and ends in front of City Hall downtown; runs through Stanley Park, crosses Lions Gate Bridge to West Vancouver, heads east to North Vancouver, then crosses back to Vancouver proper.
AIMS and BCA sanctions

1,241 entries in '91
1,500 volunteers

Voyageur Marathon
Lee Valley Road, RR #2
Massey, Ontario
Canada P0P 1P0
705/865-2736 Fax:
   705/865-2736
July
Shelda and Norm Patenaude
1977
Certified
Out and back and 2 loops:
   One-mile loop of town,
   crosses Spanish River and
   runs east for 3K and returns
   to bridge, then west for 6K,
   then back to bridge, across
   bridge and returning to
   start; course is described as
   picturesque and tranquil.
OTFA and TAC sanctions
162 entries in '91
85 volunteers

*Yukon Gold Midnight
   Marathon*
Run Yukon
Box 4502
Whitehorse, Yukon
Canada Y1A 2R8
403/668-4236
June

Note: The two national
   running magazines, *Runner's
   World* and *Running Times*
   (see Appendix III), carry
   current marathon listings in
   their monthly race
   schedules. In addition,
   Runner's World carries an
   annual marathon schedule
   in its January issue, while
   Running Times breaks the
   list in two, carrying the first
   half of the year in the
   December issue and the
   second half in the June
   issue.

II: Major
International Marathons

The riotous growth of interest in marathons in the United States in the late 1970s spread to the rest of the world at varying rates of speed. Today, marathons are staged in most major cities in the world. The largest marathons on foreign soil are in London and Berlin. The marathon runner should be cautious, however, because the quality of organization of foreign marathons varies greatly. Ironically, some marathons scheduled in very desirable tourist cities are relatively unorganized, while those held in less romanticized major cities are often well organized. There are several tour companies that offer packages to foreign marathons, the most active of which is Marathon Tours, 108 Main Street, Boston, MA 02129; 617/242-7845. It is advised that American marathoners planning to participate in a foreign marathon do so through an American tour operator. An individual dealing with the arrangements can face a nightmare in pulling all the strings together, while the tour operators, besides being familiar with how to pull the strings, are also granted blocks of entries for their clients by the marathon's race director. The automatic entry comes as part of the tour operator package.

Athens Marathon
Athens, Greece
October
Marathon Tours
Certified
Point-to-point: Begins in the

town of Marathon; course is very hilly. From mile 10 to 20 it is especially hilly, although the final 10K is slightly downhill. Race finishes inside the 1896

Olympic Stadium. Race is beset by traditionally poor organization.
S.E.G.A.S. sanction
2,500 entries in '91, 2,000 finishers
75 volunteers

Berlin Marathon
Berlin, Germany
September
Marathon Tours
1974
Certified
Loop: Passes through 10 of the city's boroughs; start is near Charlottenburg Castle. Eight miles of the course is within the former East Germany.
German Track & Field Federation sanction
19,000 entries in '91, 17,000 finishers
1,000 volunteers

Bermuda International Marathon
Hamilton, Bermuda
January
Marathon Tours
Peter Lever, race director
1978
Certified
Multiple loop: Follows picturesque South Shore Road through Mid-Ocean and Castle Harbour golf courses and onto Harrington Sound, then joins North Shore Road before passing through Hamilton. Course is hilly.
B.T.F.A. sanction
175 entries in '91, 118 finishers
200 volunteers

Dublin Marathon
Dublin, Ireland
October
Marathon Tours
Certified
Loop: Begins in the city of Dublin and loops around the city, including several miles in Phoenix Park. Finish is next to St. Stephen's Green. Some hills in the first half, flat in the second half.
Irish Track & Field Association sanction
5,000 entries in '91, 4,500 finishers
500 volunteers

Fletcher Challenge Marathon
Rotorua, New Zealand
Marathon Tours
May
Certified

London Marathon
London, England
April
Marathon Tours
or
Keith Prowse
234 West 44th Street
New York, NY 10036
800/669-8687
Alan Storey, race director

Certified

Point-to-point: Begins in Greenwich Park, with three separate groups passing through the park. Passes the *Cutty Sark,* over Tower Bridge, around the Isle of Dogs, along the Thames, past Buckingham Palace, with the finish on Westminster Bridge in the shadow of Big Ben.

A.A.A. sanction

33,000 starters in '91, 27,000 finishers

4,000 volunteers

Macau Marathon

Macau, China

December

Mary Frances Productions

7603 New Market Drive

Bethesda, MD 20817

301/320-3663

Moscow International Peace Marathon

Moscow, Russia

June

Marathon Tours

Certified

Paris Marathon

Paris, France

March

Marathon Tours

Certified

Loop: Begins at the Champs-Élysées, passes the Arc du Triomphe, through the Bois du Boulogne, past the Eiffel Tower and Notre Dame, through the Bois de Vincennes, and finishes on Avenue Foch.

Canceled for '91, expects 9,000 runners in '92

Pyramids Marathon

Cairo, Egypt

January

Mary Frances Productions

7603 New Market Drive

Bethesda, MD 20817

301/320-3663

Not certified

Stockholm Marathon

Stockholm, Sweden

May

Marathon Tours

Certified

Multiple loops: Begins outside the Olympic Stadium, passes through the Djürgarden, through Old Town, over the Vesterbron (West Bridge), does a second loop, and finishes inside the 1912 Olympic Stadium.

Swedish Amateur Athletic Federation sanction

15,000 starters in '91, 13,000 finishers

1,000 volunteers

III: Periodicals

The following periodicals are either devoted exclusively to covering running or carry material on running on a regular basis:

American Athletics
P.O. Box 1497
Los Altos, CA 94023
415/968-4419

American Health
28 West 23rd Street
New York, NY 10010
212/366-8900

California Citysports/North
123 Townsend Street,
 Suite 560
San Francisco, CA 94107
415/546-6150

California Citysports/South
215 Long Beach Boulevard,
 Suite 606
Long Beach, CA 90802
213/437-8822

California Running News
4957 East Heaton Avenue
Fresno, CA 93727
209/255-4904

Chicago Runner
459 North Milwaukee Avenue
Chicago, IL 60610
312/845-9123

The Competitor
214 South Cedros
Solana Beach, CA 92075
619/793-2711

Florida Running
8640 Tansy Drive
Orlando, FL 32819-4529
407/352-9131

Footnotes
629 South Washington Street
Alexandria, VA 22314
703/836-0558

The Harrier
P.O. Box 41
Marlboro, NJ 07739
908/308-9701

Illinois Runner
P.O. Box 53
Fairbury, IL 61739
815/692-4636

Indiana Running & Racing News
503 East Main Street
Hartford City, IN 47348
317/348-4739

Inside Texas Running
9514 Bristlebrook Drive
Houston, TX 77083
713/498-3208

Keeping Track
1012 East 21st Avenue
Eugene, OR 97405
503/344-0498

Master Pieces
P.O. Box 14668
Lenexa, KS 66285-4668
816/746-1414

Master Runner
210 7th Street Southeast, Suite
  C-23
Washington, DC 20003
202/546-5598

Mastersports
Hurley & Company
400 East 85th Street, #9-D
New York, NY 10028
212/535-7550

Metrosports
695 Washington Street
New York, NY 10014
212/627-7040

Michigan Runner
7990 West Grand River, Suite
  C
Brighton, MI 48116
313/227-4200

National Masters News
P.O. Box 2372
Van Nuys, CA 91404
818/785-1895

New England Runner
P.O. Box 252
Boston, MA 02113
617/899-0481

New York Running News
9 East 89th Street
New York, NY 10128
212/860-4455

Northern California Schedule
80 Mitchell Boulevard
San Rafael, CA 94903-2038
415/472-7223

Northwest Runner
1231 Northeast 94th
Seattle, WA 98115
206/526-9000

Ohio Runner
P.O. Box 586
Hilliard, OH 43026
614/224-7500

Oklahoma Runner
P.O. Box 2008
Tulsa, OK 74101
918/581-8306

Oregon Distance Runner
2300 Southwest Hoffman
  Drive
Portland, OR 97201
503/224-6020

Outside
1165 North Clark Street
Chicago, IL 60610
312/951-0990

Peak Running Performance
P.O. Box 128036
Nashville, TN 37212
615/383-1071

Physician & Sports Medicine
4530 West 77th Street
Minneapolis, MN 55435
612/835-3222

*Road Race Management News-
letter*
2102 Wilson Boulevard, Suite
437
Arlington, VA 22201
703/276-0093

Runner (New York edition)
6-2 Steven Drive
Ossining, NY 10562
914/961-2626

Runner's World
33 East Minor Street
Emmaus, PA 18098
215/967-8956

Runner Triathlete News
P.O. Box 19909
Houston, TX 77224
713/781-7090

Running Advice
576 Armour Circle
Atlanta, GA 30324
404/892-1158

Running & FitNews
9310 Old Georgetown Road
Bethesda, MD 20814
800/776-ARFA

Running Commentary
441 Brookside Drive

Eugene, OR 97405
503/683-2118

Running Journal
P.O. Box 157
Greenville, TN 37744
615/638-4177

Running Research News
P.O. Box 27041
Lansing, MI 48909
517/393-3150 or 800/333-FEET

Running Stats
1985 14th Street, Suite 1260
Boulder, CO 80302

Running Times
251 Danbury Road
Wilton, CT 06897
203/834-2900

Southern Runner
P.O. Box 6524
Metarie, LA 70009
504/454-8247

Sports Illustrated
Time & Life Building
Rockefeller Center
New York, NY 10020-1393
800/528-5000

Starting Line
P.O. Box 19909
Houston, TX 77224
713/781-7090

S.W.E.A.T. Magazine
4120 North 70th Street, #211
Scottsdale, AZ 85251
602/947-3900

TACStats
915 Randolph

Santa Barbara, CA 93111-1031
805/683-5868

Track & Field News
2570 El Camino Real, Suite
606
Mountain View, CA 94040
415/948-8188

Triathlete
1127 Hamilton Street
Allentown, PA 18102
215/821-6864

UltraRunning
300 North Main Street
P.O. Box 481
Sunderland, MA 01375
413/665-7573

Walking
9–11 Harcourt Street
Boston, MA 02116
617/266-3322

Women's Sports & Fitness
1919 14th Street, Suite 421
Boulder, CO 80302
303/440-5111

IV: Associations
and Organizations

Many runners find that keeping to a marathon training program is made easier when it's possible to schedule workouts—especially long workouts—with other runners, or to schedule at least one or two workouts per week with organized running groups or clubs.

Running clubs also provide a vehicle for plugging into what is happening within the running community in your area and often offer low-priced tours to major events, carpooling to local races, and ongoing feedback on which races to enter and which to avoid.

The major running organization within the United States is The Athletics Congress of the USA. TAC is charged with developing the sport of "athletics" within the United States. *Athletics* is the British term for track and field, but it has been stretched since the running revolution to include long-distance events, including those held on the roads. TAC is the U.S. governing body for participation in international events.

TAC also sanctions many races, including marathons, and it oversees prize money awarded in various events; a TAC membership is necessary to share in any prize money. Annual membership in TAC is currently (1992) $12.

TAC's *national office* is:
The Athletics Congress/USA
One Hoosier Dome, Suite 140
Indianapolis, IN 46225
317/261-0500 Fax: 317/261-0481

If you wish general membership information, you can write to the national headquarters and they will forward your inquiry to the region that services you.

TAC divides the United States into numerous geographic regions. The list that follows contains all the regional associations; since specific officers change with each election, the address listed is that of the regional office:

Adirondack
Adirondack Assn./TAC
233 4th Street
Troy, NY 12180
518/273-5552 Fax: 518/273-0647

Alabama
Alabama Assn./TAC
2301 Airport Boulevard
Mobile, AL 36606
205/434-7472 Fax: 205/478-5072

Alaska
TAC/Alaska
P.O. Box 92106
Anchorage, AK 99509
907/279-1554

Arizona
Arizona Assn./TAC
8436 East Hubbell Street
Scottsdale, AZ 85257
602/949-1991

Arkansas
TAC/Arkansas
41 White Oak Lane
Little Rock, AR 72207
501/666-1720

Border
Border/TAC
229 Arboles
El Paso, TX 79932
915/581-2962

Central California
Central California/TAC

P.O. Box 801
Wasco, CA 93280
805/758-3081

Colorado
Colorado/TAC
16842 East Brown Place
Aurora, CO 80013
303/690-1756

Connecticut
TAC/Connecticut
P.O. Box 207
Manchester, CT 06040
203/643-4096

Dakotas
Dakotas/TAC
1310 Loy Avenue
Wahpeton, ND 58075
701/642-1321

Florida
Florida Athletics Congress
1330 Northwest 6th Street,
  Suite D
Gainesville, FL 32601-4245
904/378-6805 Fax: 904/373-8879

Georgia
Georgia/TAC
506 Creekridge Court
Woodstock, GA 30188-4104
404/928-9149 Fax: 404/928-3759

Gulf
Gulf Assn./TAC
8618 Birdwood Road

Houston, TX 77074
713/777-6840 Fax: 713/541-8080

Hawaii
Hawaii/TAC
c/o Honolulu Marathon
    Association
3435 Waialae Avenue, Room
    208
Honolulu, HI 96816
808/734-7200

Illinois
Illinois/TAC
111 West Butterfield Road
Elmhurst, IL 60126
708/833-7303 Fax: 708/833-5162

Indiana
TAC/Indiana
215 Lincoln Street
Rensselaer, IN 47978
219/866-3040

Inland Empire
Inland Empire/TAC
418 Cocolalla
Cheney, WA 99004-1753
509/235-4762

Iowa
TAC/Iowa
1716 Plaza Circle
Des Moines, IA 50322-5753
515/276-2669

Kentucky
Kentucky/TAC
1515 Tyler Park Drive
Louisville, KY 40204
502/458-4989

Lake Erie
Lake Erie/TAC
4173 Wilmington
South Euclid, OH 44121
216/382-2656

Maine
Maine/TAC
18 Mayflower Road
Hallowell, ME 04347
207/623-3521 ext. 2639

Metropolitan
Metropolitan Athletics
    Congress
P.O. Box 170
Church Street Station
New York, NY 10008-0170
212/227-0071 Fax: 212/227-0756

Michigan
Michigan/TAC
10102 West Carpenter Road
Flushing, MI 48433
313/481-6887

Mid-Atlantic
Mid-Atlantic/TAC
P.O. Box 7231
Philadelphia, PA 19101
215/472-0780

Minnesota
Minnesota/TAC
1700 105th Avenue, Northeast
Blaine, MN 55434
612/785-5600 Fax: 612/785-5699

Missouri Valley
Missouri Valley Assn./TAC
620 West 26th Street
Kansas City, MO 64108
816/842-3311 Fax: 816/471-8557

Nevada
Nevada/TAC
4505 Maryland Parkway
Las Vegas, NV 89154
702/739-3256 Fax: 702/739-0989

New England
New England Athletics
  Congress
P.O. Box 1905
Brookline, MA 02146
617/566-7600

New Jersey
New Jersey/TAC
P.O. Box 6909
Piscataway, NJ 08855-6909
908/463-8444

New Mexico
New Mexico Assn./TAC
118 Amherst, Northeast
Albuquerque, NM 87106
505/255-029

Niagara
Niagara/TAC
1203 Eggert Road
Eggertsville, NY 14226
716/833-7596

North Carolina
NCA/TAC/USA
P.O. Box 10825
Raleigh, NC 27605
919/782-2896

Ohio
Ohio/TAC
P.O. Box 5848
Dayton, OH 45405-0848
513/455-6787

Oklahoma
Oklahoma/TAC
5312 North Vermont
Oklahoma City, OK 73112
405/942-6733

Oregon
Oregon Assn./TAC
P.O. Box 1133
Sandy, OR 97055
503/252-7755 Fax: 503/252-7132

Ozark
Ozark/TAC
900 Weidman Road
Manchester, MO 63011
314/434-3397

Pacific
Pacific Assn./TAC
800 Bonita Drive
Folsom, CA 95630
916/983-4622 Fax: 916/983-4624

Pacific Northwest
Pacific Northwest/TAC
4261 South 184th Street
SeaTac, WA 98818
206/PNAC-754 Fax:
  206/286-1025

Potomac Valley
Potomac Valley Assn./TAC
4007 Bateman Avenue
Baltimore, MD 21216
301/367-8862

San Diego-Imperial
San Diego-Imperial/TAC
P.O. Box 80512
San Diego, CA 92138
619/488-3960

Snake River
Snake River/TAC
425 Dubois
Twin Falls, ID 83301
208/733-2155 Fax: 208/733-4317

South Carolina
South Carolina/TAC
Asst. Athletic Dir.
South Carolina School for
   Deaf & Blind
820 Patch Drive
Spartanburg, SC 29302
803/585-7711

Southern
Southern Assn./TAC
P.O. Box 806
Port Gibson, MS 39150
601/437-4251

Southern California
Southern California
Assn./TAC
12458 Rives Avenue, Suite
204-A
Downey, CA 90242
213/869-4574 Fax: 213/862-2048

South Texas
South Texas Assn./TAC
3428 North St. Mary's
San Antonio, TX 78212
512/732-1332

Southwestern
Southwestern Assn./TAC
6606 Greenfield
Arlington, TX 76016
817/483-4598

Tennessee
Tennessee Assn./TAC
Tennessee State University
3500 John Merritte Boulevard

Nashville, TN 37209
615/320-3210

Three Rivers
Three Rivers Assn./TAC
73 Elmore Road
Pittsburgh, PA 15221
412/374-2186

Utah
Utah/TAC
1663 Moor Dale Lane
Salt Lake City, UT 84003
801/272-9316

Virginia
Virginia Assn./TAC
3122 West Clay Street, Suite 6
Richmond, VA 23230
804/353-9348

West Texas
West Texas Assn./TAC
5108 Shawnee
Amarillo, TX 79109
806/352-6200

West Virginia
West Virginia/TAC
Route 3, Box 85
Proctorville, OH 45669
614/886-5116

Wisconsin
Wisconsin/TAC
22 Lamplighter Way
Madison, WI 53705
608/266-7659

Wyoming
Wyoming/TAC
Foot of the Rockies
1740 Dell Range Boulevard
Cheyenne, WY 82009
307/778-7866

The national organization that has, from its inception, been concerned with road racing, and only road racing, is the Road Runners Club of America. The organization grew with the sport during the late 1970s and did much to help the sport grow in logical directions at a time when TAC (then the AAU) was hard-pressed to acknowledge that a road racing revolution was underfoot.

There are RRCA chapters spread throughout the United States. For information on the chapter nearest you, contact the national headquarters:

National RRCA Offices
629 South Washington Street
Alexandria, VA 22314
703/836-0558 Fax: 703/836-4430

Another valuable association, especially for those just becoming involved in running, is the American Running & Fitness Association. Its current membership dues are $25 a year, which bring a raft of benefits, including its monthly publication, _Running & FitNews._

American Running & Fitness Association
9310 Old Georgetown Road
Bethesda, MD 20814
800/776-ARFA

V: Readings on Running

The sport of running has been fortunate to attract to its ranks a small army of literate folk. Through the years, there has been a wealth of books published about the sport and avocation of running, as well as an excellent subgenre dealing with the marathon and that sport's offbeat cousin, the ultramarathon. Many of the books listed here are now out of print, but because of running's popularity, enough copies of most of these were printed that they periodically surface in used-book stores before they are once again snatched up and salted away in a running aficionado's library.

Autobiography and Biography

Benoit, Joan. *Running Tide.* New York: Alfred A. Knopf, 1987, 213 pp. A very pleasant admission inside the private world of the winner of the first women's Olympic marathon.

Benyo, Richard. *The Masters of the Marathon.* New York: Atheneum, 1983, 244 pp. Profiles of fourteen of the greatest marathoners in history.

Beyer, Jinny. *A Six-Minute Mile.* McLean, Va.: EPM Publications, 1984, 209 pp. A forty-plus mother decides to take up running and sets as her goal breaking six minutes for the mile.

Bishop, Bob. *The Running Saga of Walter Stack.* Millbrae, Calif.: Celestial Arts, 1978, 109 pp. Running legend Walt Stack, an institution in the Bay Area and one of the pioneers of women's running, is reverently portrayed.

Clayton, Derek. *Running to the Top.* New York: Collier Books, 1980, 137 pp. Clayton held the world's best marathon time for a dozen years; his story is one of single-minded determination. Begs for more autobiography and less retreaded training tips.

Coe, Sebastian. *Running Free.* New York: St. Martin's, 1981, 174 pp. The autobiography of the track runner considered "the Nureyev of the Track," this one's both readable and inspiring. (Not to be confused with Joan Ullyot's book of the same title.)

Cordellos, Harry. *Breaking Through.* Mountain View, Calif.: Anderson World, 1981, 271 pp. The extraordinary story of the famed Northern California blind athlete who not only defied the odds but excelled, with a sub-3:00 marathon to his credit.

Cragg, Sheila. *Run Patty Run.* San Francisco: Harper & Row, 1980, 177 pp. Patty Wilson of Southern California took up running in spite of her epilepsy and in the process set a number of ultradistance records.

Cunningham, Glenn. *Never Quit.* Lincoln, Va.: Chosen Books, 1981, 143 pp. Expected to be a cripple, Cunningham worked against the odds to become one of the outstanding runners of the 1930s.

Daws, Ron. *The Self-Made Olympian.* Mountain View, Calif.: World Publications, 1977, 158 pp. In 1968, Daws made the U.S. Olympic marathon team by training with attention to detail and in spite of what were up till then less than world-beating performances.

DeMar, Clarence. *Marathon.* Shelburne, Vt.: The New England Press, 1981, 156 pp. Reprint of the 1937 autobiography of the man who dominated the Boston Marathon for decades. Reissued recently by John Parker's Cedarwinds Publishing in Tallahassee, Florida. A must book for marathoners.

Giller, Norman. *The Marathon.* Secaucus, N.J.: Cartwell Books, 1983, 96 pp. Large-format book profiling thirteen famous marathoners, with plenty of photographic accompaniment.

Heidenreich, Steve. *Running Back.* New York: Hawthorn Books, 1979, 219 pp. Heidenreich was regularly breaking the 4:00 mile back in 1976, but became the victim of a hit-and-run accident; this book details his battle to relearn the basics of speech while also learning again to run.

Higdon, Hal. *The Marathoners.* New York: Putnam, 1980, 160 pp. Long profiles of marathoners Frank Shorter, Bill Rodgers, Garry Bjorklund, and Gayle Barron, with capsule profiles of other major players.

Howe, Herbert M. *Do Not Go Gentle.* New York: W. W. Norton, 1981, 187 pp. Diagnosed with a rare—and virile—form of cancer, the author decides that he's not going to allow his body to be destroyed without a fight.

Lebow, Fred. *Inside the World of Big-Time Marathoning.* New York: Rawson Associates, 1984, 288 pp. Politics and performances behind and in front of the scenes of the growing world of the marathon by someone who knows where the skeletons are kept.

Lewis, Fredrick, and Dick Johnson. *Young at Heart.* Waco, Tex.: WRS Publishing, 1992, 208 pp. The first book from Doc Wayman (Spenco) Spence's publishing company specializing in "impossible dreams," this pleasant biography of the legendary Johnny Kelley, two-time Boston winner and perennial entrant in that race, is long overdue. Besides the authors' biographical presentation, there are numerous reprints of pieces on Kelley from years past. Especially appreciated is the inclusion of Boston Marathon scribe Jerry Nason's 1935 story on Johnny's first victory in the classic race.

Liquori, Marty. *On the Run.* New York: William Morrow, 1979, 288 pp. A pleasant recounting of the road to the top of one of America's premier milers.

Magnusson, Sally. *The Flying Scotsman.* New York: Quartet Books, 1981, 191 pp. In the wake of *Chariots of Fire,* journalist Magnusson wanted to learn more about one of its heroes, Eric Liddell. Liddell proves to be as much a hero in life as he was made out to be in the film.

Marks, Rick. *More Than a Run.* Los Angeles: J. P. Tarcher, 1978, 374 pp. To celebrate the Bicentennial, fourteen members of the L.A.P.D. set out, in relay fashion, to run from Los Angeles to Montreal; could have benefited by some judicious cutting, but a good read for the hard-core runner.

Maule, Tex. *Running for Life.* London: Pelham Books, 1973, 215 pp. At the age of fifty-one, *Sports Illustrated* writer Maule suffered a massive heart attack; he took up running in an attempt to recapture his health, and his story is inspired and inspiring.

Parker, John. *The Frank Shorter Story.* Mountain View, Calif.: Runner's World Magazine, 1972, 48 pp. Parker's homage to his friend and hero, the man credited with launching the distance running craze. One of Parker's best efforts.

————. *Runners & Other Dreamers.* Tallahassee, Fla.: Cedarwinds Publishing, 1989, 178 pp. Very personalized profiles of more than a dozen running personalities, some of them done with a bit of an uncalled-for zap.

Rodgers, Bill. *Marathoning.* New York: Simon & Schuster, 1980, 326 pp. As pleasant an autobiography as Rodgers is a person.

Semple, Jock. *Just Call Me Jock.* Waterford, Conn.: Waterford Publishing, 1982, 205 pp. Most famous for attempting to pull "K. Switzer" off the Boston Marathon course in 1967, Jock was a gruff, kindhearted sub-deity in the pantheon of Boston legends.

Shepherd, Don. *My Run Across the United States.* Los Altos, Calif.: Tafnews Press, 1970, 187 pp. South African Shepherd chronicles his run from Los Angeles to New York.

Smith, David. *Healing Journey.* San Francisco: Sierra Club Books, 1983, 201 pp. Incredible physical adventures high on peak performances.

Wallach, Len. *The Human Race.* San Francisco: California Living Books, 1978, 215 pp. More than anyone would probably need to know about San Francisco's crazy Bay-to-Breakers road race and the people who helped to create and then sustain it.

Essays

Benson, Dennis C. *Making Tracks: Meditations Along the Jogging Trail.* Nashville: Abingdon, 1979, 126 pp. Benson muses as he moves through his training, finishing up each observation with a biblical paraphrase.

Kostrubala, Thaddeus. *The Joy of Running.* Philadelphia: J. B. Lippincott, 1976, 159 pp. Although the book presents facts about running and fitness, it does so in a form that Dr. George Sheehan took to the sublime.

Nelson, Bert. *Of People and Things.* Los Altos, Calif.: Tafnews Press, 1977, 64 pp. Bert is one of the founders of *Track & Field News* and his interviews, thoughts, statistics, comments, and observations are a treasure: first measured performance known to posterity—656 B.C., 23-foot-2.5-inch-long jump by Chionis of Sparta.

Parker, John L., ed. *And Then the Vulture Eats You.* Tallahassee, Fla.: Cedarwinds Publishing, 1991, 166 pp. A collection of stories dealing with ultramarathoning, although technically the final two contributions don't qualify.

Shapiro, James E. *Meditations from the Breakdown Lane: Running Across America.* New York: Random House, 1982, 239 pp. Jim Shapiro's excellent journal of his 1980 solo run across the United States.

————. *On the Road: The Marathon.* New York: Crown Publishers, 1978, 178 pp. A book on the marathon that is short on how-to and long on the people who make the sport unique; especially unusual is the "Space Travel" chapter on ultramarthoning. Joe Greene's photos of Ted Corbitt, Don Choi, Park Barner, and Nick Marshall deserve to be placed in a special archives.

————. *Ultramarathon.* New York: Bantam Books, 1980, 253 pp. Jim's unforgettable early forays into the crazy world of ultrarunning.

Sheehan, George. *Dr. Sheehan on Fitness.* New York: Simon & Schuster, 1983, 240 pp. More inspirational musings by the Good Doctor. (Read *Dr. Sheehan on Running* first, however.)

————. *Dr. Sheehan on Running.* Mountain View, Calif.: World Publications, 1975, 205 pp. George Sheehan's *Runner's World* columns from formative years of the running revolution reformated into book form; George at his best: "Tell me a man is a runner, I thought, and I know more about him than if you said he was a Christian."

————. *Personal Best.* Emmaus, Pa.: Rodale Press, 1989, 242 pp. More musings and philosophy from Doc Sheehan. Periodically, George has said that he hasn't got anything left to write about, but then the well refills. (Not to be confused with Kenny Moore's *Personal Bests.*)

————. *This Running Life.* New York: Simon & Schuster, 1980, 254 pp. Chapter 6 contains the essay that I consider George's all-time best effort, on doing his PR 3:01:10 marathon at the Marine Corps.

Fiction and Poetry

Crutcher, Chris. *Running Loose.* New York: Greenwillow Books, 1983, 190 pp. A well-written juvenile novel with a credible track race as its conclusion.

Glanville, Brian. *The Olympian.* Boston: Houghton Mifflin, 1980, 253 pp. Glanville's 1969 classic. Then editor of Houghton Mifflin Tom Hart worked as hard as Ike Low, the novel's hero, to bring this one to publication in the United States.

Higdon, Hal. *The Electronic Olympics.* New York: Holt Rinehart Winston, 1971, 106 pp. A pleasant juvenile novel that combines the Olympics and some science fiction.

Lear, Peter. *Goldengirl.* New York: Ballantine Books, 1977, 408 pp. Made into a dreadful movie with Susan Anton in the lead role; we all had a hoot at this one when it came out, but the novel's good for two rainy afternoons' slumming.

McNab, Tom. *Flanagan's Run.* New York: William Morrow, 1982, 443 pp. My favorite running novel is based upon the Bunion Derby cross-America races and is a real page-turner; while doing a good job of capturing the on-the-road "promotion" of the Bunion, the book also captures the time period. Should have been made into a major motion picture.

Parker, John L. *Once a Runner.* Tallahassee, Fla.: Cedarwinds Publishing, 1978, 225 pp. Considered by many to be the best novel ever written about the sport, and former University of Florida speedster Parker certainly knows his stuff, but high points occasionally get bogged down with Cassidy's self-absorption.

Sillitoe, Alan. *The Loneliness of the Long-Distance Runner.* New York: Alfred A. Knopf, 1959, 144 pp. Cross-country is incidental to the story of a rebellious working-class youth who finds "escape" in his running.

Teitell, Conrad. *Bedtime Stories for Runners.* Old Greenwich, Conn.: Pro Bono Publications, 1980, 48 pp. Classic bedtime stories retold with a running slant, such as Little Red Running Hood. Designed to not keep you awake.

Whiting, Nathan. *Running.* New York: New Rivers Press, 1975, 117 pp. Pleasant poems, some about running, some not, but all are marked by movement.

Watson, Richard. *The Runner.* Lakemont, Ga.: Copple House

Books, 1981, 148 pp. Middle-age personal turmoil gets
smoothed out by an increasing addiction to running; lean
writing, nicely paced, low-key novel.

History, etc.

Benyo, Richard. *The Death Valley 300.* Forestville, Calif.: Specific
Publications, 1991, 294 pp. Benyo's history of the unique
corner of California that houses the lowest point in the
Western Hemisphere (and hottest, driest place on earth)
and the tallest peak in the lower forty-eight states, and failed
and successful attempts to run from one spot to the other
in midsummer.

Campbell, Gail. *Marathon: The World of the Long Distance Athlete.*
New York: Sterling Publishing, 1977, 176 pp. Campbell
divides the book into distance runners, distance swimmers,
and distance bicycle racers, then presents short profiles of
the stars and the major events. The writing is spare, well
researched.

Cumming, John. *Runners & Walkers.* Chicago: Regnery Gateway,
1981, 177 pp. A meticulous history of the pedestrian movement of the latter half of the nineteenth century and of
running races that seemed to go on forever.

Falls, Joe. *The Boston Marathon.* New York: Macmillan Publishing,
1977, 203 pp. A lighthearted and far-ranging look at the
grandfather of all marathons, journalist Falls is not an
expert on the subject, but he's able to invest the race with
a zest sometimes missing from books by those too close to
the sport.

Fixx, Jim. *The Complete Book of Running.* New York: Random
House, 1977, 315 pp. Criticized from within running because it was written by a late-comer, the book is still a
damned good read in spite of the fact that some material is
now sorely out of date.

————. *Jim Fixx's Second Book of Running.* New York: Random
House, 1980, 240 pp. A partially unnecessary follow-up to
his best-seller (see above), this volume *does* have some new
material—and is just about as well written as they come.

Henderson, Joe. *The Running Revolution.* Eugene, Ore.: Gemini
Books, 1980, 205 pp. A hard-to-find collection of Joe's writ-

ings from 1976 to 1979, the period in which he made his way from editor of *Runner's World* magazine to the now-defunct *Running,* a time of transition and trials.

Henry, Bill. *An Approved History of the Olympic Games.* Sherman Oaks, Calif.: Alfred Publishing Co., 1984, 504 pp. Very dry reading, but most of the relevant facts are present.

Higdon, Hal. *On the Run from Dogs and People.* Chicago: Henry Regnery Company, 1971, 239 pp. When veteran running writer Higdon finds his pace, nobody can keep up with him; this is a cult classic! (See below.)

————. *On the Run from Dogs and People.* Chicago: Chicago Review Press, 1979, 223 pp. Hidgon made *major* revisions on his 1971 cult classic in order to reflect all that had happened to running during the seventies. One of those rarities: a classic that didn't go downhill with major revisions and restructuring.

Hopkins, John. *The Marathon.* London: Stanley Paul, 1966, 111 pp. A bit on the dry side, this slim volume concentrates on the Olympic marathon.

Hosler, Ray, ed. *Boston: America's Oldest Marathon.* Mountain View, Calif.: Anderson World, 1980, 180 pp. An excellent compilation of pieces on this historic race carried in the pages of *Runner's World,* and Hosler rounds out the lot with a few gems of his own.

Krise, Raymond, and Bill Squires. *Fast Tracks: The History of Distance Running.* Lexingon, Mass.: Stephen Greene Press, 1982, 282 pp. A labor of love that traces running from 884 B.C. to 1981; invaluable and highly readable.

Lucas, John. *The Modern Olympic Games.* New York: A. S. Barnes, 1980, 242 pp. Very readable history that makes the main characters come alive, in spite of the fact that to read some of the sentences out loud leaves you out of breath.

Nabokov, Peter. *Indian Running.* Santa Barbara, Calif.: Capra Press, 1981, 208 pp. A sensitive and informative book that weaves Indian running with their culture, and covers everything from running and hunting to the accomplishments of Jim Thorpe, Tom Longboat, and Billy Mills. The omission of Andy Payne, the Cherokee who won the first Transcontinental Footrace, is glaring.

Nelson, Cordner. *Runners and Races: 1500 m./Mile.* Los Altos,

Calif.: Tafnews, 1973, 326 pp. As thorough and readable a history as you'd care to find.

Osler, Tom, and Ed Dodd. *Ultramarathoning.* Mountain View, Calif.: World Publications, 1979, 299 pp. Dodd does the honors in presenting the history of the sport, and Osler deals with the training; a classic.

Osmun, Mark. *The Honolulu Marathon.* New York: J. B. Lippincott, 1979, 255 pp. Divided into two parts: personalities and then a countdown to the race; the personalities (which Osmun does very well) win. Good behind-the-scenes stuff of what goes into making a major marathon work.

Prokop, Dave, ed. *The African Running Revolution.* Mountain View, Calif.: World Publications, 1975, 112 pp. Published as No. 47 in the *Runner's World* Booklet Series, this history of the African presence in running in the decade of the sixties frequently crops up at used-book stores; grab it!

Rose, John R. *Foster Sons of Pikes Peak.* LaCrosse, Kans.: MoValley Press, 1968, 120 pp. A loving look at the early days of America's toughest marathon; plenty of stats and snapshots.

Thomas, James H. *The Bunion Derby.* Oklahoma City, Okla.: Southwest Heritage Books, 1980, 133 pp. March 4, 1928, the start of the first Transcontinental Footrace from L.A. to N.Y., with a cast of characters that proves once again truth is, indeed, stranger than fiction. (Good companion volume to Tom McNab's novel *Flanagan's Run.*)

Humor

Blaun, Randi. *The Incredibly Lazy Person's Guide to a Much Better Body.* New York: Linden Press, 1983, 208 pp. This is one of those only too-common books: a humorous title that takes its message seriously (Seriously!): that you can acquire a good body by doing almost nothing.

Lessem, Don. *Aerphobics: The Scientific Way to Stop Exercising.* New York: Morrow Quill, 1980, 146 pp. Every activity that takes itself too seriously is eventually the subject of a good-natured putdown. Lessem does just enough homework on aerobic sports to skewer it well.

Rose, Kenneth D., and Jack Dies Martin. *The Lazy Man's Guide to Physical Fitness.* Chicago: Great Lakes Living Press, 1974,

224 pp. Not really designed as a humorous book (see Randi Blaun's book above) but ends up that way.

Ziegel, Vic, and Lewis Grossberger. *The Non-Runner's Book.* New York: Collier Books, 1978, 117 pp. Long-term runners may remember this one because of its take-off of the Jim Fixx cover: red sweatpants with red running shoes attached spilling out of a garbage can. Mildly funny, but not as good as Lessem's *Aerphobics.*

Psychology

Bell, Keith F. *Championship Thinking.* Englewood Cliffs, N.J.: Prentice-Hall, 1983, 188 pp. Texas psychologist Bell puts together a very readable summation of the basics of thinking positive about your performance, including managing fatigue and pain, essentials to a successful marathon.

Benyo, Richard. *The Exercise Fix.* Champaign, Ill.: Leisure Press, 1990, 145 pp. An examination of the dark side of exercise when positive addiction is taken too far.

Csikszentmihalyi, Mihaly. *Beyond Boredom and Anxiety.* San Francisco: Jossey-Bass Publishers, 1975, 231 pp. ". . . it is vital to preserve an understanding of the active, creative, self-motivated dimensions of behavior. The study of play seems to offer such an opportunity," Csikszentmihalyi feels. His research on play and the "flow" that comes with it (primarily in dance and rock climbing) is also applicable to running.

———. *Flow: The Psychology of Optimal Experience.* New York: Harper & Row, 1990, 305 pp. Csikszentmihalyi elaborates on his theories of "flow" and extends them to all aspects of modern life. Read *Flow* and *Dr. Sheehan on Running* and call me in the morning.

Dardik, Irving, and Denis Waitley. *Quantum Fitness: Breakthrough in Excellence.* New York: Pocket Books, 1984, 191 pp. Released in time to take advantage of the 1984 Olympic Games, this book repackages old knowledge under a new name.

Garfield, Charles A. *Peak Performance.* Los Angeles: J. P. Tarcher, 1984, 219 pp. Very solid, easy-to-follow program that brings together what was known about psychological training of the athlete in this country at that time.

Glasser, William. *Positive Addiction*. New York: Harper Colophon Books, 1976, 159 pp. The seminal book on how people can continue for years to do a "seemingly boring" thing like running, and the beneficial psychological effects it bestows. A classic that examines meditation and running as addictions toward betterment.

Henderson, Joe. *Think Fast: Mental Toughness Training for Runners*. New York: Plume, 1991, 141 pp. This book might better be called Philosophy Meets Psychology on the Run. Joe brings his run-for-life philosophy to a hard edge with boxed checklists that point the way to toughness after considering why and how you are running.

Lilliefors, Jim. *The Running Mind*. Mountain View, Calif.: World Publications, 1978, 141 pp. Lilliefors, an editorial assistant at *Runner's World* in the late seventies, does a very credible job examining the psychological side of running; he adds to the then sparse literature with his own survey of the nation's runners.

Loehr, James. *Mental Toughness Training for Sports*. Lexington, Mass.: Stephen Greene Press, 1982, 191 pp. Loehr is one of our more advanced scientists in teaching the mind to lead the body toward its goals; much of his work has been with tennis players, but his information translates well to running.

Porter, Donald. *Inner Running: The Ultimate Natural High*. New York: Tempo Star Books, 1978, 221 pp. Filled with plenty of serene running photos, this book teaches the runner to slow down and maximize the good psychological effects generated by running. Nothing wrong with that, as long as you're not shooting for a time goal.

Sachs, Michael L., and Gary W. Buffone, eds. *Running as Therapy: An Integral Approach*. Lincoln, Neb.: University of Nebraska Press, 1984, 339 pp. *The* essential handbook on what psychological effects running does and does not have. Surprise: This book isn't deadly dull reading either.

Training

Alexander, Sidney. *Running Healthy*. Lexington, Mass.: Stephen Greene Press, 1980, 269 pp. Head of the vascular section of the Lahey Clinic in Boston, Dr. Alexander presents a primary case for running to cardiovascular health.

Averbuch, Gloria. *The Woman Runner.* New York: Cornerstone Library, 1984, 214 pp. Gloria Averbuch brings together many facets of the women's running movement in a well-organized, extremely readable volume.

Bailey, Covert. *Fit or Fat?* Boston: Houghton Mifflin, 1977, 115 pp. I know it isn't strictly a running book, but I always keep a few copies handy in case someone makes the mistake of saying, "But I'm too heavy to run." Bailey's informed, friendly approach is irresistible.

Barron, Gayle. *The Beauty of Running.* New York: Harcourt Brace Jovanovich, 1980, 225 pp. Attractive, intelligent, articulate, 1978 Boston winner Barron puts together a readable, insightful book. Some of the photos recall the women of the 1970s who pushed women's running a giant step forward: Jackie Hansen, Judy Leydig, Penny DeMoss, Joan Ullyot, Marty Cooksey, Miki Gorman, etc.

Benyo, Richard. *Return to Running.* Mountain View, Calif.: World Publications, 1978, 235 pp. A beginner's manual where the author makes all the mistakes for you, thereby saving you the trouble of stumbling down dark alleys.

Bloom, Marc. *Cross-County Running.* Mountain View, Calif.: World Publications, 1978, 193 pp. Cross-country running is the purest of all running, and Bloom (founding editor of *The Harrier, the* cross-country journal for the United States) has long been one of its most fervent proponents. A little dated, but it remains a fun and inspiring read.

Bompa, Tudor O. *Theory and Methodology of Training.* Dubuque, Iowa: Kendall/Hunt Publishing, 1983, 280 pp. For the more serious-minded and those who want to know why and how results occur when various work/rest applications are made to the human body. Scientific but not dense.

Bowerman, William J. *Jogging.* New York: Charter, 1967, 152 pp. Oregon coach Bill Bowerman's simple, direct, to-the-point seminal jogging program.

Bridge, Raymond. *Running Through the Wall.* New York: Dial Press, 1980, 224 pp. Good advice on pushing the physiological barriers for improvement.

Brown, Skip, and John Graham. *Target 26.* New York: Collier

Books, 1983, 300 pp. Although loaded with science, this book is very readable. Covers every aspect of the marathon you'd want to know except for proposing personal training programs. Both authors are experienced marathoners, and their more than one hundred marathons infuses the book with fascination for and respect of the distance.

Consumer Guide editors. _The Running Book._ New York: Warner Books, 1978, 223 pp. Another among the rush-to-publish onslaught of books in the wake of the running revolution; books from _Runner's World_ had covered it all before. Originally published as _Consumer Guide_ magazine No. 199 in September 1978.

Cooper, Kenneth H. _Running Without Fear._ New York: Bantam Books, 1986, 257 pp. The father of aerobics wrote this book in the wake of Jim Fixx's death to explain the incident and to assure people who wanted to take up running that it was safe to do so. A very readable and insightful book.

Costill, David L. _A Scientific Approach to Distance Running._ Los Altos, Calif.: Tafnews, 1979, 128 pp. If our philosophical guru is George Sheehan, our scientific guru is Dave Costill. Director of the Human Performance Lab at Ball State in Muncie, Ind., Dave has done many of the pioneer studies in aerobic sports—and this is where he put them together for the rest of us to benefit.

Daws, Ron. _Running Your Best._ Lexington, Mass.: Stephen Greene Press, 1985, 288 pp. Daws (see _The Self-Made Olympian_ in the Autobiography section) puts together a readable, unflinching primer for the hard-core runner who wants to improve. No wimps need apply.

Dellinger, Bill, with Blaine Newnham and Warren Morgan. _The Running Experience._ Chicago: Contemporary Books, 1978, 190 pp. A very pleasant, well-written "basics" manual raised to a higher level by the expertise of the authors, especially Dellinger, three-time Olympian and track and cross-country coach at the University of Oregon in Eugene. Warren Morgan's photos, as usual, are excellent.

Friedberg, Ardy. _How to Run Your First Marathon._ New York: Fireside, 1982, 126 pp. Brief and to the point, with no room for subtleties but competently presented, journalist Friedberg's slim book reads like a three-part magazine article.

Galloway, Jeff. *Galloway's Book on Running.* Bolinas, Calif.: Shelter
    Publications, 1984, 287 pp. Originally self-published by for-
    mer Olympian Galloway, this book has become the stan-
    dard running text of the 1980s. Jeff's advice is sound and
    sincere, although his marathon program (12-by-1-mile re-
    peats and long runs beyond marathon length) seem de-
    signed to exhaust rather than improve the runner.
Glover, Bob, and Jack Shepherd. *The Runner's Training Diary.* New
    York: Penguin, 1978, 192 pp. Bob Glover has been doing a
    series of basic running training books for Penguin since the
    late seventies. He's knowledgeable, experienced, and one of
    the country's best teachers of beginning running.
Harris, Reg. *The Part-Time Runner.* Napa, Calif.: PTR Publications,
    1983, 192 pp. In the early seventies, Reg coached in Tunisia.
    One of his athletes was Mohamed Gammoudi, who would
    win three Olympic medals. Reg put his coaching savvy into
    a book whose timing coincided with a glut of running
    books, so he published it himself. It's easily one of the best
    training books ever done. Send $10 to PTR at 1325 Imola
    Avenue West, Napa, CA 94559, and he'll send one to you.
Heggie, Jack. *Running with the Whole Body.* Emmaus, Pa.: Rodale,
    1986, 167 pp. A recreational runner while a student of the
    Moshe Feldenkrais school of body movement, Heggie ap-
    plies advanced teachings in structural movement to the
    process of running. Better than it sounds.
Henderson, Joe. *Jog, Run, Race.* Mountain View, Calif.: World
    Publications, 1977, 203 pp. This was a transitional book for
    Joe, moving as it did from the philosophy of running to the
    practical for beginners; fortunately, in spite of the many
    workout charts, the philosophy seeps through.
————. *The Long Run Solution.* Mountain View, Calif.: World
    Publications, 1976, 182 pp. My favorite of all Joe's books:
    plenty of inspiration toward perspiration, and Joe's lean,
    well-formed writing style is singing.
————. *Long Slow Distance: The Humane Way to Train.* Los Altos,
    Calif.: Tafnews, 1969, 62 pp. The year before Bob Anderson
    lured Joe away from *Track & Field News* to become the
    editor of *Runner's World,* Joe turned out this humble tome.
    It would serve as the template for *Runner's World* and the
    running revolution: You don't have to kill yourself training

to run well. The booklet profiled Amby Burfoot (the photo of him, sans beard, is a classic), Bob Deines, Tom Osler, Ed Winrow, Jeff Kroot, and Joe himself. In short, the bible of the running revolution.

————. *Run Farther Faster.* Mountain View, Calif.: Anderson World, 1984, 243 pp. This is one of the "transitional" books wherein Joe joined his unerring philosophy of running with practical tips and programs. Each chapter begins with philosophy (usually in the form of a parable) and quickly moves to the nuts and bolts.

————. *Run Gently, Run Long.* Mountain View, Calif.: World Publications, 1974, 94 pp. If you want to see the everyman approach that made *Runner's World* a success, it's all contained herein.

————. *Running A to Z.* Lexington, Mass.: Stephen Greene Press, 1983, 192 pp. Joe uses each letter of the alphabet as a launching pad for one or more essays that back their way into training principles.

————. *Running Your Best Race.* Dubuque, Iowa: Wm. C. Brown, Publishers, 1984, 190 pp. More hard-core training than in most of Joe's books, but his ability to see the philosophical sinew makes his presentation more easily understood.

Henning, Joel. *Holistic Running.* New York: Signet, 1978, 163 pp. Henning is a good writer but attempts to cover too much in too few pages; the holistic concept almost jells.

Higdon, Hal. *Run Fast: How to Train for a 5K or 10K Race.* Emmaus, Penn.: Rodale Press, 1992, 212 pp. The 5K road race is the fastest-growing running event in the country, while the 10K is the most stalwart. Long-running journalist and author Higdon knows all the training theories and presents them here in his usual readable, authoritative style. For beginning racers, this is an excellent way to break in—and to make substantial improvements once you're comfortable among the ranks of the weekend road warriors.

Hlavac, Harry F. *The Foot Book: Advice for Athletes.* Mountain View, Calif.: World Publications, 1977, 385 pp. The most readable—and useful—of the books by podiatrists that came out in the wake of the running revolution.

Homer, Joel. *Marathons: The Ultimate Challenge.* Garden City, N.Y.: Dolphin Books, 1979, 96 pp. Large-format trade paperback chock-full of great pictures but minimum text about seventeen major marathons.

Jacobs, Donald T. *Getting Your Executives Fit.* Mountain View, Calif.: Anderson World, 1981, 206 pp. This is one of those landmark books that was well researched, well written—and five years before its time. Jacobs holds a Ph.D. in health psychology and more than knows his stuff. With the rising cost of health care, Don's practical program of getting corporations to front-end get and keep key employees fit and healthy makes too much sense to be widely accepted.

————. *Ride & Tie.* Mountain View, Calif.: World Publications, 1978, 207 pp. This book is a basic manual for one of those unique sports—like orienteering—that never seems to catch on, except in little pockets of the country. Two runners and a horse compete as a team, the runners leapfrogging by taking turns on the horse. You sort of have to be there.

Jordan, Payton, and Bud Spencer. *Champions in the Making.* Englewood Cliffs, N.J.: Prentice-Hall, 1968, 280 pp. Hard-core, track and field oriented, but filled with excellent information—and with the philosophy of quality versus quantity.

Karlgaard, Richard. *The Last Word on Running.* Ottawa, Ill.: Caroline House, 1978, 300 pp. Former *Runner's World* editorial assistant Karlgaard adds one more basic running book to the avalanche that ultimately destroyed the market. Done in a Q and A format, the book offers nothing new.

Liquori, Marty, and John L. Parker. *Marty Liquori's Guide for the Elite Runner.* Chicago: Playboy Press, 1980, 166 pp. Extremely well written and instructive, although the breakdown of runners by ability into categories doesn't necessarily jive with standard performance translators of mile and 10K performances to the marathon; for example, Category B: Mile under 5:00, 10K under 38:00, marathon under 2:50; Jeff Galloway's Predicting Race Performance chart predicts a 2:57:45 off a 37:49 10K, which is much more realistic.

Lydiard, Arthur. *Running with Lydiard.* Auckland, New Zealand: Hodder and Stoughton, 1983, 209 pp. What Arthur Lydiard doesn't know about distance running ain't worth knowing.

Miller, Joe. *Burst of Speed.* South Bend, Ind.: Icarus Press, 1984, 106 pp. Five methods of improving running speed. My favorite is Tow Training: running behind a moving vehicle.

Milvy, Paul, ed. _The Long Distance Runner: A Definitive Study._ New York: Urizen Books, 1978, 621 pp. Primarily for the scientific market, this is the reformated anthology of scientific papers originally presented by the New York Academy of Sciences (vol. 301) as _The Marathon: Physiological, Medical, Epidemiological, and Psychological Studies._ A landmark volume by Professor Milvy.

Myers, Larry. _Training with Cerutty._ Mountain View, Calif.: World Publications, 1977, 174 pp. Percy Cerutty was a unique man, inspiring either awe or incredulity. His greatest claim to fame is having coached Herb Elliott, arguably the world's greatest miler. Some say Elliott would have been great with or without Cerutty's help. Larry Myers carries a strong inclination toward the former.

Nelson, Cordner. _Advanced Running Book._ Mountain View, Calif.: Runner's World Books, 1983, 192 pp. A long-running observer of the sport, Cordner wastes no time cutting to the theories behind top-level training and racing.

Noakes, Tim. _Lore of Running._ Champaign, Ill.: Leisure Press, 1991, 804 pp. If you have space in your library for only one book on the physiology of running, and you'd like it to double as a doorstop, Tim's book is your book. An updated version of his 1986 Oxford University Press tome. If a study of a specific aspect of running exists, it's digested and interpreted for you here.

Osler, Thomas J. _The Conditioning of Distance Runners._ Long Distance Log Publication, 1967, 29 pp. More a booklet than a book, Osler's primer on distance running is still viable today. By studying running and applying what he learned, Osler was able to progress from a 5:00 high school miler in 1957 to AAU 25K champ in 1965 and 30K champ in 1967; he later applied his studies to pushing back the barriers in ultrarunning. This deserves to be reprinted somewhere. The theories and applications still hold.

——. _Serious Runner's Handbook._ Mountain View, Calif.: Anderson World, 1978, 187 pp. If you could get Osler to sit down long enough to ask him 255 questions about moving your running from intermediate to advanced, this would be the transcript.

Rodgers, Bill, and Priscilla Welch. *Masters Running and Racing.* Emmaus, Pa.: Rodale, 1991, 178 pp. In deference to the Baby Boomers who fueled the running revolution, this volume is a readable, knowledgeable, practical guide to running—and then sprinting—through the middle years. The basic lesson: As you age, you don't slow much, but it takes longer to recover from your efforts.

Runner's World editors. *The Complete Marathoner.* Mountain View, Calif.: World Publications, 1978, 425 pp. A massive anthology of articles from the magazine on every conceivable aspect of the marathon. Most of the material is still applicable, especially chapters like Ted Corbitt's excellent primer in "Course Measurement."

————. *The Complete Runner.* Mountain Views, Calif.: World Publications, 1974, 391 pp. Before there was *The Complete Book of Running,* there was *The Complete Runner,* a collection of valuable training articles from *Runner's World* magazine. Should read Joe Hederson, editor, since at that point he *was* the *Runner's World* editorial department.

————. *Complete Runner, Volume Two.* Mountain View, Calif.: Runner's World Books, 1982, 465 pp. The one regret with this book is that the editors were forced by simple economics to hold half of the pieces from the magazine that they had hoped to include; what did get in, however, outweighs the regrets. As opposed to *The Complete Runner,* this volume contains as much feature material as training advice.

————. *The Complete Woman Runner.* Mountain View, Calif.: World Publications, 1978, 441 pp. Unlike most of the *Runner's World* anthologies of this period, the sixteen chapters in this volume were specifically commissioned. Part four contains the results of a major survey of *Runner's World*'s female subscribers, and fifty profiles of female runners who ranged from rank beginner to national-class level.

————. *New Exercises for Runners.* Mountain View, Calif.: World Publications, 1978, 155 pp. They worked then, they work now. Just don't try to bend the way yoga coach Jean Couch does in some of the photos.

————. *New Guide to Distance Running.* Mountain View, Calif.: World Publications, 1978, 381 pp. Overshadowed by the magazine's highly successful *The Complete Runner,* this volume of well-organized pieces from the magazine is a better read. Jim Lilliefors did the editing honors.

———. *Running After 40.* Mountain View, Calif.: Anderson World, 1980, 164 pp. An excellent compilation of essential information for the person who wants to get better with age.

Running Times editors. *The Adventure of Running.* New York: Dale Books, 1978, 131 pp. Primarily a guide culled from *Running Times* pieces, the book is now well out of date, but it serves as good archival material.

Schreiber, Linda. *Marathon Mom.* Boston: Houghton Mifflin, 1980, 178 pp. An inspiring story of a previously sedentary mother of five (including a set of quadruplets) who decided to take up running and uncorked a 2:54:33 at the 1978 New York City Marathon!

Schreiber, Michael. *Training to Run the Perfect Marathon.* Sante Fe, N.M.: John Muir Publications, 1980, 189 pp. Schreiber's approach to marathon training is to avoid the "No pain, no gain" philosophy. His program is sound, and the graphic presentation of this large-format book is very pleasant.

Sheehan, George. *Medical Advice for Runners.* Mountain View, Calif.: World Publications, 1978, 307 pp. On the—thankfully—few occasions when the ol' running machine breaks down, I still find myself reaching for this book. Dr. Sheehan tells it like it is, but even better. Compiled from his Medical Advice column in *Runner's World.*

Shephard, Roy J. *The Fit Athlete.* London: Oxford University Press, 1978, 214 pp. Physiologist Shephard uses Olympic athletes under various training and racing conditions to discuss—and illuminate—the physiology of exercise.

Sleamaker, Rob. *Serious Training for Serious Athletes.* Champaign, Ill.: Leisure Press, 1989, 247 pp. If you want to know how and why training works, this is your book.

Sparks, Ken, and Garry Bjorklund. *Long-Distance Runner's Guide to Training and Racing.* Englewood Cliffs, N.J.: Prentice Hall, 1984, 242 pp. This solid book made the mistake of coming out when the bookstores were overwhelmed with running books—and promptly got lost. Would have been even leaner and meaner without the unnecessary—and now dated—forty-seven files on name runners. Both authors were world-class runners.

Squires, Bill. *Improving Your Running.* Lexington, Mass.: Stephen Greene Press, 1982, 206 pp. The onetime coach of Bill Rodgers and Alberto Salazar takes the reader from rank beginner to hoary veteran in fifteen readable chapters.

Steffny, Manfred. *Marathoning.* Mountain View, Calif.: Anderson World, 1977, 194 pp. The personable editor of the German running magazine *Spiridon,* Manfred offers a concise and didactic course in how to train for and run the marathon. The chapters on sub-2:40, sub-2:20, and sub-2:10 marathons are especially interesting to those of us who will run that fast only in our dreams.

Subotnick, Steven I. *Cures for Common Running Injuries.* Mountain View, Calif.: Anderson World, 1979, 158 pp. Basic advice, but with too much attention to first-person.

————. *The Running Foot Doctor.* Mountain View, Calif.: World Publications, 1977, 147 pp. Podiatrist Subotnick takes runners through the potential foot problems encountered in running by using case studies. Runners weren't shy about sharing their aches and pains.

Temple, Cliff. *Challenge of the Marathon.* London: Stanley Paul, 1981, 174 pp. Cliff is an accomplished British coach, and in the wake of the running revolution striking England, he put together a very readable guide to the marathon for the English market.

Tyus, Wyomia. *Inside Jogging for Women.* Chicago: Contemporary Books, 1978, 60 pp. A lightweight, thrown-together effort to fill out Contemporary's "Inside" *(fill in sport here)* series. Contemporary would have better served women runners to ask 1964 Olympic gold-medal winner Tyus to write her autobiography.

Ullyot, Joan. *Running Free.* New York: Putnam, 1980, 287 pp. San Francisco's Dr. Ullyot recycles much of what she presented in her earlier classic, *Women's Running.* (Not to be confused with Sebastian Coe's *Running Free.*)

————. *Women's Running.* Mountain View, Calif.: World Publications, 1976, 155 pp. One of the most successful books *Runner's World* ever published: Dr. Ullyot tapped into the growing women's running movement and served it well. A national-class marathoner, Ullyot was a staunch devotee of Dr. Ernst Van Aaken (see *Van Aaken Method*).

Van Aaken, Ernst. *Van Aaken Method.* Mountain View, Calif.:

World Publications, 1976, 135 pp. German physician and coach van Aaken was a moving force behind bringing women's running along in the seventies. His theories that the fat stores of women will eventually catapult them beyond men in performance have proved wrong, but most of his teachings still ring true.

Wassersug, Joseph D. *JARM: How to Jog with Your Arms to Live Longer.* Port Washington, N.Y.: Ashley Books, 1984, 101 pp. Dr. Wassersug's theory is that you can benefit more from using your arms than your legs in exercise. The book contains excellent arm exercises that would benefit runners by *complementing* their running workouts.

Wood, Peter. *Run to Health.* New York: Charter, 1980, 351 pp. Stanford University's Peter Wood is one of those rarities: a scientist who translates research for the layman into wonderfully effective prose. Everything you need to know about taking up running—and how to keep at it.

Index

ABOUT THE AUTHOR

RICHARD BENYO, former executive editor of *Runner's World* magazine (1977–84), is the author of more than a dozen books in the areas of health, fitness, and sports. A veteran of more than thirty marathons, several of them under three hours, he has also experimented with ultramarathoning. In 1989 he and running partner Tom Crawford became the first and remain the only athletes to run from Badwater in Death Valley (at −282 feet below sea level, lowest point in the Western Hemisphere and hottest and driest place on earth) to the summit of Mount Whitney (at 14,494 feet, highest point in the contiguous United States) and back in the middle of summer, a distance of 300 miles.

Mr. Benyo lives in Sonoma County in California, and is a member of the board of directors of the Napa Valley Marathon and the starting-line coordinator of that race.

ABOUT THE TYPE

This book was set in Garamond, a typeface originally designed by the Parisian type cutter Claude Garamond (1480–1561). This version, called Stemple Garamond, was modeled on a 1592 specimen sheet from the Egenolff-Berner foundry, which was produced from types assumed to have been brought to Frankfurt by the punch cutter Jacques Sabon (d. 1580).

Claude Garamond's distiguished romans and italics first appeared in *Opera Ciceronis* in 1543–44. The Garamond types are clear, open, and elegant.